Nobunoni Book Of Shadows

By
Tata Nganga Nobunoni

MAPLE
PUBLISHERS

Nobunoni Book Of Shadows

Author: Tata Nganga Nobunoni

Copyright © 2025 Tata Nganga Nobunoni

The right of Tata Nganga Nobunoni to be identified as author of this work has been asserted by the author in accordance with section 77 N 78 of the Copyright, Designs N Patents Act 1988.

ISBN 978-1-83538-461-9 (Paperback)

Book Cover Design N Layout by:
    White Magic Studios
    www.whitemagicstudios.co.uk

Published by:
    Maple Publishers
    Fairbourne Drive, Atterbury,
    Milton Keynes,
    MK10 9RG, UK
    www.maplepublishers.com

The views expressed in this work are solely those of the author N do not reflect the opinions of Publishers, N the Publisher hereby disclaims any responsibility for them. This book should not be used as a substitute for the advice of a competent authority, admitted or authorized to advise on the subjects covered.

Welcome to the jungle

NATURAL SELECTION.

LIFE, DEATH N THE BITS IN BETWEEN.

THE VIEW SEEN FROM ANOTHER PERSPECTIVE IS ALWAYS DETACHED FROM THE TRUE FEELINGS, FELT N EXPERIENCED.

THE BEAST, THE ANIMAL, THE TAMED, THE MAN.

THE MAN SEEMS OUT OF THE ABOVE SELECTION TO BE THE ONLY ONE THAT SEARCHES FOR AN IDENTITY N, WITH THE CREATION OF THAT IDENTITY, SEEKING POWER N CONTROL.

THE ANIMAL THE BEAST LIVES IN IGNORANCE OF THESE HIERARCHY PROBLEMS.

CREATIVITY.

IMAGINATION.

THE GREATEST TOOL. MIND.

THE REALISATION N UNDERSTANDING OF DIFFERENT STATES.

STATES OF AWARENESS.

STATES OF CONSCIOUSNESS.

AS KIDS IN A TATTERED, BEATEN N RAIN SOAKED, BICYCLE SHED.

SMOKING TAILOR-MADE CIGARETTES.

OUR FIRST RECOGNISED EFFECT WAS DIZZINESS.

A KIND OF NUMBNESS OVER THE BODY.

I AM SOON TO REALISE, TOO MUCH TOO QUICK N I NEARLY PASS OUT, THROW UP N GET SENT HOME FOR THE DAY.

LIKE ALL GOOD THINGS, THEY DO NOT LAST.

ONE GETS USED TO THEM.

WELL THE BODY DOES ANYWAY.

SOON SMOKING FIVE CIGS A DAY N NOT EVEN THINKING ABOUT IT.

THE BRASH OF THE YOUNG.

AT THE AGE OF FOURTEEN, I LIVE IN A QUAINT LITTLE SOUTH DORSET TOWN, RINGWOOD.

SET ON THE RURAL OUTSKIRTS OF "THE NEW FOREST" AMONGST TREES, FIELDS N HORSES.

ENDLESS MILES OF HORSE GRAZING LANDS, HEATHER N FORESTRY RESERVES, DOTTED WITH MEANDERING BROOKS N STREAMS FULL OF TINY BROWN BLACK MINNOWS, RED BELLIED BABY PIKE N VIBRANTLY SPOTTED BROWN TROUT.

THE NEAREST SO-CALLED ENTERTAINMENT TO ME IS 12 MILES AWAY, ON THE COAST.

SO I BUNK OFF SCHOOL N GO TO BOURNEMOUTH.

WHERE I CAN BUY CIGARETTES.

STUFFING MY SCHOOL UNIFORMS INTO RUCKSACKS, N JUMPING INTO THE MORNING TRAIN.

THIS IS ACHIEVED BY JUMPING ON THE MOVING TRAIN AT THE BACK N OPENING THE DOOR.

JUST BEFORE THE TRAIN PULLS INTO THE STATION, I WILL JUMP OFF AGAIN.

SOMETIMES I GET CAUGHT N HAVE TO PAY A FINE.

WHICH I GET A SEVERE STROPPING FOR, FROM MY FOSTER FATHER, WITH HIS BELT.

NOT VERY OFTEN THOUGH.

NOT OFTEN ENOUGH TO STOP ME FROM ACQUIRING A TASTE FOR THIRTY FAGS A DAY.

I GET THE SMOKES FROM A VENDING STALL THAT SELLS NEWSPAPERS, ON THE PROMENADE SEAFRONT.

ONE OF THOSE LITTLE WOODEN HUT NEWS STANDS, WITH GLOSSY MAGS, POST CARDS, SWEETS N CIGS.

BALLOONS, BUCKET N SPADE N CANDY FLOSS.

FIVE FOR FIVE PENCE.

THE VENDOR WAS A FAT BLACK HAIRED GREASY MAN, CALLED PEDRO, WITH GREEK PARENTAGE.

I CALL HIM PEDS, COS HE PEDDLES LOTS OF STUFF.

LADIES STOCKINGS, PORN MAGS.

WHISKEY.

NEWSPAPERS, N OF COURSE, CIGARETTES.

HE HAS NO CARE HOW OLD YOU ARE.

HE JUST WANTS TO SELL THE CIGS.

SCHOOL DINNER MONEY WILL SUFFICE.

PEDS IS RUMOURED TO HAVE STABBED A LOCAL BARMAN IN THE HAND FOR REFUSING TO PAY HIM HIS WINNINGS, FROM A HORSE RACE.

THIS IS ANOTHER OF HIS TALENTS.

HE TAKES MONIES FOR BETS N THEN SCRIMS OFF THE TOP.

HE CALLS IT HIS PERCENTAGE.

P.

YOU GOT TO PAY P.

HE ALWAYS GRINNED N THEN GIVE I A KIND OF PIGGY STARE ACROSS THE TOP OF SPECTACLES.

I JOKE N CALL HIM P. P.

A REFERENCE TO THE EXTREMELY SMALL SIZE OF HIS PENIS.

PUNY.

SO I HAVE BEEN INFORMED BY THE LOCAL WORKING GIRLS.

THESE GIRLS FREQUENTED THE BARS N LOCAL HOTELS ON THE SEA FRONT N PLIED THEIR TRADE WITH LAUGHING ABANDON.

IT COMES TO PASS THAT I GET ANTIQUATED WITH MANY OF THESE LADIES IN THE COURSE OF MY YOUTH.

LEARNING MANY WAYS TO DUCK N DIVE N LIVE OFF THE STREETS N THE GOOD WILL OF FRIENDS.

I HAD BEEN SMOKING N DRINKING BEER FOR A COUPLE OF YEARS BEFORE I GOT INTO OTHER THINGS.

I AM AT SCHOOL AT THE TIME.

TRYING TO FIND A QUIET PLACE TO SMOKE.

AT THE BACK OF THE KITCHENS, FACING THE SCHOOL PLAYING FIELDS STANDS A LARGE WASTE BIN.

THE KIND YOU SEE THE CORPORATION LIFT UP WITH TWO FORKS ON THE BACK OF A LORRY.

THIS IS ALWAYS PUSHED SNUG AGAINST THE WALL, NEXT TO A YELLOW SKIP.

THIS GAVE GREAT PROTECTION FROM THE WIND IF NOT THE RAIN.

PLUS IT IS QUIET THERE.

I WALK AROUND THE CORNER OF THE KITCHEN WALL N HEAD FOR THE BACK OF THE SKIP.

WIND N RAIN TEARING AT MY FACE.

I CROUCH ALONG THE OTHER SIDE N AM STARTLED TO SEE GARY, HUDDLED N WHITE FACED, KNEELING ON THE GROUND WITH HIS BACK AGAINST THE COLD IRON.

GARY IS A YEAR OLDER THAN I, N HAS MOUSE BLONDE, UNKEMPT HAIR.

BROWN DARK EYES, WHICH SEEM TO ALWAYS BE FOCUSED ON SOMETHING ELSE.

HE HAS THIS KIND OF NERVOUS TWITCH, WHICH SEEMS TO AFFECT HIS WHOLE BODY, EVERY SPACE HE FLICKS HIS HEAD TO CLEAR HIS EYES TO SEE.

"YA ALRIGHT?" HE MUMBLES N SUCKS ON A POORLY MADE UP ROLL.

"WHAT YOU UP TO?" I SAY.

"OH, TRYING TO STAY FUCKIN WARM N OUT OF ANYONES WAY,

YOU KNOW."

HE GRINS.

HIS TEETH, BLACKENED N STAINED, BREATH SALLOW.

"WANT TO TRY SOME?"

"WHATS THAT?" I REPLY NERVOUSLY.

"KEEPS YOU WARM," HE GRINS N STICKS A PAPER TUBE IN HIS MOUTH.

REACHING INTO HIS PANTS POCKET HE PRODUCES A SMALL PIECE OF TIN FOIL N A TIN.

THE TIN CONTAINED A BROWN CRUMBLY SUBSTANCE, WHICH HE COMMENCED TO POUR, LIBERALLY, ONTO THE SILVER PAPER.

I VAGUELY KNEW WHAT IT WAS.

HE PRODUCES... AS IF OUT OF THIN AIR... A GREEN LIGHTER N PROCEEDED TO HEAT N BURN THE FOIL, PRODUCING A FAIR AMOUNT OF SMOKE, WHICH HE SUCKED INTO HIS LUNGS THROUGH THE TUBE IN HIS MOUTH.

"HERE TRY IT. GO ON."

I TAKE THE TUBE N PLACE IT IN MY MOUTH.

IT TASTES SWEET, KIND OF GREEN, BUT BITTER.

HE BURNS THE GEAR N INSTRUCTS ME TO FILL MY LUNGS N HOLD MY BREATH.

"GOOD EH?"

"FUCKIN HELL," I EXCLAIM. "NASTY SHIT."

"HERE TRY AGAIN," HE SAYS GRINNING.

"YOU GOT TO SUCK UP THE SMOKE N HOLD IT DOWN. YOU NO TASTE IT SO MUCH THEN."

I SUCK THROUGH THE TUBE N HOLD MY BREATH.

I FEEL KIND OF FUZZY.

A WARMTH CLIMBING.

MY HEAD STARTS TO GET HOT N PRICKLES.

"PHEW, SHIT.

"WHAT A FUCKING EVIL TASTE!"

"YOU GET USED TO IT."

"HERE GIVE ME THAT TUBE."

I NO REALISE IT BUT I HAVE JUST THEN STARTED TO DRIFT OFF.

DETACH FROM MY SURROUNDINGS.

A GLOW THAT I CAN ONLY DESCRIBE WITH A BLOOD RED TINGE CRAWLING OVER MY BODY...

THE JOLT OF HIS VOICE STARTLES ME.

I AM VERY HOT.

I HAND THE TUBE BACK N TRY TO STAND UP.

MY HEAD ITCHING N FUZZY, BEGINNING TO SWIM.

RAIN DRIZZLED COLD DOWN MY SOAKED HAIR N DOWN THE BACK OF MY NECK.

MY LEGS FAIL ME.

SWEAT BURSTS OUT ALL OVER MY BODY, N I START TO FEEL REAL SICK.

VERY SICK.

I VOMIT ON N OFF FOR NEARLY HALF AN HOUR, I FEEL I AM GOING TO DIE.

VOMIT N SWEAT STREAKING MY FACE.

UNABLE TO MOVE OR REALLY EVEN THINK, I LEAN BACK AGAINST THE SKIP.

PRAYING NOT TO DIE.

"OH FUCK," I GROAN.

I NEED A DRINK.

I LAY HALF-SLUMPED AGAINST THE SKIP, RAIN SWEAT N VOMIT MINGLED WITH MY ALREADY RAIN SOAKED CLOTHES. I USE MY P. E. VEST TO CLEAN UP A BIT.

GAS GOES TO THE NEWSAGENTS TO GET FAGS N COCA-COLA.

I SPEND THE NEXT HALF-HOUR DROOLING N DISAPPEARING IN N OUT OF WAKEFUL CONSCIOUSNESS; UNABLE OR WISHING TO FEEL MY COLD SHAKING BODY.

WHEN HE RETURNS, I AM KIND OF SERIOUSLY UNTOGETHER, BUT NOT SO NAUSEOUS.

MY HEAD IS VERY CLOUDY N MY INNER SELF FEELING WARM N SECURE.

"WOW FUCK YOU ARE BOMBED," HE COMMENTS N HANDS ME A COKE.

I TEAR OPEN THE CAN N GULP THE ICE-COLD FIZZ FOR ALL MY LIFE.

"STEADY, YOULL CHUCK UP AGAIN. JUST SIP IT."

I AM BEYOND CARING FOR NOW.

THE ICE-COLD COKE SLIDES DOWN SLICK AS CAN BE, BURNING MY THROAT WITH EXQUISITE PAIN N COOLING RELIEF, N THEN SLOWLY WARMS WITHIN MY GUT.

EYES SHUT, GREEN, BLUE, PURPLE N RED LIGHTS WRESTLED ABOUT UNCONTROLLABLY.

LIKE SOME SURREAL FIREWORK DISPLAY, BUT THE ROCKETS ARE GOING UP N DOWN.

MY WHOLE WORLD SHATTERING WITH COLOURS N BODY SHAKING,

OUT OF CONTROL.

I CRUMPLE TO THE FLOOR, BELCH OFF THE GAS N VOMIT HIGH INTO THE AIR.

VOMIT COKE COMES DOWN ON MY COAT N RUCKSACK, SPLATTERING THE BLUE MATERIAL N SLOPPING ON THE SIDE OF THE SKIP, LIKE SOME APPARITION OF SELF-MADE LIFE FOR ONE SECOND.

FIZZLING N GROWING IN THE AIR, LANDING N COVERING EVERYTHING IN FRONT OF ME.

THEN DISAPPEARING IN THE RAIN SOAKED TARMAC.

I HAVE NO CLUE ONE CAN COULD CHUCK SO FAR N SO MUCH.

GETTING TO MY FEET, I STAGGER FOR THE GRASS PLAYING FIELD, TO LIE DOWN.

THE GRASS WET ON MY CHEEK, SMELLS FRESHLY MOWN N SLIGHTLY OF DEAD ROTTING CUTTINGS.

A FRESH LOAM EARTHY CLEAN SMELL.

REASSURING.

I LAY LIKE THAT FOR MOST OF THE REST OF THE AFTERNOON.

SOAKED, SICK, BUT STRANGELY CONTENT.

THE WET GRASS N SOIL PRESSED CLOSE AGAINST MY FACE.

I PEER HORIZONTALLY AT A CLOVERLEAF N WONDERED IF IT TOO HAD EVER EXPERIENCED SUCH ANGUISH N PLEASURE.

THE WIND N RAIN BLOWING SOFTLY OVERHEAD, I DRIFT OFF TO SLEEP, NOT CARING FOR BEING WET N COLD.

JUST LYING THERE IN THE PEACE OF THE MOMENT.

LIVING WITH FOSTER PARENTS IS HELL.

I AM SICK A LOT OF THE SPACE N ARGUE ABOUT GOING TO SCHOOL, OR TAKING A JOB.

"A GOOD PAID, RESPECTABLE JOB," HE WILL SAY.

IN THE MACHINE SHOP WHERE HE WORKED FOR THE LAST 24 YEARS AS A CNC LATHE OPERATOR.

I REQUIRE TO GO TO SEA, EITHER ON FISHING BOATS OR DEEP SEA.

"THAT IS NOT RESPECTABLE."

EVEN THOUGH THE PAY TURNS OUT TO BE QUITE GOOD FOR ME SOME YEARS LATER.

I CAN NEVER SEEM TO PLEASE OR FULFIL A DREAM THAT ALREADY HAS BEEN LOST ON HIS OWN TWO CHILDREN.

TRYING ENDLESSLY TO RE-MOULD ME N MAKE ME FIT HIS VIEW, IS NOT CONDUCIVE TO ONES MENTAL STATE, SO, ONE EVENTFUL NIGHT, IT ALL EXPLODES N I LEAVE...

I HAVE BEEN OUT ON THE FIELD AT THE FOOT OF THE ROAD.

NEXT TO WHERE I LIVE IS A GARAGE, N AT THE BACK OF THE GARAGE IS A FIELD FULL OF SCRAP MOTORS.

FROM MY BEDROOM WINDOW I CAN SURVEY THE RED BROWN RUSTY TOPS OF CARS THAT HAVE BEEN LEFT,

WITH DAMAGED PAINTWORK, IN THE RAIN TOO LONG.

WEEDS OF GORSE N FERNS, PURPLE HEATHER, GROW IN BETWEEN,

WITH THE ODD SCATTERED TREE FOR SHADE.

I HAVE AN OLD BLUE FORD ANGLIA CAR,

PARKED IN THE BUSHES AT THE FAR END OF THAT FIELD.

IF NO ONE KNEW I AM THERE NO ONE COMES DOWN.

SECLUDED UNDER THE PROTECTING BRANCHES OF AN OLD OAK TREE N ALSO OVERGROWN WITH BINDWEED,

I HAVE QUITE A SECLUDED SPOT.

EVEN FROM THE GRAVEL PATH THAT RAN BESIDE THE CAR,

ONE CAN NO SEE THE OLD FORD ANGLIA BLUE THROUGH THE LEAVES.

A DEN FOR SURE.

I TAKE GIRLS THERE AFTER SCHOOL.

OR JUST SKIVE OFF.

THE CAR HAS BEEN HAND PAINTED MANY TIMES.

I JOKE THAT THE PAINT HELD THE CAR TOGETHER.

ONLY THE REAR N FRONT WINDSCREEN REMAINED.

WOODEN BOARDS PLACED ALONG THE SIDES PREVENTED THE WIND COMING THROUGH THE OPEN WINDOWS.

I SPEND MOST OF THIS FRIDAY AFTERNOON IN THE DEN.

SMOKING N DRINKING BEER N LISTENING TO SMALL RED TRANSISTOR RADIO,

I FIND IN AN OLD CAR.

I LIKE TO WATCH THE SPARROW HAWKS, AS THEY HOVER AGAINST THE CLOUDS IN A BLUE GREY SKY.

HANGING N DIVING.

SEEMINGLY MOTIONLESS ONE MINUTE N THEN AS BLINDING JAVELINS THE NEXT,

RACING TOWARDS THE EARTH THE NEXT.

I OFTEN WONDER AT THE FEAR OF THE UNSUSPECTING PREY,

WHEN, A VAST FAST MOVING SHADOW ENGULFS ALL THE SURROUNDING LIGHT,

N THE IMMINENCE OF DEATH IS NEAR.

A TENDER MOMENT OF INNER SILENCE ENVELOPS ME N HOLDS ME IN AWE, AT THE POINT OF DEATH.

DO THEY KNOW?

FOR ONE INSTANT.

DO THEY KNOW THAT ALL IS LOST?

OR IS DEATH SWIFTER THAN THAT?

CAN DEATH SNATCH AWAY EVEN THE EVENT?

THE CONCEPT,

OF THE MOMENT.

ANNIHILATING THY EXISTENCE.

COMPLETELY.

UTTERLY.

WITHOUT RECORD?

THE BOARDS AT THE LEFT HAND SIDE OF THE CAR MOVE N JED N GAS ROLL IN.

"HEY GOT A BEER! YOU GOT A BEER FOR ME THEN?"

SHOUTS JED. GASS OLDER BROTHER.

HE SNATCHES AT MINE TO NO AVAIL

I'LL SAVE YOU SOME, OK?

HE SHRUGS.

ARE YOU SORTED? I ASK.

I KNEW JED USUALLY CARRIED SOMETHING WE COULD SMOKE.

"YES. I'LL SORT IT IN A MO."

"WHAT YOU DOING LATER, AT ABOUT 4 OCLOCK?"

I GOT TO GO SEE PED N SORT SOME SHOTS FOR THE WEEKEND."

"ILL BE HERE," I SAY.

JED HAD BEEN SHOOTING GEAR FOR SOME 3 YEARS NOW N WAS PROUD OF THE SCARS N CALLING HIS HITS HIS SHOTS.

HE ALWAYS MANAGED TO GET TWO A DAY, ON WEEKDAYS N THREE A DAY FOR SATURDAY N SUNDAY.

HE RUNS SOME SCAM WITH PEDS N THE BOOKIES.

IT TURNS OUT THAT PEDS STABBED A BARMAN MANY YEARS BEFORE N HAD GOTTEN DONE BADLY,

SOME 8 MONTHS LATER.

HE GAVE UP THE NEWS STAND N TOOK TO HIS BED.

FROM WHERE HE NOW CONDUCTED HIS BUSINESSES.

JED BEING 4 YEARS GASS SENIOR IS EXTREMELY SKINNY FOR HIS YEARS N ALWAYS SEEMS TO LIVE ON CIGS N BEER.

I BOUGHT HIM A BURGER ONE EVENING.

HE THANKED ME KINDLY.

THEN PROMPTLY GAVE IT TO POPPY, HIS BITCH, GERMAN SHEPHERD DOG, SAYING "A DOGS GOT TO EAT, YA KNOW."

"YES RIGHT," I SAY.

"WHAT ABOUT YOU?"

HE JUST SHRUGS IN HIS USUAL MANNER, LIFTING HIS SHOULDERS IN A HIGH SHRUG, BREATHING IN.

DROPPING HIS SHOULDERS N EXHALES.

"PHEW!"

"THE FOOD BRINGS ME DOWN MAN."

"TWILL BRING YOU SIX FOOT DOWN IF YOU NO EAT IT." I RETORT.

HE JUST LAUGHS N SWIGS THE REMAINDER OF MY CAN OF BEER, BELCHES, LOBBING THE EMPTY HIGH IN THE AIR, LAUGHS N THEN BOOTS IT OVER A FEW WRECKED CARS OUT OF SIGHT, UPON ITS RETURN TO EARTH.

WE ALL SMILE AT THAT ONE.

EVER SINCE FINDING LITTLE PINK DICONAL TABLETS IN HIS FATHERS BEDSIDE CABINET, JED HAD BEEN INTO OPIATES.

ON THE DAY HE FOUND THEM, HE BROUGHT A GLASS SYRINGE N SAT IN ONE OF THE CARS IN THE SCRAP YARD N DONE TWO OF THEM UP HIS ARM. WE DIDNT GET ANY PEACE FOR A MONTH AFTER THEY RAN OUT. HE SEEMED TO LIVE N BREATHE THEM, EVEN TO THE POINT OF NAMING HIS DOG AFTER THE FLOWER THAT IN HIS WORDS, GAVE HIM SO MUCH LOVE.

THE WORDS "THINK PINK" WERE TATTOOED ON HIS FOREARM, NEXT TO ANOTHER OF A SET OF WORKS STUCK IN HIS ARM WITH SPOTS OF BLOOD RUNNING FROM THE ENTRANCE HOLE.

WE MINGLE AROUND N SMOKE CIGS THEN JED GOES OFF TO GET HIS SHOTS.

I AM SITTING IN THE OLD ANGLIA TRYING TO DUCK THE RAIN THAT THE WIND KEEPS BLOWING THROUGH THE CRACKS WHERE THE WOOD DOES NOT COVER PROPERLY, WHEN I HEAR JED N TWO GIRLS TALKING.

"AH COME ON J, YOU PROMISED ME 3, I GIVE YOU MY MOTHERS MOGGIES."

"DONT FUCK ABOUT, I'LL CUT YOU, YOU BASTARD."

"IM SICK GIVE ME MY FUCKIN GEAR."

JED STARTS DANCING.

"OOOOOOOOOOH! IM REALLY SCARED."

"I'LL GET MY SISTER TO FUCK YA FACE UP FOR YA, MASH UP THEM PRETTY LOOKS FOR YA."

"GONNA CUT ME ARE YA, GO ON THEN, DO IT!"

"GO ON THEN!"

HE BEGINS TO SPIN LIKE A WHIRLING TOP, KICKING DUST N STONES HIGH IN THE AIR.

MILLI SLAPS HIM HARD IN THE FACE.

"EH!" JED RETORTS, "WHAT YOU DO THAT FOR?"

FUCKIN BITCH!

HE STANDS DANGLING A BAGGY OVER MILLIS HEAD, TEARS BEGINNING TO SPROUT AT EYE CORNERS.

"AH COME ON," MILLI RETORTS. "LETS NOT FIGHT, GIVE ME TWO N YOU CAN HAVE ONE. I DIDNT MEAN TO HIT YOU, YOU JUST WINDING ME UP LIKE ALWAYS."

MILLI IS NOW NEARLY IN TEARS N SHAKING.

"I NEED A HIT J," SHE WINES.

"COME ON JED," I SHOUT, "STOP FUCKIN ABOUT N GET OVER HERE, I AM GETTING WELL DRENCHED WAITING FOR YOU.

DID YOU GET ME ANYTHING?"

JED AMBLES OVER, "DONT I ALWAYS?"

SO MILLI, HER FRIEND, JED N MYSELF PILE INTO THE OLD ANGLIA CAR N GET DOWN TO BUSINESS, SEE WHAT JED HAS FOR US.

HE PRODUCES A ZIP LOCK BAG WITH NINE LITTLE SILVER PAPER BAGGIES IN.

PULLS OPEN THE GLOVE BOX N LAYS OUT A SPOON, A LITTLE BOTTLE OF WATER N A NEW ONE-MIL SYRINGE.

"LET ME GET SORTED FIRST N THEN YOU CAN SHARE THE WASH WITH MILLI.

"THANKS J," SAYS MILLI.

YOURE A STAR!

JED TAKES THREE OF THE TINY WRAPS FROM THE BAG N PROCEEDS TO EMPTY THE CONTENTS INTO THE SPOON ALONG WITH A PINCH OF CITRIC, FILLS THE ONE MIL FROM THE BOTTLE N FIRES THE WATER INTO THE SPOON.

TAKES A LIGHTER FROM HIS TOP LEFT POCKET N COOKS THE MIX UNTIL IT HAS MELTED N DROPS ATOP A PIECE OF CIGARETTE FILTER.

HE REMOVES THE CAP N STABS THE SPIKE INTO THE FILTER N DRAWS UP ALMOST ALL THE COOK.

"STEADY ON MAN," I SHOUT, "YOU DO ALL THAT, YOU GOING TO BE PUSHING UP DAISIES."

"ILL BE ALL RIGHT."

FLICKING THE AIR BUBBLE OUT HE ROLLS UP HIS LEFT SLEEVE.

"HERE HOLD MY ARM, WILL YA."

I GRAB HIS BICEP TO PUMP HIS VEINS N HE BEGINS TO DIG THROUGH YELLOW RED SCABS FOR THE LINE HE KNOWS SO WELL.

FLUSH, THE SYRINGE FLOODS WITH BLOOD N I RELEASE MY GRIP SLIGHTLY.

JED SQUEEZES HARD ON THE PLUNGER, FIRING THE COOK DEEP INTO HIS VEIN.

"AH THATS THE COOKIE," HE EXCLAIMS N SAGS BACK INTO THE PASSENGER SEAT.

"GOT A CIG?"

MAN I NEED A SMOKE.

JUST LIKE JED!

I REACH OVER N COLLECT THE SPOON N A NEW SET OF WORKS N ORGANISE A HIT FOR MILLI N MYSELF.

I GIVE HER HERS N THEN DO MY SHOT.

I SLIP OFF INTO A QUIET WARM SPACE OF NO CARES OR WORRIES.

SLOWLY GAINING DISTANCE FROM THE HARSHNESS OF NORMAL REALITY.

SOME THREE HOURS LATER I COME TOO.

"GROGGY N EXTREMELY STONED," I EXCLAIM.

"FUCKIN HELL MAN!

YOU NEARLY KILLED ME, HOW FUCKIN STRONG IS THAT STUFF?"

I BANG JED ON THE ARM N HE JUST SLUMPS FORWARD LIFELESS.

I LOOK AT MILLI N HER FRIEND; THEY ARE OK, BUT WELL BOMBED.

I JUMP OUT OF THE CAR LITERALLY FALLING FLAT ON MY FACE GRAZING HANDS N KNEES UPON THE GRAVEL N RUN AROUND TO THE PASSENGER SIDE.

RIPPING THE WOOD BOARDING OFF OF THE SIDE OF THE CAR, I GRAB JED BY THE SCRUFF OF HIS JACKET N HEAVE HIM OUT ONTO THE GROUND.

HE IS DEATHLY GREY N NO BREATHING.

SOMETHING IN ME SNAPPED.

BEADS OF SWEAT ICE COLD N BURNING FORMED UPON MY BROW N MY EYESIGHT BEGAN TO SWIM.

"FUCK, HE'S OD'D."

I SCREAM AT THE GIRLS TO GET OUT N HELP TRYING TO PULL MY FRIEND TO HIS FEET.

JED CANNOT MOVE OR EVEN TRY TO HELP ME.

I GIVE UP ON THIS IDEA AS MILLI N HER FRIEND PILE OUT OF THE CAR.

"MILLI CALL AN AMBULANCE, HE IS FUCKIN DYING." TEARS NOW STREAM DOWN MY FACE.

"COME ON FUCKIN PHONE NOW."

I CANNOT SEE, MY WORLD IS EXPLODED WITH TEARS N PAIN,

MAKING FOR DIFFICULTY IN EVEN BREATHING.

BUT I KNEW JED HAD TO BREATHE.

I GRAB AT THE BUTTONS ON HIS DENIM JACKET N FUMBLED TO GET THEM OPEN, TEARING AT HIS SHIRT BENEATH.

I LOWER MY HEAD TO HIS CHEST TENTATIVE TO LISTEN.

NOTHING.

I HAVE NO CLUE OF OR KNOW CPR..

I PINCH HIS NOSE N FILL HIS LUNGS, N THEN PROCEEDED TO KIND OF THUMP HIM IN THE CHEST.

I FILL HIS LUNGS AGAIN; HE COUGHS N STARTS TO VOMIT.

TURNING HIM OVER I GRAB HIM UNDER HIS ARMS N HOLD HIM AS HE EXHALES N VOMITS SOME MORE, GROANING, WE BOTH FALL ONCE AGAIN TO THE GRAVEL FLOOR.

I LOOK UP N THE TWO GIRLS ARE GONE.

IT IS JUST YOU N ME NOW, BUD.

I AM CRYING BADLY, BUT MY FRIEND NEEDS MY HELP.

HE IS NOW BREATHING IF SOMEWHAT VERY SHALLOW N DROOLING SPITTLE N VOMIT DOWN HIS BARE CHEST, MUMBLING INCOHERENTLY.

I GRAB HIM BY HIS LEFT ARM PULLING HIM TO HIS FEET, HIS ARM OVER MY SHOULDER

N WE STAGGER UP THE FIELD TOWARDS THE HOUSING ESTATE.

FUCKIN MILLI N HER FRIEND JUST RAN OFF.

IT TAKES ME SOME TWENTY MINUTES TO DRAG HIM N MYSELF TO THE ROADWAY N THERE IS NO ONE ABOUT.

I PROP JED AGAINST A GARDEN WALL N START TO BANG ON DOORS.

FOR WHAT SEEMS LIKE AN ETERNITY NO ONE COMES.

THEN THIS CHAP COMES OUT OF HIS HOUSE INQUIRING.

I TOLD HIM THERE HAD BEEN AN ACCIDENT N TO PHONE THE AMBULANCE.

INSTEAD HE SAID, "WHATS UP?

IS HE ALL RIGHT?"

BIT OF A DUMB QUESTION I FEEL..

I RETURN TO WHERE I LEFT JED AS HE HAD SLUMPED DOWN THE WALL.

I SIT WITH HIM FOR A FURTHER 20 MINUTES SOAKED THROUGH TO THE SKIN WITH FEAR N RAIN.

THE AMBULANCE ARRIVES.

HE IS VERY LUCKY TO BE ALIVE.

THEY TAKE JED OFF ON A GURNEY. I SIT IN THE BACK OF THE AMBULANCE WITH HIM SORELY SHAKEN

IN THE HOSPITAL I AM BASICALLY DISMISSED, STILL PINED UP, WHITE N SHAKING "HE SHALL BE OK "GO HOME."

UPON I RETURN HOME THAT NIGHT MY FOSTER FATHER STOOD AT THE DOOR TO GREAT ME.

"FUCKIN DRUGS!" HE RETORTS, "TOLD YOU, YOU ARE NO GOOD."

HE PROMPTLY TURNS, GOES INDOORS.

N NEVER SPEAKS WITH ME AGAIN.

IT IS SOME MONTHS BEFORE I TRY AGAIN, N I MIGHT SAY, WITH SOME CAUTION.

BY, NINETEEN, I WAS USING REGULAR N EVENTUALLY MOVED AWAY FROM HOME TO LONDON TO FULFIL MY DREAMS.

DREAMS OF GEAR.

HOW TO GET IT N HOW TO USE IT.

I FIRST FIND DIGS, AT THE BACK OF EARLS COURT UNDERGROUND STATION.

FOR A MEAGRE SEVEN POUNDS A NIGHT, I MOVED INTO BRAMHAM GARDENS.

WHERE I GOT WELL ACQUAINTED WITH THE LADY'S DAUGHTER THAT OWNED THE HOUSE.

SHE IS A BUXOM GIRL OF SOME 24 YEARS OF AGE.

RED, LONG FLOWING HAIR, WITH GREEN EYES.

SHE LIKED TO HANG AT THE BACK OF THE STATION N TEASE THE YOUNG LADS COMING TO N FRO IN THE BUSTLE OF THE LUNCH TIMES N EVENING RUSH HOURS.

MANY LADS KNOW HER.

MY ROOM CONSISTS OF A LARGE ROOM N BED, WITH A CUBBY-HOLE ATTACHED AS A KITCHEN.

A SMALL SINK, FRIDGE N COOKER WERE PRECARIOUSLY PLACED ON A DILAPIDATED TABLE. TWO OF THE LEGS HAD FALLEN OF SO ONE END IS PROPPED UP ON SOME TEA CHEST LIKE BOXES, COVERED WITH A CLOTH.

MY VIEW CONSISTS OF PEERING THROUGH THE SQUARES OF A SASH WINDOW, INTO THE SIDE ALLEYWAY N THE WALL OF THE ADJACENT BUILDING.

THE WINDOWSILL IS CAKED IN PIGEON SHIT N THE ROOM HAS A STRANGE MOULDY SMELL.

I RAISE THE WINDOW, SHOOING OFF THE BIRDS N TAKE A BREATH.

WET, SMOKEY.

THE SMELL OF CURRY N TARMAC MIXED WITH CAR FUMES.

I HAVE NOW MY OWN PLACE TO LAY MY HEAD.

I SIT ON THE BED N ROLL A CIGARETTE N PONDER MY SITUATION.

YOUTHFUL FANTASIES.

PICTURES OF PUBS, CLUBS N GIRLS.

THE GIRL I MET DOWNSTAIRS FLOATED IN MY MIND.

I FALL ASLEEP N DREAM.

DREAM OF THE GIRL WITH THE LONG FLOWING RED HAIR.

SHE SEEMS TO WANT TO TELL ME SOMETHING.

A KNOCK ON THE DOOR AWAKENS ME.

IT IS 8.30 IN THE MORNING N I SLEEP ON THE BED ALL NIGHT.

I MOVE ACROSS THE ROOM N OPEN THE DOOR.

STANDING IN THE DOOR, IS SIOUX.

SHE LOOKS STUNNING, BUT ALSO KIND OF SCARY.

SHE IS WEARING A LEATHER JACKET N EXTREMELY TIGHT BLACK JEANS.

BLACK CALF BOOTS, PURPLE EYE SHADOW, N BLACK LIPSTICK.

SHE HAS PAINTED FINGERNAILS ON HER LEFT HAND BLACK N THE RIGHT HAND RED.

HER HAIR IS TIED UP IN A KIND OF KNOT BUN ON THE TOP OF HER HEAD N SHE HAS A CIGARETTE IN HER MOUTH.

"JUST LIKE THE INDIANS." SHE SMILES, "GOT A LIGHT? MY MOTHER TELL ME TO BRING YOU THESE."

SHE HANDS ME CLEAN SHEETS.

"SORRY, LIKE THE INDIANS?"

I TAKE THE BUNDLE N TURN N WALK INTO MY ROOM.

"THE NAME SILLY."

"OH," I SAY AS SHE FOLLOWS. "WHERE YOU FROM?"

I EXPLAIN THAT I HAVE COME UP FROM DOWN SOUTH N THAT CHAOS REIGNS WITHIN MY LIFE. N I HAVE DECIDED TO GET OUT ON MY OWN.

AWAY FROM ALL THE MAD FAMILY N THAT I WAS HOPING TO FIND A JOB,

IN ONE OF THE LOCAL RESTAURANTS.

I HAVE FRIENDS IN THE RESTAURANT BUSINESS.

SHE REPLIES,

"I CAN HAVE A WORD IF YOU LIKE."

"YOU NO MIND A K. P. JOB OR SOMETHING LIKE THAT?

THE MONEY IS NOT BRILL, BUT IT PAYS."

"SWEET, SOUNDS GREAT."

"HOW LONG YOU LIVE HERE THEN?" I SAY.

SHE EXPLAINS THAT HER MOTHER DIVORCED HER IRISH HUSBAND WHEN SIOUX HAD BEEN NINE N SHE N HER MOTHER HAVE MOVED FROM DUBLIN TO LONDON, FOURTEEN YEARS PREVIOUS, TO RUN THIS HOUSE.

I SENSE SOME BITTERNESS IN HER WORDS, LIKE, IT IS HER MOTHERS FLAT THAT SHE IS STUCK HERE IN LONDON N NOT BACK IN DUBLIN.

SHE N I SIT FOR HALF OF THE MORNING, CHATTING ABOUT HOW BEAUTIFUL OUR RESPECTIVE HOME TOWNS ARE N OUR DREAMS OF GOING BACK HOME.

SIOUX SAYS SHE MISSES THE BAKERY AT THE END OF THE STREET WHERE SHE GREW UP.

THE SMELL WAFTING THROUGH HER BEDROOM WINDOW IN THE MORNINGS DOES AWAKE HER.

SHE DESCRIBES THE BUSTLE ON THE STREET BELOW HER WINDOW N HOW THE SMELL OF THE FRESH BREAD ACTED AS A CLOCK FOR HER N SHE ALWAYS KNEW WHAT TIME OF DAY IT WAS BY THE SMELLS RISING FROM BELOW.

I LIKE THIS GIRL.

SHE IS WILD N FREE.

A BIT LIKE ME.

AT ABOUT 11.30 AM SHE N I PART WITH PROMISES OF GETTING TOGETHER LATER.

I HAVE BUSINESS TO ATTEND.

AS IT HAPPENS I NEVER SEE SIOUX FOR NEARLY ANOTHER TWO YEARS LATER.

I GET ON THE TUBE TRAIN N TRAVEL TO THE WEST END N GET BUSTED.

ONE GRAM A CLASS POSSESSION WITH A BUM RAP, INTENT TO SUPPLY.

I AM FUCKED.

TWO YEARS BORSTAL TRAINING,

FOLLOWED BY THREE MONTHS,

HMP FOR TRYING TO GET MYSELF WELL FOR A FEW HOURS.

HEROIN IS A BITCH! I AM RELEASED SOME 19 MONTHS LATER INTO A COLD HARSH CRUEL WORLD.

I FEEL LIKE A CHILD WITH TOO MANY ADULT EXPERIENCES EXPERIMENTS GONE BAD (KIETH) (FINDING SEXUALITY)

AH, HELL IT IS SOME SORT OF MASOCHISTIC LOVE OF PAIN THAT KEEPS ME FROM REACHING FOR THE GEAR.

THIS LADY BROWN SUGAR THAT RAILS HER CLAWS SO DEEP WITHIN MY VERY SOUL.

I KNOW FROM EXPERIENCE.

I KNOW NOW, I KNOW HER WELL.

I KNOW HER TOO WELL.

I SORTED IT LAST TIME, I CAN SORT IT NOW.

AH, BUT DO I REALLY GET WHAT I AM LOOKING FOR, OR AM I STILL A SLAVE TO SOMETHING?

A SLAVE TO DRUGS,

A SLAVE TO THE GOVERNMENT,

A SLAVE TO THE SYSTEM,

A SLAVE TO SOCIETY.

AAAAAAAHHAA! I SIGH N STRETCH MY UPPER BACK BACKWARD OVER THE CHAIR WITH ARMS STRETCHED HIGH.

MY NECK N HEAD BEING PULLED DOWN MY BACK,

WITH THE STRESS OF WITHDRAWAL.

HEAD IS CRACKING.

SKIN CRAWLING, GOOSED, FREEZING TO THE BONE, I REACH FOR MY BACCY.

AT LEAST A SMOKE WILL CALM ME.

I PULL OUT RIZLAN BACCY N HANDS SHAKING I MAKE A BAD ATTEMPT AT ROLLING IT.

MY EYES ARE EXTREMELY SENSITIVE N MY BODY ACHES AS IF TOTALLY DRAINED.

I NEED HEAT FROM THE INSIDE, NOT OUTSIDE IN,

SWEATING TOO MUCH.

THE BEAST IS UPON ME.

IT IS EARLY IN THE DAY.

MARCH TIME.

THE LIGHT THROUGH MY LIVING ROOM WINDOW SLATE GREY N COLD.

TOO COLD FOR ME TO VENTURE OUTSIDE.

I STAND N STRETCH ONCE AGAIN SEEING THE BIN MAN AS HE COMES COME UP THE PATH.

AH CRAP, THE BINS. I EXCLAIM TO MYSELF N GRAB SOME JEANS N A JACKET.

GRABBING THE BINS IN MY BACK PORCH AREA I OPEN THE BACK DOOR.

THE WIND CHILLS ME TO THE BONE N MAKES ME MOAN.

GOOSE FLESH TIGHTEN N MY MUSCLES BEGIN TO SPASM.

WITH A SUPREME EFFORT I STRUGGLE UP THE GARDEN PATH WITH THREE BLACK BAGS N I AM GREETED WITH A SMILE FROM THE BIN MAN.

CAN NO SEE WHAT THERE IS TO SMILE ABOUT.

I GRUMP.

IT IS BLOODY FREEZING.

I DUMP THE BAGS AT HIS FEET WHILST HE INSPECTS ME QUIZZICALLY.

I SHUFFLE OFF N SLAM THE DOOR,

RELIEVED TO BE ONCE MORE OUT OF THE COLD WIND.

I AM AT THIS NOW NEARLY THREE MONTHS.

I AM GOING TO BEAT THIS BITCH THIS TIME.

NO METHADONE SINCE SUNDAY MORNING N IT WAS NOW FRIDAY.

"CAN NO TAKE THIS NO MORE."

I MOAN AGAIN.

I SHUFFLE OFF TO THE KITCHEN TO LOOK FOR CODEINE N A CUP OF STRONG TEA.

EVERYTHING LOOKS STRANGE.

SPARKLY LIKE, N MY HEAD IS THUMPING LIKE A JACK HAMMER.

MY BODY FEELS LIKE IT IS BEING RUBBED WITH SANDPAPER N BEATEN WITH BIG STICKS.

I SWITCH THE KETTLE ON N LEAN ON THE WORK SURFACE POPPING OPEN A POT OF DF118S 60S, TIP OUT 6 N POP THEM IN MY MOUTH, CHEWING ON THE BITTER PILLS INTENTLY AWAITING THE COMING RELIEF. MY HEAD N PSYCHE ARE SHATTERED LIKE SOME BROKEN JIGSAW.

THE KETTLE GURGLES N POPS.

I GRAB A WOODEN STOOL N CROUCH CLOSE TO THE WARMTH OF THE KETTLE POURING WATER IN MY SILVER TEAPOT.

THE STEAM N WARMTH FEEL GOOD UPON MY FACE,

BUT THE REST OF ME IS STILL FREEZING.

POURING MILK INTO MY TEA I PONDER USING SOME "H" FOR RELIEF.

YES, NO!

YES, NO!

YES!

THIS TIME THE CODEINE IS NO WORKING.

BEDROOM.

I GRAB THE LIGHTER OFF MY COMPUTER TOP, WITH THE PICTURE OF "SCRATCHY" ON IT N WONDER N KNOW OF HIS PAIN WITH "ITCHY" TORTURING HIM ALL THE DAY.

I SIGH, CUDDLE N DRINK MY TEA N AMBLE TO THE BEDROOM.

I AM SHAKING N SWEATING BAD NOW, VERY DIFFICULT TO SEE.

I PUSH MY HAND UNDER THE BED MATTRESS N PULL OUT A FLATTENED TUBE WITH SILVER PAPER TRAY.

THE TRAY STREAKED IN BROWN SHINY STREAKS SHOWED IT WAS NOT ALL USED UP.

LITTLE BIT OF CODEINE N A FEW LINES.

I PULL THE QUILT OFF OF THE BED N WRAP IT ROUND MY SHOULDERS.

BETTER, BUT NO MUCH.

I FLICK THE LIGHTER N INHALE DEEPLY OF THE THICK WHITE SMOKE,

HOLDING I BREATH UNTIL I NEARLY BURST.

I EXHALE N CHASE ANOTHER LINE.

NO WHERE NEAR THE AMOUNT OF METHADONE I AM USING, BUT SLOWLY WARMTH RISES THROUGH I BONES.

THAT IS ENOUGH.

NO MORE.

GOT TO MAKE IT LAST.

I ROLL OVER ON MY SIDE ON THE BED STILL WRAPPED IN THE QUILT N SLOWLY FEEL THE MUSCLE TENSIONS EASE.

HOW LONG CAN I TAKE THIS, I PONDER?

DYING, USING TO DIE, DYING TO USE.

I TAKE A DEEP DRAG UPON MY ROLL UP SIGH N EXHALE AT THE CEILING.

I DRIFT OFF FITFULLY DREAMING OF ARGUING WITH PEOPLE OVER GEAR N MONEY.

A FEW HOURS PASS N I AWAKE TO A SOAKED N SCREAMING BODY.

SELF-EXAMINATION ONLY MAKES THE EXPERIENCE WORSE.

I QUESTION WHAT I AM FEELING.

I FOCUS ON MY BODY, N WHAT I FOCUS ON HURTS.

INTENSE EXPLORATION, PAIN, TOO MUCH INPUT.

WOW! HEAVY WAVES OF THE BEAST OF CRAVING NOW.

THERE I GO.

FOCUS ON IT N, BANG! THE PAIN GOES TO MY HEAD N STARTS A FIRE BURNING.

DO YOU REMEMBER, WHEN IT ALL COMES ALL AROUND AGAIN?

WOW MY ARMS HURT.

WELL OF COURSE THEY DO.

I THINK OF THEM.

ALL MY SKIN DAMP WET COLD N BURNING.

I HURT.

EVEN TO TOUCH A SMOOTH SURFACE BRINGS PAIN.

I LIE THERE N TRY TO FOCUS ON NOTHING.

IT WORKS A LITTLE.

REACHING FOR THE BEDSIDE TABLE I GRAB MY ROLL UP, LIGHT IT.

THE SMOKE TRICKLES UP MY RIGHT NOSTRIL N I BEGIN TO SNEEZE.

MY WORLD EXPLODES IN AN AURA OF DISTORTED RED GREEN N BLACK TRIANGLES.

THE SNEEZING CAUSING STARS TO EXPLODE WITHIN MY HEAD.

BODY DAMP N SHAKING, I WRAP I DRESSING GOWN AROUND MY SHOULDERS N WALL WALK TO THE BATHROOM.

I SIT UPON THE LOO TO CATCH MY BREATH.

WOW! IM COLD, BUT STILL NOT COMPLETELY WITHDRAWN.

THE CODEINE N LINES MUST HAVE HELPED.

NOSE DRIBBLING, I CRAWL OVER TO THE BATH N TURN ON THE HOT TAP.

THIS IS THE ONLY WAY I AM GOING TO GET WARM ENOUGH TO FEED MYSELF.

I DRAG MYSELF UP FROM THE COLD BATHROOM FLOOR N GO TURN THE CENTRAL HEATING UP TO FULL.

I AM NOW ACHING IN THE BACK, GROIN OUTWARDS.

I NEED A REAL FIRE IF I REALLY WISH TO STAY WARM KICKING A JONES.

RADIATORS JUST NO CUT IT.

YOU CAN WRAP YOURSELF IN A QUILT N SIT ON THE DAMN THINGS N ALL YOU GET IS BURNS FOR ONES TROUBLE.

THE WATER IN THE BATHROOM BECKONS NOISILY N I LOWER MY WEARY BODY INTO THE WARM WATER.

THE TAP OF THE KEYS ANNOYS TO THE POINT OF WANTING TO SMASH THE COMPUTER, BUT THAT IS ILLOGICAL.

I AM ONLY IN PAIN.

MENTAL N PHYSICAL.

I HAVE NOTICED THE WITHDRAWAL HAS CHANGED FROM THE METHADONE WITHDRAWAL.

COLD N FREEZING YES,

ALL BODY FLUSHING N SWEATING, COLD.

BUT LESS PAIN.

MORE PAIN IN MY PSYCHE, COLD TWISTED PAIN THAT JUST SITS N TWISTS I MUSCLES INSTEAD OF FINDING RELEASE.

EAT.

I MUST EAT.

WARM FOOD.

I LIE IN THE WARM SUDS OF MY BATH PONDERING THIS THOUGHT.

THE KITCHEN WILL BE FREEZING.

THE GARDEN EVEN COLDER.

HAVING NO ROOM IN MY LITTLE ROOM FOR A LARGE FRIDGE FREEZER, RUN ELECTRICAL CABLE DOWN THE BACK YARD TO THE DIS-USED OUTHOUSE TOILET,

N THEN PLUG THE REFRIGERATOR IN OUT THERE.

THE ONLY PROBLEM BEING IT IS LIKE HIKING THROUGH A WET N MISERABLY COLD MINI JUNGLE OUT THERE N THERE IS NO WAY THAT I WISH TO GET COLD.

THE SPASMS OF SUCH SHIVERS WILL MAKE ME ACHE ALL DAY.

I LAY IN MY BATH, WAIT FOR THE HEATING TO CLEAR SOME OF THE COLD FROM THE ROOMS,

THEN GRABBING PURPLE FLOWERED BATH TOWEL N DRESSING GOWN N SLIPPERS, I JUMP FROM MY BATH N RUN TO THE KITCHEN TO LIGHT THE GAS STOVE.

PLACING A PAN ATOP THE STOVE WITH WATER TO BOIL I RUN N JUMP BACK IN MY BATH.

COLD YES, BUT NOT TOO BAD.

STAY FOCUSED ON OTHER THINGS NOT THE BODY.

GOOD MEDICINE.

NOW I HAVE TO BRAVE THE GARDEN.

I TURN THE HOT TAP ON FULL N LIE BACK IN MY BATH, THE HOT WATER SLOWLY FILLING TO OVER FLOW UPON THE FLOOR.

THAT IS BETTER, I AM NOW PINK ALL OVER N THE BATHROOM IS DRIPPING CONDENSATION FROM THE WALLS WITH STEAM.

I GRAB MY TOWEL N DRESSING GOWN N JUMP INTO THE HALL.

PLACING MY CAMOUFLAGE JACKET OVER MY HEAD N SHOULDERS I DIVE BRISKLY OUT THE BACK DOOR TO THE OUTHOUSE TOILET.

GRABBING MILK BREAD N EGGS I RUN AS FAST AS ... TRIPPING OVER MY SLIPPERS ... WILL ALLOW N ARRIVE BACK IN MY KITCHEN SHAKING, N OUT OF BREATH.

SHIT!

THE LAST TIME I FELT LIKE THIS IS WHEN I HAD TO JUMP INTO A HOLE CUT IN THE ICE ON A LAKE IN REYKJAVIK, ICELAND, WHEN I WAS DOING A SURVIVAL COURSE THERE.

THAT TIME I JUMPED IN N I SWEAR I PASSED OUT MOMENTARILY, THE WATER SO SHOCKING THAT I SWALLOWED A MOUTH FULL N COULD NO BREATHE PROPERLY TO SWIM.

SUFFICE TO SAY I WAS HAULED OUT BODILY, ROLLED IN SNOW N STRIPPED NAKED N THEN RUN NEARLY A QUARTER OF A KILOMETRE IN THE SNOW BEFORE BEING THROWN IN A WARM SHOWER.

THE WATER WAS ACTUALLY COLD, BUT BECAUSE I WAS SO FROZEN IT FELT QUITE WARM TO ME...

THESE TWO GUYS WERE SCREAMING AT ME ALL THE TIME.

COME ON!

COME ON!

ROLL IN THE SNOW,

RUN!

ALL I WANTED WAS FOR ALL THE PAIN TO STOP RIGHT THEN.

I WANTED TO BE IN THE WARM SHOWER NOT OUT NAKED IN THE SNOW.

THEIR VOICES SEEMED VERY DISTANT TO ME IN THAT SPACE AS I RAN, STUMBLED N FELL IN THE SNOW.

I JUMP ONCE MORE FROM MY BATH SPILLING WATER ON THE FLOOR N RUN TO THE BEDROOM FOR BACCY.

RETURNING TO THE BATHROOM I PULL THE PLUG N SIT ON THE LOO SEAT DRAPED IN SODDEN TOWELS.

KNOWING THE WARMTH GAINED FROM THE BATH WILL NO LAST LONG, I SMOKE A ROLL-UP N AS BRISKLY AS POSSIBLE DRY MYSELF N DRESS IN JEANS N TWO JUMPERS SOCKS N A BLACK WOOLLEN BENNY HAT.

WARM NOW, I MAKE MY WAY TO THE KITCHEN, OPEN THE WINDOW TO LET OUT ALL THE STEAM N PREPARE MYSELF SCRAMBLED EGGS ON TOAST N A LARGE MUG OF VERY STRONG MATE TEA.

RETIRING WITH THE SAID TEA, BACK TO BED FULLY CLOTHED.

MY BRAIN IS FRYING, NOT ADRENALINE, COURSING THROUGH MY BRAIN, TELLING MY BODY IT HURTS.

I LEAN ON THE SIDE OF THE BED N PLACE MY MUG OF TEA ON THE BEDSIDE TABLE, MISS N IT FALLS BANG SMACK ON THE TOP OF MY RIGHT BIG TOE.

WITHDRAWAL NOW COMPLETELY FORGOT FOR THAT MOMENT AS REAL PAIN FLOODS TO MY HEAD.

I CURSE N GRAB MY FOOT N ROLL ONTO THE BED.

"AH!" I GROAN.

"NOW I HAVE TO GET COLD AGAIN N MAKE MORE TEA."

LIFE IS LIKE THIS WHEN YOU GOT A JONES, CLUMSY WHEN STONED N TWISTED N TIGHT OF MOVEMENT WHEN SICK.

IT ALL ADDS TO DISASTER IN THE END.

I MAKE A SECOND CUP OF MATE TEA N RETIRE MUNCHING ON A SCRAMBLED EGG SANDWICH N RETURN BACK TO BED.

SLEEP FITFULLY.

UP CONFUSED. WHY IS IT WHEN YOU HAVE A JONES UNDER CONTROL, THE WORLD EXPLODES AROUND YOU LIKE SOME LUNATIC CATHERINE WHEEL FIREWORK.

CRACKLING N SPITTING AT ME...

HANDS ON HEAD WALKING IN CIRCLES.

WOW! I NEED SOME VALIUM.

I AMBLE TO THE KITCHEN N RUMMAGE IN A DRAWER, FINDING A POT WITH STILL THREE BLUES WITHIN. I FIND ONE N DRINK SOME ORANGE JUICE.

WEED.

GOOD FEELING.

I LOAD MY BONG N INHALE DEEPLY.

SLOWLY EXHALING, MY BODY BEGINS TO THUMP RHYTHMICALLY WITH MY HEART N I FEEL THE FIRST TENDRIL LIKE FINGERS OF THE DOPE HITTING ME.

WOW..

I MUST RELAX.

MY HEAD HURTS REALLY BAD.

THE COMBINATION OF VALIUM N WEED ONLY COMMENCE TO CONFUSE ME EVEN MORE N CREATE MORE CHAOS.

DOOR!

PHONE!

BANK!

DOOR, PHONE.

NO ONE AT DOOR WHEN I ANSWER IT.

SOMEONE IS FUCKING WITH ME!

AH SHIT! THAT IS FUNNY.

I AM PLAYING WITH MYSELF.

SLOW DOWN.

AH! THAT IS BETTER.

SMOKE SOME "H" MAN, SLOW DOWN.

I TELL MYSELF.

NOT FOR THE PLEASURE OF DOING IT MIND, BUT JUST SO I CAN OPERATE, JUST SLOW DOWN.

OFF TO THE BEDROOM FOR A TOOT.

I SMOKE APPROXIMATELY 7.5MG OF VERY FINE GREY BROWN "H" FROM IRAN.

SOME STREET GEAR A FRIEND HAD ACQUIRED FOR ME WHILST ON ACTIVE DUTY.

RUNNING THE SAID IN THREE LINES, INHALING DEEPLY

THE SMOKE WARMING ME ALMOST INSTANTLY.

"PHEW, THIS IS HARD WORK."

I LIE BACK ON THE BED N DRIFT OFF FOR A WHILE.

AWAKING TO THE SOUND OF THE POSTMAN KNOCKING ON THE DOOR.

I DRAG MYSELF OFF OF THE BED N GO OPEN THE FRONT DOOR TO BE GREETED BY THE ICY TEETH OF DRIVING SLEET N SNOW.

THE POSTMAN SO WRAPPED UP IN ORANGE WEATHER GEAR SO AS NOT TO BE REALLY RECOGNISABLE UNDER HIS HAT N HOOD.

"SIGN N PRINT HERE," HE MUMBLES IN BROKEN ENGLISH WITH A VERY DISTORTED CHINESE ACCENT.

I FUMBLE WITH THE PEN TRYING TO KEEP THE WIND N SNOW OUT OF MY HOUSE N SIGN HIS LITTLE PIECE OF PAPER.

HE HANDS ME A BOX N TURNS SWIFTLY; LEAVING MY GARDEN GATE OPEN I MIGHT ADD, N SWIFTLY DISAPPEARS AFTER WALKING ONLY TEN YARDS INTO THE HOWLING BLIZZARD.

HOP SKIP N BY JIGGERDY, ITS FREEZING OUT THERE.

I THINK OF ARCTIC EXPLORERS N HOW THEY MANAGE IN SUB MINUS TEMPERATURES, THE BOX WARM N BROWN IN MY HANDS.

I TURN N SHUT THE DOOR FIRMLY N SCREAM AT MY TWO DOGS TO BE QUIET.

THEY PICK UP TERRIBLY ON THE STRESS YOU GO THROUGH, USING N TRYING NOT TO USE.

BEING SICK ALL THE TIME MAKES ONES FUSE VERY SHORT.

THE DOGS BECOME EASY TARGETS WHEN THINGS GO WRONG.

STILL I AM BLESSED, I DEARLY LOVE DOGS N THEY LOVE ME.....

I HAVE BEEN STUDYING WAYS N MEANS OF TRYING TO GET HEALING OF ANY KIND FOR THIS ADDICTION. HOSPITALS, INSTITUTIONS, AGENCIES, THE LIKES, I HAVE TRIED THEM ALL.

IT WAS TIME TO TURN TO OLDER MORE TRADITIONAL METHODS OF TRYING TO GET A HANDLE ON MY PROBLEMS.

I START TO READ ABOUT HEALING PLANTS LIKE AYAHUASCA, A SERIOUS CONCOCTION OF BETA-CARBOLINES N PLANTS AS ADD MIXTURES CONTAINING ALKALOIDS THE LIKES OF NN DMT, 5MEO DMT N BUFOTENINE.

I THEN FIND A REFERENCE IN A GLOSSY MAGAZINE OF "THE TREE OF LIFE" THAT WILL STEP ON MAD MONGOLIAN EYES. THE REFERENCE WAS TO A POTION USED BY MONKS TO HELP CURE OPIUM ADDICTION, BUT THERE WAS NO REFERENCE TO THE HERBS USED.

SO I CHOOSE AYAHUASCA.

I KNEW A CHAP ABOUT 4 MILES FROM WHERE I LIVE THAT HAS EXPERIENCE OF THE SAID BREW N IS WILLING TO BREW ME SOME IF I GET THE VINE N THE OTHER HERBS REQUIRED.

I HAVE EVEN TASTED THE BREW A FEW TIMES, BITTER N EARTHY, BUT NEVER PARTOOK OF ENOUGH TO POSSIBLY HELP WITH THE WITHDRAWAL SYNDROME OF METHADONE N OPIATES METH-AMPHETAMINE VALIUM N MANY OTHER SMARTIES N ALCOHOL.

I READ THAT IT CAN WORK THOUGH.

I ORDER THE HERBS ONLINE N THESE HAVE JUST ARRIVED IN THE BOX IN THE POST.

IT IS SPACE TO SEE JOSÉ.

I DON THREE T-SHIRTS N TWO QUILTED LUMBER-JACK SHIRTS, I COMBO JACKET BOOTS N HAT.

UP MY HOOD, STICK MY TWO JACK RUSSEL DOGS ON THEIR LEADS N FALL OUT OF THE FRONT DOOR.

THE WIND N SNOW IS BLINDING.

MY DOGS EVEN HESITATE TO WANDER IN THE STORM.

I WONDER IF THIS IS AN OMEN OF THINGS TO COME.

I BEND MY HEAD INTO THE ICY TEETH OF THE WIND N SLEET N HEAD ACROSS THE FIELDS AT THE BACK OF MY HOUSE TOWARDS THE OLD SIDE OF THE RAILWAY YARDS.

ICICLES STAND ALMOST HORIZONTAL, STREAMING FROM A CHAIN LINK FENCE MAKE AN EERIE PING NOISE AS I BREAK THEM OFF BRUSHING BY.

MY DOGS LITTLE LEGS ALMOST COMPLETELY DISAPPEAR IN THE SNOW UNDER FOOT.

I TRUDGE ON THROUGH THE WHITE VEIL OF SNOW WITH FACE N BODY FROZEN N WET.

JOSÉ IS A NOMAD KIND OF TRAVELLER, LIVING IN BENDERS N TRAILER VANS WHERE HE CAN.

THIS TIME OF YEAR HE IS ALWAYS AT THE RAILWAY YARD.

HE COULD GET COAL FROM THE YARD TO FILL HIS CAST IRON WOOD BURNER N ALSO SLEEP IN AN OLD CARRIAGE OUT OF THE WORST OF THE WEATHER.

WE USED TO GO ON EXPEDITIONS TOGETHER TO THE CITY AT NIGHT TIME, EARLY EVENING, N RAID THE DUST BINS OUT THE BACK OF SUPERMARKETS.

THEY THROWING THE OUT OF DATE PRODUCTS OUT IN BLACK PLASTIC BIN BAGS AT THE END OF THE DAY.

THIS IS WHERE I FIRST MET HIM.

HE OFFERING TO JUMP IN THE SKIP N PASS FOOD OUT SO WE COULD BOTH INSPECT N TAKE THE HEALTHY LOOKING GOODS.

HE IS AN ARTIST, TRAVELLER TATTOOIST WITH MARKINGS ON HIS BROWN WITHERED CHEEKS N A LONG BROWN PONY TAIL.

HE HAS VERY INTIMIDATING EYES.

SMALL, BRIGHT BLUE N PIERCING.

HE TELLS OF TALES OF TRAVELS IN SOUTH AMERICA N MEXICO WHERE HE MET N LOST HIS WIFE TO TYPHOID.

I TRAMP FOR WHAT SEEMS LIKE AN ETERNITY.

SNOW STICKING TO MY FACE N GLASSES, COATING MY JEANS JACKET IN POWDER WHITE THAT MY BODY HEAT IS BEGINNING TO MELT.

THE COLD IS BITING.

I STUMBLE OVER MY OWN STEPS ONLY FORWARD BECAUSE MY DOGS PULL ME ALONG A PATH I CAN NO SEE.

BY THE TIME I REACH THE TOP OF THE HILL OVERLOOKING THE OLD RAILWAY YARD WITH THREE RED BLACK FURNACE CHIMNEYS SILHOUETTED AGAINST THE EVENING SKY. I AM SOAKED TO THE SKIN N SHAKING BADLY.

I TUMBLE DOWN THE HILLSIDE N INTO THE SIDE OF A LARGE CREAM N BROWN RED PASSENGER CARRIAGE.

THERE IS A LOW LIGHT SHINING THROUGH A WOOD BOARD PLACED OVER A BROKEN WINDOW IN THE GUARD SECTION OF THE CARRIAGE.

JOSÉ IS HOME.

I KICK MY BOOTS AGAINST THE SIDE OF THE CARRIAGE SENDING COAL BLACKENED SNOW ALL OVER THE SIDING N HEAR HIS DOG BARK ANGRILY AT THE WINDOW.

"QUIET."

"WHOS THAT?" HE RETORTS STRAIGHT AFTER QUIETING THE DOG.

"IT IS ONLY I," I SAY AS HE SEES I THROUGH THE OPENING DOOR.

"WOW BRO, GET IN HERE BEFORE YOU DIE," HE EXCLAIMS N HEAVES THE TWISTED CREAKING DOOR UPON RUSTY HINGES.

SENDING A SHRILL PIERCE SCREAM THROUGH THE EVENING STORM.

I WINCE INWARDLY AT THE NOISE

"YOU ALRIGHT?" JOSÉ ASKS.

"YES, CLUCKING."

I CLIMB INTO THE GUARD SECTION OF THE CARRIAGE N SURVEY A MOST HOMELY BUT CRAZY SITE.

THE WHOLE CARRIAGE IS FURNISHED WITH NEWSPAPERS, STACKED INTO CHAIRS N WALLS, INSULATING THE CARRIAGE FROM MOST OF THE COLD.

IN THE MIDDLE OF THE CARRIAGE STANDS A BLACK IRON POT BELLY STOVE, N HAS LION SHAPED FEET SPREAD OUTWARDS AT ALL FOURS TO STAND UPON WHAT I CAN ONLY DESCRIBE AS A MAGIC CARPET.

THE CARPET IS WORN, BUT OF VERY FINE DESIGN OF REDS N BROWN SCROLLS OF BAROQUE DESIGNS.

I GAZE AT THE PATTERNS IN THE WEAVE N THEY SEEM TO COME ALIVE, MOVE ABOUT N REALIGN.

I AM VERY TIRED.

I TIE MY DOGS TO THE ONLY WOODEN CHAIR IN THE CARRIAGE, HAND JOSÉ THE BOX OF HERBS N SAG ONTO THE FLOOR IN FRONT OF THE POT BELLY STOVE.

OPENING THE DOOR I PLACED MORE WOOD INSIDE N KNOCKED IT ABOUT A LITTLE WITH A SPRING COIL HANDLED FIRE POKER UNTIL IT LIGHTS.

THE WARM GLOW OF THE FLAMES HYPNOTISING ME N LULLING ME TO FALL ASLEEP.

I DRIFT ABOUT IN DREAMS OF WALKING ENDLESSLY LOST IN THE SNOW WHEN JOSÉ NUDGES ME TO WAKE UP.

"HERE DRINK THIS."

"HOT MATE N MUSHROOMS."

"THANKS BRO." I SNIFF AT A WET DRIBBLING NOSE, GRAB THE BATTERED WHITE BLUE RIMMED ENAMEL MUG N HOLD IT IN BOTH HANDS TO MY LIPS.

THE STRONG EARTHY BREW SLIDES DOWN EASY WARMING N CALMING, SHATTERED NERVES N POUNDING BODY..

"ARE THE HERBS OK?" I ASK AS I GULP DOWN MORE.

"NICE VINE MAN, NO KNOW ABOUT THE LEAF THOUGH."

"SO HOW WE GOING TO TELL THEN?"

"MAKE IT."

HE LEAVES ME PONDERING THIS THOUGHT N WANDERS OFF TO THE OTHER END OF THE CARRIAGE BANGING N CLATTERING, LOOKING FOR A POT N LID.

"YOU HAVE TO BUST ALL THAT VINE UP REAL GOOD."

"HERE USE THESE."

HE HANDS ME A PAIR OF RED HANDLED ROSE CLIPPERS N A HEAVY WHITE PLASTIC BAG.

"CUT IT UP SMALL N STICK IT IN THERE, ILL GO N GET SOME WATER."

THE VINE I HOLD IN MY HAND IS KIND OF BIG.
THE BARK SCRAPED OFF N IT IS BROWN RED.
IT HAS A DEEP DUSTY LINES ALONG ITS SIDES N THE END LOOKED LIKE SOME SPONGE I WOULD IMAGINE.
THE INSIDE LOOKED KIND OF POURRIS.
I SIT CROSSED LEGGED IN FRONT OF THE LITTLE STOVE N BEGIN TO CUT N BREAK THE VINE.

JOSÉ PULLS OUT AN ORANGE FOUR POUND LUMP HAMMER N A SHEET OF STEEL N STARTS TO POUND THE LITTLE CUTTINGS UNTIL THEY ARE FIBROUS N DUSTY.
HE SCOOPS UP ALL THE DUST N WOOD FIBRES N PLACES THEM IN THE IRON POT, EMPTYING THE CARRIER BAG N POURS IN SOME WATER.
PUTS THE LID ON THE POT N PLACES THE PAN ON THE STOVE TO BOIL.

"MAN, I LOVE YOUR TEA," I SAY WITH A BIG GRIN ON MY FACE.
"SWEET," JOSÉ REPLIES.
THE MUSHROOMS WERE NOW BEGINNING TO WORK THEIR MAGIC N BRING ME DOWN FROM MY SHIVERING PSYCHOTIC STATE.

I LOOK AROUND N SURVEY JOSÉS LITTLE HOME.

ALL THE PILES OF NEWSPAPERS ARE COVERED IN COLOURED BLANKETS, REDS, YELLOWS N BLUES.

A TABLE HAS BEEN FASHIONED OUT OF A BIG PILE OF THEM ATOP WHICH IS PLACED A SHATTERED TV.

ATOP OF WHICH STANDS A CANDLE ON A SAUCER.

TWO MORE CANDLES LIGHT THE CEILING AREA BY BEING HUNG IN JAM JARS FROM WASHING LINE COPPER WIRES THAT ALLOW FOR THE JARS TO BE SLID ALONG N MOVED.

A BED HAS BEEN FASHIONED ALSO OUT OF PAPERS N IS COVERED IN A VERY THICK BRIGHT BLUE QUILT COVER.

DUCK FEATHERS SCATTERED THE FLOOR N FLOATED IN THE AIR FROM HOLES WITHIN THE QUILT.

I SIT N WATCH A FEATHER FLOAT LAZILY BY N MY THOUGHTS DRIFT OFF WITH ITS MOVEMENT.

COLOURS OF BLUES N SUBTLE ORANGES N REDS BEGIN TO TWINKLE AT THE EDGE OF MY VISION.

MY BODY SLOWLY MELTING INTO THE RUG I SIT UPON, I SEE WISPS OF SILK RED N GOLD HANGING AS IF IN THE AIR. EVERYTHING LOOKS ALIVE N IS SHIMMERING WITH ELECTRIC LIGHT.

NOW FLASH STROBES FLY ACROSS MY EYES N I CLOSE THEM TO SEE INTRICATE DELICATELY DRAWN FLOWERS OF MAUVE N BLUES FLOWING IN THE WIND. SPIRALLING N CHANGING FORM AS I LOOK.

LIKE A KALEIDOSCOPE FOR ONLY MY MINDS EYE TO SEE.

PATTERNS FLOAT ABOUT WITHOUT REAL FORM.

I GAZE AT THEM BLANKLY N THEY DISAPPEAR ONLY TO BE REPLACED BY WAVES OF SEAWEED N PATTERNS ON THE CARPET IN FRONT OF ME.

THE FLOOR BEGINS TO TAKE ON LIFE, THE CARPETS DESIGN GROWING N MOVING ON ITS OWN GENERATING AN ENERGY THAT SEEMS TO MAKE EVERYTHING VIBRATE SLIGHTLY.

OH, THIS IS BETTER I NOW FEEL PEACEFUL.

I GAZE AT A LITTLE CLOCK ON TOP OF A BOX TO THE SIDE OF THE BURNER.

MICKEY MOUSE HANDS, THEY START TO GO BACKWARDS.

LOOKING INTENTLY, I CAN STOP THEM N MAKE THEM GO THE PROPER WAY.

"NICE CLOCK EH?" SAYS JOSÉ MAKING ME JUMP AS IF I HAD BEEN MILES AWAY DREAMING.

"UH YES, I LIKE IT.

I AM JUST PLAYING WITH IT"

"I KNOW," HE SAYS WITH A BIG GRIN ON HIS FACE.

HE REACHES INTO HIS LEFT TOP POCKET N BRINGS FORTH A GOLD COLOURED COIN.

"FOUND THIS THE OTHER DAY," HE SAYS.

"WHAT YOU THINK?"

HE LEANS FORWARD SLIGHTLY TO HAND ME THE COIN N DROPS IT TUMBLING TO THE CARPET.

I TURN N PICK IT UP BUT CANNOT TOUCH THE COIN IT HAS NO SUBSTANCE.

I LOOK AT HIM THEN BACK TO THE COIN N IT IS GONE.

"ER WOW!" I EXCLAIM.

NOW JOSÉ BEGINS TO DO A LITTLE GIG N JUMP AROUND SWINGING HIS HAIR HIGH IN THE AIR.

"CATCH," HE SHOUTS.

N FLICKS THE COIN HIGH IN THE AIR TOWARDS ME...

THE COIN SPINS LAZILY THROUGH THE AIR AS IF TIME HAS BEEN SLOWED DOWN N I REACH TO CATCH THE COIN.

I MISS COMPLETELY N THE COIN VANISHES IN MID AIR.

I TURN N SEE THE COIN INSTANTLY APPEAR OUT OF NOWHERE IN JOSÉS HAND.

"HOW THE HELL DID YOU DO THAT?" I RETORT.

"GOOD EH!" HE SMILES N PUTS THE COIN BACK IN HIS POCKET.

"WOULD YOU LIKE SOME MORE TEA?"

NOW I AM SEEING A SIDE TO THIS MAN I HAVE NEVER SEEN BEFORE.

HE IS ANIMATED WITH ALL BODY MOVEMENTS FLOWING.

"PLEASE," I MUMBLE.

HE GLIDES ACROSS THE CARPET EFFORTLESSLY N COLLECTS A LITTLE BLUE N YELLOW TOPPED TEA POT FROM THE BACK OF THE STOVE N POURS ME MORE TEA.

"HOWS YOUR LEGS NOW AFTER THE TEA?"

VERY ASTUTE OF HIM I FEEL.

I HAVE NO REALLY LOOKED TO MY BODY N HOW I AM FEELING SINCE ENTERING INTO HIS WORLD.

MY LEGS FEEL GOOD, NO PAIN N I AM EXTREMELY WARM N FUZZY OF FEELING.

"I AM GOOD," I SAY.

"THE MUSHROOMS KILL THE PAIN."

"YES THEY ARE GOOD FOR THAT AMONGST OTHER THINGS."

WE SIT SILENTLY THEN N DRINK SOME MORE TEA SMOKING DANK ROLL UPS.

"YOULL DO IT BRO," HE SAYS SUDDENLY AS IF HE HAD BEEN DEBATING SOMETHING VERY DEEP.

"DO WHAT?" I SAY.

"BEAT THIS FUCKIN BITCH BEAST YOU ARE WRESTLING WITH, THAT IS WHAT," HE RETORTS...

HE SEEMS SLIGHTLY ANGRY AT MY NOT COMPREHENDING AT FIRST, WHAT HE SAYS...

"YOU WILL LEARN TO LEAN ON THE LIANA.
LIANA IS THE LADY OF THE VINE.
SHE WILL BRING TO YOU HEALING N GREAT WISDOMS OF LIFE DEATH N ALL THE PLANTS.
THROUGH LIANAS TEACHINGS YOU WILL BE ABLE TO COMMUNICATE WITH ALL PLANTS N ALSO LEARN IN THE USE OF THOSE PLANTS TO SPEAK WITH SPIRIT ANIMAL N ALL LIFE."

I AM STUNNED HE IS CHANGED COMPLETELY.
STILL RESPECTFUL BUT NOW DEADLY SERIOUS.

"HOW DO I SPEAK WITH LIANA?" I SAY HESITANTLY.

"YOU MAKE TEA LIKE WE ARE HAVING N THEN DRINK HER, ADD OTHER PLANTS, KIND OF BRING THEM ALONG TO THE PARTY.
LIANA WILL BRING ORDER N DIRECTION N STRENGTH TO YOUR JOURNEYS.
ALWAYS LEAN ON THE LIANA.

SHE WILL BRING YOU SHADE ALSO.
WE NEED TO ADD THE LEAF NOW
GET THE BOX."

I REACH OVER INTO THE BOX N HAND HIM A BIG BAG OF BROWN BLACK GREEN LEAVES.

"HERE TAKE A HANDFUL N HOLD THEM IN YOUR RIGHT HAND N BREATH ON THEM, CRUSH THEM N PUT THEM IN THE POT.

NOW THE LEFT HAND N BREATHE ON THEM.

SPEAK YOUR INTENTIONS AS YOU DO IT."

"WHAT SHOULD I SAY?"

"IT IS UP TO YOU MY FRIEND, YOU WISH TO FIND THE STRENGTH TO KILL THE BEAST, ASK!"

SO I DO WHAT HE SAYS N TAKE THE LEAVES N CRUSH THEM INTO THE POT, BREATHING ON THEM, N SAY ALOUD,

"I ASK OF THESE PLANTS TO GIVE ME THE STRENGTH TO KILL THIS BEAST I STRUGGLE WITH."

"NICE ONE, NOW WE LET HER COOK UNTIL TOMORROW."

"YOU BETTER GO N GET SOME SLEEP. ONLY EAT RICE N PLENTY OF WATER."

"WOW YES, CHEERS BRO!" I EXCLAIMED, REALISING I HAD YET TO TRUDGE HOME IN ALL THIS AWFUL WEATHER.

MY DOGS ARE CURLED UP SOUND ASLEEP N VERY WARM BY THE SIDE OF THE STOVE.

THEY ARE GOING TO LOVE ME.

THE FOLLOWING MORNING I ARISE TO BE GREETED BY THE SIGHT OF MY OWN BREATH PLUMING ABOVE THE COVERS.

THE GAS HAS RUN OUT OVERNIGHT.

I NO DOUBT FORGETTING TO TURN IT OFF WHILST I AM OUT.

I NO FEEL TOO BAD.

THE SUN IS SHINING SILVER GOLD ON THE HORIZON N EVERYTHING OUTSIDE IS WHITE N FROZEN.

THE SNOW HAS STOPPED.

I NO REQUIRE ANY GEAR JUST YET.

I AM STILL WITHDRAWN BUT COMFORTABLE.

JOSÉ MAKES GOOD MEDICINE, I SMILE ROLLING A BIG SPLIFF BEFORE BREAKFAST.

SMILING I GO DOWN THE GARDEN TO COLLECT BACON, EGGS, TOMATOES N CHEESE N REALISE I HAVE NO GAS.

I THEN REMEMBER JOSÉ HAD TOLD ME TO ONLY EAT RICE N PLENTY OF WATER.

SO RETURNING TO THE HOUSE I GET DRESSED, GO GET THE GAS N BY CHANCE MEET JOSÉ AT THE SHOP.

"HERE," HE SAYS HANDING ME A VODKA BOTTLE HALF FULL OF A GOLDEN BROWN LIQUID.

"THERE IS YOUR TEA. NO EAT ANYTHING FOR AT LEAST FOUR HOURS BEFORE YOU DRINK IT.

DRINK HALF OF IT N WAIT AN HOUR,

IF NOTHING HAPPENS DRINK THE REST,

I TASTED IT N IT TASTES GOOD TO ME.

STILL DON'T KNOW ABOUT THEM LEAVES THOUGH, YOU WILL SEE."

"WOW THANK YOU BRO, HOW DID YOU KNOW I WOULD BE HERE?" I MUMBLE.

HE SMILES N JUST SAYS, "BUSY, MAN, GOT TO GO."

"DRINK THE TEA. SEE YOU LATER."

HE UNTIES HIS DOG FROM THE BICYCLE RACK N WALKS OFF TOWARDS THE TOWN.

WAVING BEHIND HIM AS HE GOES.

OK I HAVE GOT MY TEA BUT I AM NOT FEELING TOO BAD AT THE MOMENT SO I SHUFFLE HOME OVER ICY PAVEMENTS TO FIND SOME WHERE WARM TO SIT.

IT IS NEARLY DARK N I AM IN PAIN.

I HAVE BEEN LYING IN BED DRIFTING WITH MY THOUGHTS, FLOATING IN A WARM VOID WHEN I AWAKE COMPLETELY TO FIND MYSELF ONCE AGAIN SWEATING N ICY COLD.

I HAVE TO TRY THIS TEA.

I GRAB A TOWEL FROM THE FOOT OF MY BED N PROCEED TO DRY MYSELF WITH IT. WHILST CHANGING I SWEAT SOAKED CLOTHES.

G.O.D.. I PRAY THIS HELPS.

I TAKE THE BOTTLE N UNSCREW THE TOP GIVING IT A SNIFF.

NO MUCH THERE SO I POUR HALF OF THE GOLDEN BROWN LIQUID OUT OF THE BOTTLE N RETURN THE TOP.

I SIP THE BREW HESITANTLY.

IT TASTES EARTHY N QUITE BITTER.

I TRY TO DRINK SOME N IT MAKES ME GAG.

SO I SPLIT THE GLASS INTO TWO N TAKING A DEEP BREATH, I DOWN IT ALL IN ONE.

NOT SO BAD, NO GAG THIS TIME.

WOW, BITTER!

ERR!

NEED A ROLL UP!

I GO TO THE LIVING ROOM N ROLL MYSELF A ROLL UP LOWERING MYSELF INTO MY FAVOURITE CHAIR.

SMOKING IT SLOWLY AWAITING ANY SIGNS THAT THINGS MIGHT BE HAPPENING.

I SIT N SMOKE.

I WATCH THE CLOCK.

FORTY MINUTES N NOTHING.

I GET UP QUICKLY N GO TO THE KITCHEN

IS THIS DUD, IS IT GOING TO DO ANYTHING FOR ME.

MY LEGS ARE REALLY HURTING BY NOW N I FEEL NO DIFFERENCE WHATSOEVER.

SO I TAKE THE BOTTLE N POUR SOME OF THE GOLDEN TEA ON TOP OF WHAT I HAVE IN THE GLASS ALREADY N DOWN IT IN TWO GULPS.

I NEARLY THROW IT UP.

THE LIANA, TEA DRIBBLING DOWN THE BACK OF MY NOSE N BURNING MY THROAT.

BESIDES THE DRY BITTER TASTE THERE IS A STRANGE SMELL IN THE AIR LIKE OLD BURNT PLASTIC BUT SWEETER SOMEHOW LIKE JASMINE.

THE BITTER TASTE SLOWLY TURNING WOODY, EARTHY.

MY BODY BEGINS TO VIBRATE SLIGHTLY N A NUMBNESS SLOWLY CREEPS ACROSS ME...

I FEEL I SHOULD LIE DOWN.

I ROLL WITH A KIND OF MOTION SICKNESS TOWARDS MY BEDROOM, BEGINNING TO FEEL VERY SICK.

I RUN FOR THE BATHROOM N VOMIT BROWN TEA DOWN THE LOO.

I BEGIN TO SHAKE N BEADS OF SWEAT FORM UPON MY SKIN.

I VOMIT AGAIN N HANG THERE, KIND OF DEAD OVER THE TOILET GASPING FOR BREATH.

MY WORLD AS I KNOW IT BEGINS TO COLLAPSE BEFORE MY VERY EYES.

I FEEL SUDDENLY AS IF I HAVE BECOME VERY SMALL N EVERYTHING ELSE IS INCREDIBLY HUGE.

THE TILES ON MY BATHROOM FLOOR SEEM TO BE LIKE HUGE GREAT LANDING PLATFORMS ON SOME GIANT AIRBASE SOMEWHERE.

THE CORNERS JAGGED N ELONGATED SO AS TO SEEM STRETCHED.

MY WORLD EXPANDS.

SOUND SEEMS TO ECHO N BOUNCE AROUND THE WALLS.

I CRAWL ON ALL FOURS TO MY BED N THROW MYSELF ATOP CURLING UP IN A BALL.

NO SICK ANY MORE JUST COMPLETELY BLASTED, FINDING IT EXTREMELY HARD TO OPEN MY EYES BECAUSE OF THE COLOURS N THE AWESOME INPUT.

BUT CLOSED EYES, IT IS BEGINNING TO GET EVEN WORSE.

MY MIND'S EYE EXPLODES IN AN OUTWARD SPIRAL FULL OF PINK BLUE YELLOW RED N GREEN FLASHES N A MOST DISCONCERTING WHOOSHING STARTS IN MY EARS.

I TRY TO STAND SWEAT POURING OFF MY BODY SHAKING.

BOY, YOU GONE N DONE IT NOW!

I INWARDLY WINCE.

I DRAG MYSELF OFF THE BED FEELING VERY SICK.

ALL OF MY BEDROOM N THE DOORWAY TO THE HALL ARE RIPPLING.

IT IS VERY HARD TO LOOK AT ONE THING.

THE FOCUS JUST MAKES THE OBJECTS SEEM TO WARP N MOVE.

I FALL TO THE FLOOR N CLOSE MY EYES VERY TIGHT.

IT NO HELPS ONE BIT.

SWEAT BEADS BEGIN TO RUN DOWN MY FACE N NECK N I KNOW I NEED TO THROW.

CRAWLING ON KNEES N GRABBING FURNISHINGS FOR SUPPORT I DRAG MY NOW BURNING BODY BACK TO THE BATHROOM N PROMPTLY COLLAPSE UPON THE COLD FLOOR.

I TRY TO PEER AT THE TOILET BUT IT SEEMS TO BE JUST A WHITE KIND OF BLOB IN THE DISTANCE.

MY STOMACH TIGHTENS.

I HEAVE MYSELF TOWARDS THE LOO N VOMIT AGAIN, DRIBBLING DOWN MY CHIN.

MY BODY IS NOW BURNING, SWEATING N COMPLETELY NUMB.

I GASP FOR AIR N RAISE MYSELF TO MY FEET WITH THE AID OF THE BATHROOM SINK.

TURN ON THE COLD TAP FULL N SPLASH MY FACE.

I LOOK UP IN THE MIRROR AT MYSELF N AN OLD MAN WITH LONG WHITE HAIR N LONG GREY BEARD PEERS BACK AT ME WITH INTENSE BLUE EYES.

WOW! I DUCK THE MIRROR CLOSING MY EYES N SPLASH MORE WATER ON MY FACE.

THEN THE FULL FORCE OF THE BITTER BREW HITS ME....

THE WORLD EXPLODES LIKE A STAR IN EVERY COLOUR CONCEIVABLE N I COLLAPSE ONTO THE FLOOR.

WOW! THIS IS TOO STRONG.

CURLING ON THE FLOOR I SLOWLY TUNNEL OUT OF MYSELF N DRIFT AWAY FROM MY BODY COLD N SWEATING ON THE BATHROOM FLOOR.

BY NOW HAVING NO MUCH CARE IF I LIVE OR DIE, MY BODY WRETCHED, I FLOAT SLOWLY OFF AS IF LOSING CONSCIOUSNESS.

IT IS WARM N COMFY HERE, ALL I NEED TO DO IS BREATHE.

I FAINTLY KNOW MY BODY IS STILL THERE BUT CAN NO MOVE AS SUCH.

FACES LOOM OUT OF THE DARKNESS, JESTER LIKE N JEER AT ME.

ONE, SUCH A CLOWN WITH BLUE WHITE STRIPED BAGGY PANTS, RED TOP, ORANGE WIG, WHITE FACE.

SILLY LONG BLACK SHINY BOOTS N HE KEEPS JUST LOOMING IN MY FACE LIKE A BIG BALLOON BEING THUMPED OFF ME...

THUMP! THUMP! THUMP!

HIS LIPS PAINT BRIGHT RED AROUND BROKEN WHITE JAGGED TEETH.

WHITE CHEEKS TWISTED LIPS IN AN EVIL GRIN.

HE FLOATS OFF N THINGS BEGIN TO MOVE VERY FAST.

NO REDS N BLUES N GREENS, I SEE NOW SWIRLING N EVOLVING THROUGH MY PSYCHE, YELLOWS N WHITE, WHITES AS BRIGHT AS ARC LIGHTS.

FLASH!

THE RIGHT SIDE OF MY SKULL SMASHES OPEN LIKE I HAVE BEEN STRUCK BY LIGHTNING.

NO PAIN JUST A GENTLE TEARING SENSATION AS IF SOMETHING GENTLY SNAPS.

MY BODY BEGINS TO JUMP N THRASH ABOUT AS IF I HAVE BEEN HIT BY A TRUCK.

LIGHT THUNDERING OUTWARDS FROM A CENTRE, ALL ENERGY POINT INWARDS.

THERE IS NO PAIN JUST A FEELING OF MY SKULL BEING CRACKED OPEN FROM THE INSIDE.

Nobunoni Book Of Shadows

ALL OF MY SKIN BEGINS TO MELT N PEEL OFF.

THE FEW TEETH I HAVE LEFT IN MY MOUTH SEEM TO WANDER ABOUT WITHOUT KNOWING WHERE TO SIT.

EYES OPEN, EVERYTHING TUNNELLING DOWN MASSIVE VORTEXES EVERYWHERE I LOOK.

INCREDIBLY HARD TO FOCUS.

THERE IS AWESOME BEAUTY WITHIN THIS CHAOS I REMIND MYSELF AS I TRY TO HOLD ONTO THE LAST REMNANTS OF MY REMEMBERED SELF.

I PEER AT THE SHOWER CURTAIN N WATCH AS IF TRANSFIXED PATTERNS, SYMBOLS N THE LITTLE DUCKS RUN AROUND AS IF ALIVE, THE FISH ALSO SWIMMING WITHIN THE CURTAINS SEA SCENE.

THE CRAB WINKS AT ME...

THIS IS TOO MUCH, I TRY TO STAND.

THE GROUND SLANTS AWAY FROM ME N THE PICTURES N PATTERNS TURN 6 D N BEGIN TO FLOAT IN THE AIR.

I STARE AT THE FLOOR N WATCH IT SLOWLY DISSOLVE AS IF MADE OF WATER CLAY BEING STIRRED WITHIN SOME GREAT SOUP POT..

I FEAR I MIGHT FALL INTO MY OWN INSIDE WORLD, INSIDE OF THIS PERCEIVED VORTEX N VANISH.

I RAISE MY HEAD N VOMIT AGAIN RATTLING MY BODY N THE WATER IN THE LOO.

SPINNING UNCONTROLLABLY NOW, I KIND OF TRY TO STAND N GET HIT BY A WAVE OF POWER THAT SHAKES ME TO THE FLOOR AGAIN.

A GREAT RED EYED SLOBBERING GREY HULK LOOMS OVER ME N TRIES TO PICK ME UP.

I NEED TO RUN, GET OUT OF THE WAY.

WAVE AFTER WAVE OF FEAR RIPPLES THROUGH MY BODY.

I SPIN MINDLESSLY IN A VOID, BEING RIPPED N MAULED AT BY MANY EXTREMELY DISGUSTING ARMS OF OTHER CREATURES WITH RED GREEN N BLUE EYES.

I LIE ON A SLIDING CLIFF OF MUD BEING MAULED N GRABBED BY ARMS FROM BELOW.

IN SLOW MOTION THE CREATURES BULKING SLIMY WET HULKS RISE FROM THE DEPTHS OF THE DEAD N TRY TO DRAG ME DOWN INTO A REDDISH BROWN BOILING SOUP FROM WHICH THEY MATERIALISE.

NOW MY HEART IS POUNDING N I MANAGE TO GET UP OFF THE COLD N NOW VOMIT SOAKED FLOOR N LOOK AROUND.

IT IS AS IF THESE GREAT BEASTS STAND IN FRONT N BESIDE ME DISTORTING MY VIEW OF THE OPEN DOORWAY N THE HALL BEYOND.

EVERYWHERE I LOOK I SEE VINES N TREES WITH THESE CREATURE LOOMING IN-BETWEEN.

I CRAWL OUT OF THE BATHROOM N TO MY BED TRYING TO CURLING UP UNDER MY QUILT HEAD N ALL.

N STILL THESE CREATURES ATTACK ME...

I AM HURLED N WRENCHED BY GROSS SLIMY GREEN GREY DEAD ARMS.

LEGS OF HUNDREDS OF WARRIORS STOMPING TO A WAR CHANT BATTER AT ME...

OTHER ROUND BALL LIKE CREATURES SLAVER ON ME WITH GAPING MOUTHS TRYING TO BITE LUMPS OUT OF ME N SCREAM IN TORMENT IN MY FACE ONE AFTER ANOTHER RELENTLESS.

I CAN SMELL DEATH N DECAY EVERYWHERE.

I TRY N JUST GIVE IN.

A PART OF ME KNOWING ONLY SURRENDER.

I AM PICKED UP N HURLED THROUGH A BLINDING VORTEX OF SCREAMING HEADS N UPPER TORSOS. THE BODIES OF THESE APPARITIONS STOP AT BELLY BUTTON LEVEL N SEEMED TO JUST MELT INTO THE MUD WALLS OF THE SPINNING VORTEX. ALL GRABBING AT ME N HITTING ME. I CURL UP IN A BALL UNDER MY QUILT N EVENTUALLY POP OUT OF THE END, LIKE BEING SHOT OUT OF A CANNON.

FREE FALL.

FOR A SHORT MOMENT I AM EJECTED OUT INTO A WARM BUBBLE OF GOLDEN ROSE LIGHT THAT BATHES ME N KIND OF HOLDS ME, TELLING THAT EVERYTHING IS ALRIGHT...

THEN THE CHAOS STARTS AGAIN.

I BEGIN TO SPIN AS IF BEING SUCKED DOWN A DRAIN HOLE, SOMEWHERE BELOW RED BROWN TENTACLES REACH UP N

POP MY BUBBLE N SUCTION SUCKERS HOLD N DRAG ME DOWN TOWARDS THE BEAKED MOUTH OF A GREAT OCTOPUS.

THE BULGING BLUE GREY EYE OF THIS CREATURE SLOWLY N OMINOUSLY GETTING CLOSER.

THE GREAT BEAKED MOUTH OPENS SHOWING ROW UPON ROW OF BACKWARD FACING TEETH N I AM LOWERED WITHIN.

I HOLD MY BREATH N CLOSE MY EYES AS TIGHT AS CAN BE.

FROM BELOW A GREAT VAT OF PUTRID GREEN YELLOW PUSS ENVELOPES ME N I BEGIN TO SPLUTTER..

N CHOKE UPON MY OWN VOMIT.

THE SMELL SO OVERPOWERING FROM THIS BUBBLING BOILING MESS THAT I THROW UP MANY MANY SPACES....

BEADS OF SWEAT DRIBBLING DOWN MY FACE N BODY LIKE ICE COLD NEEDLES, N MY HAIRED IS SOAKED TO MY FACE.

I TASTE BILE N CAN SMELL PUTREFACTION LIKE I HAVE BEEN SQUASHED DOWN AN UNCLEAN DRAINPIPE.

I DIE AS IF A TINY STAR TWINKLING OUT IN THE NIGHT BLACK SKY.

I FALL THROUGH THIS MID-AIR OF DEATH N JUST SWITCH OFF, BECOME AS SMALL AS A SEED BLOWING IN THE VORTEX OF A TYPHOON.

I BEGIN TO MUMBLE N CHANT INCOHERENTLY, EYES OPEN EYES CLOSED, ALL IS THE SAME.

A BLINDING TWISTING VORTEX OF ANIMALS N DEMONS.

I CRAWL OFF MY BED N STAGGER TO THE BATHROOM WHERE I PROMPTLY THROW UP AGAIN.

MOTION SICKNESS FROM I MOVING N TRYING TO NAVIGATE THE INSIDE OF A DEMONIC KALEIDOSCOPE... WHILST SLIDING MY HANDS ALONG THE WALLS I CAN BARELY SEE, SO AS TO STAND UP.

I TURN ON THE HOT N COLD TAPS IN THE BATH N PLUNGE MY HEAD INTO THE STREAMING WATERS.

IT HELPS, MY EYES BEGIN TO FOCUS.

I DO IT AGAIN, THIS TIME TURNING THE TAPS ON FULL N FUMBLE WITH THE PLUG IN THE BATH.

NOT CARING IF I LIVE OR DIE I SLIDE MY EXHAUSTED BODY OVER THE EDGE OF THE BATH N PLOP INTO THE WATER, CLOTHES AN ALL.

I CAN HEAR A VOICE IN THE DISTANCE PROCLAIMING,

(WHAT THE F---K) OVER N OVER AGAIN N I SLOWLY COME TO REALISE IT IS ME DOING THE MUMBLING.

THROWING WARM WATER OVER MY HEAD WITH EYES SHUT TIGHTLY I SEE VISIONS OF BEING WITHIN MY MOTHER'S WOMB.

ALL THE LIGHT REDS N ORANGE COVERED EVERYWHERE IN BLOOD VESSELS THAT SLOWLY PUMP TO THE BEAT OF MY HEART.

MY HEAD N CHEST N STOMACH HURT.

TOO MUCH RETCHING.

THE WATER IN THE BATH SEEMS TO HAVE A LIFE OF ITS OWN, AS IF I CAN SEE THE MOLECULES/ATOMS JOINED, THE SHAPE THEY MAKE TO FORM THE WATER.

I TRY TO PEER AT THE BLUE WALLS OF MY BATHROOM BUT THEY JUST LOOK AS THOUGH THEY HAVE BEEN WRITTEN ON WITH A SILVER N BLACK PEN.

SYMBOLS EVERYWHERE.

I LOOK AT THESE SYMBOLS N FEEL MY HEAD, MY BRAIN BEGIN TO CRAWL AS IF MY BRAIN IS FULL OF WORMS,

LIGHTS FLASH N BANG AROUND MY HEAD WITH EVERYTHING VIBRATING.

COMPLETELY FUCKED UP FOR SURE, BUT,

NO SICK

LYING IN THE WATER SOMEHOW FEELS INCREDIBLY SECURE,

MY BODY NUMB N KIND OF MELTING IN THE WARMTH OF THE WATER.

AT LEAST I NO WISH TO VOMIT ANY MORE.

WOW, WHAT THE FUCK JUST HAPPENED IS ALL THAT SEEMS TO UTTER FROM MY LIPS.

I PULL THE PLUG FROM THE BATH, GRABBING ALL THE TOWELS AROUND ME N STUMBLE TO MY BED,

CRAWL UNDER THE QUILT N DIE.

I ACTUALLY SLEEP,

PASS OUT SOAKING WET IN ALL MY CLOTHES

UPON AWAKING THINGS LOOKED KIND OF DIFFERENT, BUT I AM STILL COLD, BUT NO SO.

I NOW FEEL I SHOULD HAVE THE BOTTLE TO TRY THAT AGAIN. I MUMBLE N FUMBLE UNDER MY MATTRESS FOR MY LITTLE TIN TRAY.

IT IS EMPTY N ALSO SOAKING WET WITH MATE TEA.

NOW I HAVE TO START THIS SHIT ALL OVER AGAIN,

HEROIN IS A BITCH FOR SURE.

STEADY STEADY STEADY

AH, HELL IT IS SOME SORT OF MASOCHISTIC LOVE OF PAIN THAT KEEPS ME FROM REACHING FOR THE GEAR. I KNOW FROM EXPERIENCE. I KNOW IT WELL. YES I KNOW IT WELL. I SORTED IT LAST TIME I CAN SORT IT NOW.. AH, BUT DID YOU REALLY GET WHAT YOU WERE LOOKING FOR, OR ARE YOU STILL A SLAVE TO SOMETHING? A SLAVE TO DRUGS, A SLAVE TO THE GOVERNMENT, A SLAVE TO THE SYSTEM, A SLAVE TO SOCIETY. (AHHHHHHHH GOT TO STRETCH MY UPPER BACK, NECK N HEAD ARE BEING PULLED DOWN MY BACK, WITH THE STRESS OF WITHDRAWAL. HEAD IS CRACKING. SKIN CRAWLING, GOOSED, FREEZING TO THE BONE, NEED HEAT. FROM THE INSIDE, NOT OUT, SWEATING TOO MUCH.

THE BEAST IS UPON ME. IT IS NOW 21.00HRS 08TH OF MARCH. I HAVE BEEN AT THIS NOW. COMING OFF METHADONE, SINCE THE 27TH OF JANUARY. NO METHADONE SINCE SUNDAY THE MORNING OF THE FIFTH OF MARCH.) LITTLE BIT OF CODEINE N

A FEW LINES. NOWHERE NEAR THE AMOUNT OF METHADONE. I STOPPED ON SUNDAY. (30MG-25MG THEN ABSTAINED FROM ALL OPIATES FOR 30 HOURS. TOOK 900 MG DF118 MONDAY. TOO MUCH. NO CODEINE SINCE. A LITTLE BIT OF STREET GEAR SMOKED OVER PAST TWO DAYS (APPROX. 100MG EACH DAY)

A SLAVE TO ONE'S SELF. WORK, HOME, WIFE, PEER GROUPS, HOUSEWIVES, HUSBANDS ETC. THE POINT IS, IS ONE REALLY HAPPY WITH ONE'S LIFE? HOW LONG ARE THEE PREPARED TO JUST HANG AROUND, AS IF ON THE STREET CORNER, AFTER SCHOOL. STATIC, STARING, SMOKING COLD. THERE IS A PICTURE OF A POTENTIAL ADDICT. LOOKING, WANTING, HUNGRY (AH SHIT GIVE ME FIVE)!! DIMETHILTRIPTAMINE, WONDER WHY I THOUGHT OF THAT? WISH TO SEE GOD, N ASK, WHY. WHY DO I KEEP DOING THIS N JUST GETTING OLDER? NO WISER, TO THE PAIN, THE FEAR, THE BEAST OF ADDICTION!!

I AM 41 YEARS OLD MALE WHITE, CAUCASIAN, FUCKED UP, INSANE IDIOT, THAT IS VERY GOOD AT TOTAL SELF-DESTRUCTION ON DRUGS. PLUS ALSO THE ENERGY N STUBBORNNESS, TO TRY N DETOX N STAY CLEAN, SOME THIRTY TIMES. THIS IS MY THIRTY FIRST ATTEMPT. THIS TIME THOUGH I HAVE A PLAN. (AAAAAAAAAHHHHHHHH) NO PAIN, BLASTED OUT OF THE COSMOS N-------------------- NO PAIN. I PRAY, BUT FOR NOW, SELF-EXAMINATION ONLY MAKES THE EXPERIENCE WORSE. I QUESTION WHAT I AM FEELING LIKE. I FOCUS ON MY BODY, N WHAT I FOCUS ON HURTS. INTENSE EXPLORATION, PAIN, TOO MUCH INPUT. WOW HEAVY WAVES OF THE BEAST OF CRAVING NOW. THERE I GO. FOCUS ON IT N, BANG THE PAIN GOES TO MY

HEAD N STARTS A FIRE BURNING. DOES ONE REMEMBER, WHEN IT ALL COMES ROUND AGAIN? WOW MY ARMS HURT. WELL OF COURSE THEY DO. YOU THOUGHT OF THEM. THOUGHT HE HAD A BICYCLE BUT ONLY HAD A FRONT WHEEL.

ALL MY SKIN HURTS. EVEN TO TOUCH A SMOOTH SURFACE BRINGS PAIN. THE TAP OF THE KEYS ANNOYS TO THE POINT OF WANTING TO SMASH THE COMPUTER, BUT THAT IS ILLOGICAL. I AM ONLY IN PAIN. MENTAL N PHYSICAL. HAVE NOTICED THE WITHDRAWAL CHANGED FROM THE METHADONE WITHDRAWAL. (COLD N FREEZING N ALL BODY, FLUSHING N SWEATING, COLD). COLD. EAT. WARM FOOD, NO MILK, TOO GUMMY. NO GOOD FOR SNOT N ALL THAT (NOTE TO EDITOR, LOOK UP ALL DOWNSIDES OF MILK N WHEEZING. ASTHMA). WARM NOW, IN MENTAL N PHYSICAL PAIN. MY BRAIN IS FRYING. NORADRENALINE, COURSING THROUGH MY BRAIN, TELLING MY BODY IT HURTS. HOW CAN MY BODY HURT WHEN I HAVE NO DONE THE USUAL LIKE I HIT THUMB WITH A HAMMER, ASK MYSELF. BUT I KNOW THE ANSWER TO THAT. MANY YEARS OF HITTING MYSELF WITH A SLEDGE HAMMER EVERY DAY. THAT IS WHY IT HURTS... I IS AN IDIOT. WHO, I? I AM FAR FROM AN IDIOT, JUST INSANE.

THAT IS ALL.

BOUGHT UP WITH SEXUAL N PSYCHOLOGICAL ABUSE I AM UNABLE TO CLEAR ALL OF MY BODY MEMORY..

I SLEEP FITFULLY. UP CONFUSED. WHY IS IT THAT WHEN ONE HAS A JONES UNDER CONTROL, IN DETOX, THE WORLD EXPLODES AROUND ONE LIKE SOME LUNATIC CATHERINE

WHEEL FIREWORKS. CRACKLING N SPITTING AT ME. HANDS ON HEAD WALKING IN CIRCLES. WELL, SUPPOSE THAT IS THE LAW OF AVERAGES. ONE TRIES N LIVES A QUIET LIFE N ONE IS, RECLUSE. I GO OUT ALL THE SPACE N IS NEVER THERE. THEE IS? ALL SORTS N EVERY KIND OF FREAK THING IMAGINABLE, TRYING TO FIGHT FOR A SCRAP OF MEAT. LET THEM HOUND LIKE WOLVES. LET THEM GRUDGE FOR MEAT, IF THEY NO FIND IT, LET THEM HOUND N SNIVEL, FOR THEY ARE ONLY ANIMALS, LIKE MYSELF. SURVIVING PAIN. AH!! THAT WATER IN THE TAP STINKS. FLUORINE, CHEMICAL SHIT. IT IS BROWN N IF YOU PUT IT IN A GLASS N STAND IT ON THE WINDOWSILL FOR TWO DAYS, IT GROWS WHITE FUNGUS LIKE SPORE STRANDS THROUGH THE WATER. DEFINITELY ALIVE N ACTIVE N LIVING WELL IN THE WATER OF NORWICH. WOW, MY HEAD HURTS.

VALIUM I HAD 3 HOURS AGO ONLY PROCEEDED TO CONFUSE ME EVEN MORE N CREATE MORE CHAOS. DOOR!! PHONE!!! BANK!!!!!!! DOOR, PHONE. NO ONE AT DOOR WHEN I ANSWERED IT. SOMEONE IF FUCKING WITH ME LOL. AH SHIT THAT IS FUNNY. I AM PLAYING WITH MYSELF. SLOW DOWN. AH! THAT IS BETTER. SMOKE A SMALL AMOUNT OF H. NO FOR THE PLEASURE OF DOING IT MIND, BUT JUST SO I CAN OPERATE N MAINTAIN MY LIFE, FOR THE MOMENT. (I SMOKE APPROX. 75MG STREET GEAR. SMOKE IT COS IT MIGHT HAVE DOWNERS IN THE CUT. SMOKING IT SHOULD DESTROY THEM)

I HAVE A COLD. WHY DOES THE IMMUNE SYSTEM GO OUT OF WHACK WHEN ONE COMES OFF. PROBABLY BECAUSE THE OPIATES ARE A HEAVY SUPPRESSANT OF CNS, SO IT REALLY

SLOWS DOWN THE METABOLISM. WHEN ONE NO TAKES THEM, N ALREADY HAS A PHYSICAL ADDICTION, THE METABOLISM SPEEDS UP N DOES QUITE A GOOD JOB OF CHUCKING OUT THE RUBBISH THAT HAS BEEN BACKLOGGED FOR MONTHS. THIS ALSO GOES FOR ONES FEELINGS. THEY GET BLUNTED N IGNORED WHEN YOU USE OPIATES. HENCE A HELLISH CIRCLE OF PAIN, TRYING TO COME OFF N THE PSYCHOLOGICAL SIDE OF THE EFFECT ON THE VENTRAL TEGMENTAL AREA OF THE BRAIN N BRAIN REWARD CASCADE. IF THE CASCADE IS HIGH, AN URGE IS TRIGGERED (INVESTIGATE), CHEMICAL BIOLOGICAL, PSYCHOCHEMICAL REWARD. IN ORDER FOR THIS PROCESS TO BE MAINTAINED THE TRIGGER OF DOPAMINE HAS TO BE IMPLEMENTED, BY THE USE OF OPIATES, OR IF YOU ARE CLEAN, HARD EXERCISE.

AH, SORRY ABOUT THAT, FELT AS THOUGH I HAVE LEFT ONE HANGING. WELL I DID COS I AM ILL. ALRIGHT.. HAVE A COLD FOR TWO DAYS. NO TAKING METHADONE NO MORE. FEEL LIKE SHIT. LOL

NO SHITTING THOUGH, COS OF THE GEAR. (ONE G OF CRAP STREET GEAR, GONE IN, MON -FRI) JUST NECKED 220 MG DF118, PRAYING THAT IT WORKS, COS GOT TO GET TICKET FOR, I JOURNEY). HE HE HE HE.. I STILL HAVE NOT TOLD THEE WHAT I AM UP TO HAVE I! WELL JUST WAIT N SEE. ALRIGHT.. ONE WILL JUST HAVE TO READ ON.

NOW I AM SWEATING. EAT, DIAZEPAM. SIGH! IS THIS GOING TO GO ON FOREVER! GOT TO GET OUT THE DOOR N

GET A TICKET YET. FOOD IN MICRO-WAVE, ALL FRESH, MINCED CHICKEN BREAST N, WELL I DON'T KNOW YET.

GOT LOTS OF THINGS.

COOK THE MEAT FIRST.

THE NEXT DAY I FLY TO EUROPE.

FOREWARNING TO READERS

A LOT OF MADNESS AHEAD

I KICK 150MG OF METHADONE 90 MG OF VALIUM, HEROIN, SYNTHETIC OPIATES, COCAINE, SPEED, ANTI-DEPRESSANTS N ALCOHOL IN 3 MONTHS N PARTAKE OF IBOGA THERAPY AT THE END OF 3 MONTHS... I AM NO SO CRAZY ANY MORE. I FLY FOR 11 WEEKS AFTER MY FIRST INITIATION, GET SOME COHERENCE AT 12 WEEKS.

I STOP DRINKING N DROP THE METHADONE, USE A LITTLE BIT OF HEROIN N CODEINE CUT THE HABIT BY ¾. THAT REALLY HURT, I LOSE MOST OF MY TEETH KICKING VALIUM, FITTING N SCRAPING FACE ON CONCRETE N CARPETS. ONE FEELS LIKE A DONKEY IS KICKING THEE IN THE BACK OF THE HEAD, THE BODY JERKS N HEAD EXPLODES INTO LIGHT, WITH WEIRD ELECTRICAL ZIGZAG ZAPS RIPPING UP N DOWN THE SPINE ACCOMPANYING THE COLOURS.

I THROW THE PILLS N REST DOWN THE TOILET, STOP STICKING NEEDLES IN MY GROIN.

I GET UP EARLY ONE MORNING N GRAB A CAN OF SPECIAL BREW FROM THE FRIDGE, TAKE THE METHADONE BOTTLE OUT OF THE BATHROOM CUPBOARD. I CRACK THE CAN N

AS I DO, A BOOMING VOICE SAYS TO ME, ECHOING AROUND THE BATHROOM, "HAVE YOU NO HAD ENOUGH YET?" I JUMP CLEAN OUT OF MY SKIN N TURN N LOOK IN THE MIRROR. MOMENTARILY I HAVE NO REFLECTION TO SEE. I QUICKLY DUCK THE MIRROR, SHAKING I POUR THE CAN OF BEER DOWN THE TOILET N CRUMPLE TO THE FLOOR IN BROKEN TEARS. THEN ANGER SURGES THROUGH MY VEINS. I GRABBED THE BOTTLE OF METHADONE N SMASHED IT AGAINST THE BACK WALL OF THE BATH. "ENOUGH!" I SCREAM AT IT. THE GREEN SYRUP SPATTERED, SLOWLY RUNNING DOWN THE WALL N BATH. I FLY OUT OF THE BATHROOM N RUN BLINDLY INTO THE LIVING ROOM, SIT N ROLL A SPLIFF. I THEN TAKE MOST ELSE OF THAT WHICH I CAN FIND N FLUSH IT, LEAVING SOME "H" N CODEINE FOR THE CLUCK. IT TAKES FIVE DAYS BEFORE I COLLAPSE N HAVE TO CALL SOMEONE.

ANY WAYS I DIGRESS.

IBOGA TREATMENT

I LOOK N TRY EVERYTHING TO BEAT THE RETARDANT WITHDRAWAL OF METHADONE.
FLY GARLIC MUSHROOM WORKS WELL, BUT THEY ARE NO STRONG ENOUGH TO GET YOU THROUGH THE TREE TOP EFFECT N GET YOU PAST THE PAIN THRESHOLD, ALSO THEY DO NOT LAST LONG ENOUGH. AMANITA IS A MOST WONDERFUL PAIN KILLER.

BEFORE IBOGA N TRYING TO GET PAST OPIATE WITHDRAWALS, I EAT NEARLY 20 GMS OF AMANITA N ONLY MANAGED TO FALL ASLEEP FOR 3 HOURS, N GET RELIEF FROM THE INCESSANT PAIN FOR 8 HOURS.

ONE HELL OF A HIGH DOSE OF MUSCIMOL. I DID NOT GET ANY VISUALS INTERNAL OR OTHERWISE. THE POOR MUSHROOMS HAVE ALL THEIR WORK CUT OUT TRYING TO GET PAST THE METHADONE. MUSHROOMS WORK WELL FOR A LITTLE HABIT, BUT WHEN IT COMES TO METHADONE, ONLY IBOGA IS STRONG ENOUGH.

AS FOR PERSONAL INSIGHT N SELF-AWARENESS,

THE IBOGA IS THE TOOL.

53 HOUR I AM GONE,

THEN SLOWLY BUT SURELY A RISING OF ENERGY THAT IS SUSTAINED BY GOOD FOOD N WATER.

AS TO TAKING IT FOR SELF-EXPLORATION, I THINK THAT ONE WILL HAVE TO BE GUIDED N PREPARED TO JUST ACCEPT N FORGIVE. A BIT LIKE TAKING AYA, BUT ONE MUST BE PREPARED FOR ALL KINDS OF PERSONAL CONFLICT. I HAVE TAKEN N USED MANY ENTHEOGENS IN MY LIFE, BUT NO TRIP GETS EVEN NEAR TO THE EXTREMES THAT IBOGA GETS YOU.

OTT EXTREME.

I INGEST 5.2 GRAMS OF 10/1 EXTRACT, N EXPERIENCE A VERY COLOURFUL INTERNAL SCENERY, AT FIRST SOMETHING LIKE AN ARCHWAY WITH BLOOD DRIPPING DOWN IN DROPLETS N THEN

SLOWLY CHANGING TO ALL THE COLOURS OF THE RAINBOW. A BIT LIKE TETRIS, BUT DISSOLVING INTO WHAT SEEMED LIKE EARTH AT THE BOTTOM ALIVE N WRITHING. I FIND IT BEST TO KEEP THE EYES CLOSED AS THE VISUALS ARE QUITE NASTY. BLACK, RED N WHITE JAGGED TRIANGLES, N LOTS OF LEAVES N TREES.

AS I TRY TO COPE WITH NOT CHUCKING UP THE FLOOD DOSE, BY LYING ON MY BACK IN THE DARK N BREATHING THROUGH THE NAUSEA, THE TRIP GETS STRONGER AS I FIGHT WITH THE NAUSEA. AS I BREATH MY CONSCIOUSNESS BREATHES N EXPANDS, ROLLING SLOWLY BUT SURELY OUTWARD, UNTIL I BECOME AS A FLAT GALAXY OF REDS N BROWNS. I BECOME A GALAXY, EXPANDING N SPIRALLING, CENTRED AROUND A BLACK HOLE. CLOUDS AS MY FEELINGS N THOUGHTS N EMOTIONS ROLL THROUGH THIS FLAT PLAIN LIKE IMMINENT STORMS, ROLLING N FOLDING AMONGST EACH OTHER.

THE ONLY REAL WAY TO EXPLAIN THIS IS - THE LASERS IN NIGHT CLUBS THAT FIRE A FLAT BEAM/TRIANGLE ACROSS THE CLUB, PINK N RED WITH SMOKE ROLLING THROUGH THE LIGHTS.

Nobunoni Book Of Shadows

I SEEM TO BE LYING FLAT, FACE DOWN ABOVE THIS PLAIN, N
TRAVELLING ACROSS IT AT GREAT SPEED. I TRAVEL ACROSS THE

CENTRAL BLACK VORTEX, LOOK IN, BACK OFF N TRAVEL ON. I REMEMBER LOOKING N SAYING TO MYSELF. NO HERE FOR THIS. UNKNOWN. UN-CHARTERED. NO FEAR, BUT, NO HERE TO GET LOST. I FEEL THE VORTEX SUCK AT ME N I GLIMPSE MANY MASKS, FACES, WOMEN, CHILDREN, WHITE WISPY BIRDS, SPIRALLING DOWN N IN. AS I LOOK I FEEL ENTITIES PULL GENTLY AT ME. I BACK OFF N TRAVEL TO THE EDGE OF MY CONSCIOUSNESS, THE EDGE OF MY COSMOS. STAND, LIKE A WARRIOR AT THE EDGE OF SPACE ON SENTRY DUTY. MANY, MANY MORE SPIRALLING GALAXIES SURROUND ME, BUT EACH IS TOO FAR A DISTANCE FOR ME TO STEP OFF OF MY EDGE N REACH. I TURN N TRAVEL BACK.

I AM IN THE JUNGLE. EVERY ANIMAL CONCEIVABLE GALLOPS ACROSS THE GROUND BELOW ME N THE NOISE IS AWESOME. BIRDS, MONKEYS, INSECTS. I AM LEANING AGAINST A TREE N PEERING AT THE SUN THROUGH THE LOFTY HEIGHTS OF TREES N VINES. THE SUNLIGHT SEEMS TO DAPPLE ME, SPARKLE N DANCE THROUGH THE LEAVES, LIKE WATER IN A BUBBLING STREAM. I FEEL LIKE A WET PEBBLE BEING CARESSED BY WARM BUBBLING EARTHY WATERS. BIRDS EVERYWHERE ALOFT.

I SEE MANY LITTLE JUNGLE CHILDREN WITH LITTLE SQUARE HATS ON THEIR HEADS N OYSTER SHELLS AT THE SIDE OF THEIR EYES,. EACH HAS A STICK IN THE RIGHT HAND N THEY ARE RUNNING THROUGH THE TREES, PRANCING, DANCING N SINGING, N HERDING MANY MANY LITTLE FURRY ANIMALS IN FRONT OF THEM. THE FOREST FLOOR IS ABSOLUTELY WRITHING IN LITTLE FURY ANIMALS.

WHEN I ROAR AT THE JUNGLE, A MASSIVE TREE COMES OUT OF MY MOUTH, N I SEEM TO MELT N MOULD AS ONE WITH ALL THE LIFE OF THE JUNGLE.

EVERYTHING IS WRITHING WITH LIFE. I AM SURROUNDED BY TREES, VINES, BUSHES N WHAT SEEMS LIKE EVERY LIVING THING ON THE PLANET, SURROUNDS ME N SLOWLY N GENTLY CARESS MY INNER BEING. I COME ACROSS A POOL (SAME ONE I USED TO FISH WHEN I AM A CHILD) N PEER IN AT THE BABY CARP. (THIS IS A SPECIAL PLACE FOR ME AS A CHILD). I TENTATIVELY LEAN FORWARD N TOUCH THE WATER N GET FLOODED WITH BITTER SWEET N LOVING MEMORIES. ALL OF THEM MAKING ME. I FOLD OUT THROUGH THE SURFACE OF THE POOL N FEEL AS IF I AM THE POOL N MYSELF ALL AT THE SAME SPACE...

I HAVE LOTS OF VISIONS OF MY CHILDHOOD, BUT THE REAL EXPERIENCE STARTS ABOUT A WEEK AFTER.

THE IBOGA REDUCES ME TO AN ATOM, MOLECULE, DIVIDES MY CELLS (SHOWS MY CONCEPTION) THEN SPLITS ME INTO SEVEN N THEN MAKES ME DO EVERYTHING IN THREES.

MIND, HAND, HEART.

THREE DAYS INTO THE SECOND WEEK, I AM LYING IN MY BATH, N I HAVE THE MENTAL IMPRESSION OF BEING BORN N HAVING MY UMBILICAL CORD CUT. BEING DRAGGED FROM THE WARMTH INTO A HARSH WHITE N COLD N PAINFUL PLACE.

ANOTHER REASON FOR MY EXPLORATION WITH IBOGA IS THAT I DO NOT KNOW MY MOTHER AS SHE GAVE ME UP AT BIRTH. HAVING A PROPENSITY FOR OPIATES, I WONDER IF MY

MOTHER GAVE ME UP AT BIRTH, BECAUSE SHE WAS AN ADDICT N I AM BORN ADDICTED TO OPIATES.

THE INITIAL THREE WEEKS OF PAIN N CHAOS IS IDENTICAL (IBOGA SHOWS ME) TO THE BLINDING PAIN N SHOCK I EXPERIENCE AT BIRTH. SO I GET MY ANSWER.

THE PERSONAL CONFLICT IS IMMENSE. IT IS AS IF I HAVE BEEN CRUCIFIED, MENTALLY, N IF I TRY TO GO AGAINST MY CONSCIENCE I GET DISCIPLINED. WITH FEELINGS OF IMMINENT (STOP, NON-EXISTENCE, SELF- IMPOSED FEAR (DEATH OF MY BODY). I DO NO FEAR DEATH AS I NO DIE, BUT TRANSCEND INTO A SPIRITUAL FORM, WHEN I LEAVE THIS VESSEL. MY CONSCIENCE EVEN THREATENS TO KILL I IF I TAKE VALIUM AGAIN. A VERY HEAVY KIND OF, YES. NO GAME, THAT IF I TRY TO GO AGAINST, I GET SLAPPED HARD). I TAKE A MOGGY ONE NIGHT TO GET SOME GREATLY NEEDED SLEEP, N AFTER NINETY MINUTES IBOGA HAS ME OUT OF BED, NAKED N DRUMMING ON A STOOL IN MY HALL WAY. I REMEMBER TRYING TO NO BE DIRECTED BY THIS FORCE, BUT FOUND IT TOTALLY IMPOSSIBLE, EVEN TO THE POINT OF BEING HIT WITH BLINDING LIGHTNING N THUNDER THAT MAKES ME SHAKE N RATTLE UNCONTROLLABLY. I DID NO DISOBEY AGAIN. IMMENSE POWER.

I SPEND THREE DAYS ON MY BATHROOM FLOOR BEING FED HONEY N BREAD N TEA, BY MY WIFE.

I HAD TO EAT EVERY TWO HOURS OTHERWISE IBOGA MAKES YOU FEEL LIKE YOU ARE GOING TO DIE.

MY REVELATIONS LAST WELL OVER SIX WEEKS, N I CAN STILL GET UP WITH GOOD FOOD N WATER.

IT IS NEARLY 8 WEEKS SINCE I SESH N I AM STILL OUT IN THE COSMOS.

AS TO TAKING IBOGA FOR SELF-EXPLORATION, I WOULD DO IT. MY VIEWS HAVE CHANGED, COS I ONLY USED THE PLANT TO HEAL ME OF VERY BAD PROGRAMMING. THE SPIRIT IS CALLING ME, THE SPIRIT OF THE PLANT (NOW I AM ACQUAINTED), IS NUDGING ME. I STILL DREAM OF MY EXPERIENCE. N AFTER AWAKING I SEEM TO GET THE IMPRESSION THAT I AM NO ALONE ANYMORE.

MEMORY.

FREAKING NATURALLY.

SOME 8 WEEKS LATER N I CAN STILL FEEL IBOGA. I AM COMPLETELY GONE FOR 6 WEEKS +.

WHEN I AM A CHILD I HAVE THE SAME OPENNESS N PSYCHIC ENERGY, BUT I AM SCARED OF IT.

NOW I CAN USE THESE ABILITIES N FEEL VERY CALM N AT PEACE IN KNOWING THERE IS NOTHING TO FEAR.

THE POINT OF TAKING IBOGA FOR THE ADDICTION OF OPIATES IS THAT THE IBOGA REWIRES THE BRAIN N ENABLES ONE TO GET OVER THE RETARDANT WITHDRAWAL SYNDROME VERY QUICKLY. WHAT WOULD TAKE SOME THREE YEARS IS ACHIEVED IN 7 WEEKS.

WHEN I IBOGAD I AM ONLY 8 STONE 3LB,

I NOW WEIGH 12 STONE 4LB.

TO GET ONESELF EMOTIONALLY, MENTALLY, SPIRITUALLY SORTED AFTER 23 YEARS OF HELL IS NO DONE NATURALLY, BY JUST GIVING UP.

I HAVE LEARNT TO LISTEN TO MY BODY N ALLOW MY LIFE N ENERGIES TO FLOW LIKE WATER.

I HAVE A GREAT COMPASSION FOR MY FELLOW MAN.

ESPECIALLY THOSE THAT REQUIRE GUIDANCE N ASSISTANCE.

MEMORY SERVES TO BRING IBOGA CLOSER TO MY HEART N MIND N ALSO GIVES ME GREAT INSIGHT INTO THE WORLD AROUND ME...

PHEW!

HEAVY FLOOD OF EMOTIONS, GOING BACK THROUGH THAT, BUT SOMEHOW REASSURING, AS A SIGN THAT THE PAIN N DISTRESS IS OVER.

SIX MONTHS AFTER TAKING IBOGA I AM STILL GOING THROUGH A KIND OF GATHERING PROCESS, ASSIMILATING, KIND OF LIKE BUBBLES RETURNING TO ME THAT HAVE BEEN BLASTED OUTWARD INTO THE COSMOS N ARE SLOWLY RETURNING TO UNTO ME...

THE MOST ASTOUNDING THING IS THAT MEMORY OF MY IBOGA SESH PUTS ME BACK IN TOUCH WITH THE SPIRIT OF THIS WONDERFUL PLANT N MAKES MY HAIR STAND ON END WITH INCREDIBLE POWER.

AEEEHYAAA!!!

BASSE

WOW! WHAT A JOURNEY N IT IS NOT OVER YET!

I AM CONCEPTION BRANCHED.

IMAGINATION EVOLVED.

LIFE SEEKING LIFE N COMPLETENESS.

FULFILMENT.

I AM DESIRE..

APE;)~~~

COME SIT PARTAKE!!!

PARTAKE ... SIT DOWN. ONE REQUIRES THE SPADE. IT IS A TOOL. REMEMBER. PLEASE REMEMBER. NO TICK TOCK. BUT. FREE LIFE GIVEN. TAKE OF THE FRUITS MY SON, I GIVE YOU SON!... DO NO WHIP AT THE WIND. HOWL OR GRUDGE FOR MEAT THAT YOU CAN NO FIND. THE FRUITS OF LIFE ARE FREE. I REMEMBER OTHER SONG LYRICS N SEE. THE COSMOS! EXPANDING. BREATHING. PARTAKE. ARISE SLOWLY LIKE THE MORNING RAIN... NE NE NO ... THE MORNING SUN. THEE IS A CHILD OF THE LIGHT. DO NO QUESTION THIS. SIT .. DO NO THINK. STAND N BE, FEEL N FILL THE APPLES OF LIFE N THE FRUITS ARE FREE. SLOW DOWN. LOOK. DO NO TARRY. LOOK ... FEEL PARTAKE. DO NOT TRY TO ORDER. BE. SERIOUS.

YES BE.

SLOW DOWN, PEACE. SLOW DOWN. EXPAND FILL... PARTAKE. REFRESH. STAY COOL. BODY NUMB .. MIND EXPANDING. FEEL. OH BLESS! MY LORD OF THY BODY OF THEE, EARTH. THE GIFT OF LIFE IS GIVEN FREELY. COMMAND ONLY WHAT IS REQUIRED... QUESTIONS... NO! SIT.. FILL.. RISE LIKE THE MORNING SUN. FILL, RISE ENERGY.

KICKECK.

DRINK THE WATER. THE WATER IS THY LIFE. LIFE IS FREE, SIT PARTAKE .. TRY THE BANANA. SIT IN PEACE N FEEL. EXPAND FILL. SIT IN PEACE. SACRED PEACE.. DO. YES.. NOW ONE CAN SEE. ALL RIGHT...

FUNNY LITTLE CREATURE DOES NOT KNOW HOW TO CARE FOR ONESELF. FILL. BANNANNANANAAAA FILL. PEACE. AMINO ACID BLAST. I GOT THE HANG OF THIS NOW. GOT THE SUN GLASSES OFF N SLOWLY RISING FOR THE DAY. BANNANAAN!!!!!!!!!!!!!!!!!!!! OHYA IOYA UIIA OYYOH AEEHEO HUYA AYEAYE HEE. PEACE.

SLOWLY FILL EXPAND SIT DO NOT THINK DO NO TARRY THE MIND WITH RUBBISH. THROW OUT THE GARBAGE. SERIOUS. YES. YOU JUST FIGHT FOR YOUR LIFE... N ???

NOW ONE HAS THE GIFT GIVEN FREELY. SLOW DOWN. SLOW DOWN. NO PAIN.... WHY? NO QUESTIONS... SEE... FEEL... RISE... FILL N KNOW... THY SELF.. BE ... THESE ARE THE TOOLS TO LIFE... SLOW DOWN. WHY SO FAST? WONDERING DAZZLES. NO

LIKE NALTREXONE... EXPANDING WITH LIFE. WITHDRAWALS NO THERE... JUST LIVING FREE. DYSLEXIC. COULD NEVER TYPE. NO MATTER. YOU ARE CLEAN. VALIUM IS ONES SLAVE.. SIT.. PARTAKE.. SLOW DOWN. PEACE FILLS. BANANAS? YES BANANA COS? NO QUESTIONS FEEL ONLY I LIFE FORCE. EXIST. FILL MORE? AH GO FOR IT, GARY YOU ROCK THE COSMOS. HA HA HA QUESTIONS. YES OF COURSE QUESTIONS. FILL. BE. THANK YOU. ONES WILL CONTROLS. CONTROLS? HA HA G.O.D. SHUFFLES THE PLANET .. N ? REFRESH. COR. SLOW DOWN... UNDERSTAND... DO NO GRAPPLE .. ONE IS THE NATURE.. THE ANIMAL. FURRY. FREE. SLOW DOWN .. BE. THANK YOU LORD I BODY. BLESSINGS MY DEAR ONE, SAYS MY SOUL. FILL, PARTAKE, BE. AH. MOST BEAUTIFUL. EXIST N BE. BUT MY EYES SEE TOO MUCH. THAT IS WHY THEY BLINDED THEE WITH THE TAL. 26 LETTER 9 NUMBER N A 0.. CREATING MENTAL STATE OUT OF EMPATHY N CUTTING HEART CHAKRA N CLOSING THE 3RD EYE... CUT NATURAL PSYCHIC BORN FROM 9TH DENSITY EXTERNALISED OF CONSCIOUSNESS DOWN TO THE DENSITY WITHIN MOTION.. THINK.. THE INK OF WITCH WRITES RNA TO DNA BODY MEMORY RIGHT SIDE.. CREATING MIND.. THE ND IS PROGRAMMED WITH NUMBER N LETTER MAKING THE RIGHT PILLAR OF POWER DENSER OF BODY MEMORY THAN THE LEFT PILLAR.. CREATING INTERNALIZED ID BOUND EGO CENTRIC TICK TOCK HEAD. ONES QUEST FOR MEANING. MEANING YES. GO ORDER N COMMAND WHAT ONE WILL. BE FREE. BUT GOVERNMENTS? HA HA HA QUESTIONS. THE GIFT OF LIFE IS GIVEN FREE. PARTAKE N FILL. THANK MY SOUL. NOW ONE CAN SEE. YES. SLOW DOWN... NO WORRY ONESELF...

SLOW DOWN. SO TIME IS COMPLETE ILLUSION N CUTS THE TOP OF THE HEAD CLEAN OFF...

WEARY N EXHAUSTED.. AGHAST N BLIND. PARTAKE. GO NOW. COMMAND. EXIT.. GO. DO. NOW. BANANA.. YES.. WATER IS LIFE ALSO GO. LIVE. LIVE FOR LIFE... SLOW DOWN DO NO STOMP... FILL. SLOW DOWN. SIT. HA HA, QUESTIONS? DO AS ONE COMMANDS. NO AS ANYONE ELSE COMMANDS... ELSE??? I AM THE ONLY BEING UPON THIS PLANET. I CREATE OF EVERYTHING THROUGH MY DNA THAT BENDS SPACE NOT MY PERCEPTION OF REALITY..

AH, CONFLICT. THIS IS MY ONLY TASK. LIVE ... DETACHED. NUMB. YES FOR SURE ALIVE... YES. MANY BLESSINGS LORD, MY BODY. NOW I SEE THE GIFTS. OF LIFE. YES I SEE ... SLOW DOWN. TIME IS NO MY ENEMY. COSMIC CONSCIOUSNESS HAS NO LIMITER, SORCERY OF 3 6 9 3 WITHIN A CIRCLE..

TIME..... HA HA HA AHA AHA AHA HA AHA AHA AHA AHA AHA AHA AHA ASHE AHA ASHE A. DO IT IN THREES N ONE STAYS ALIVE. I GET IT NOW. YES... AWESOMENESS INDEED...

FILL PARTAKE.

FILL GO.

NOW?

YES GO. EXERCISE YOUR OWN FREE WILL.

GO.

AH WHY DO THEY NO FEED THE CHILDREN THE TRUTH MY DEAR SOUL....?

LIKE THE BIRDS.

THE BIRDS N THE BEES ARE FREE. HOW COME MAN IS NO GOOD... AS NATURE....? QUESTION. THAT IS WHY THEE IS MADE SON OF MAN. SON OF THE SUN.. AHHHHHHHHHHHHH!!!

SIGH RELIEF. SECURE. FOR SURE. NOW FOREEVER. BOSHA LI

O O O O O O O P O O O O O O O H O O H O H O H H O H O H O H O H O H O H O H O H O H O H O H O H O H O H G O H O H O H O H O H O H K L K JJKKJKKJK,KKKKKKKKLKKKKLK NO KICKECK... SLOW DOWN. FILL WITH PEACE.. DO NO TARRY WITH HASSLES.. SLOW DOWN... PEACE N FILL. WHY DO I FEEL LIKE THIS? ONE HAS BEEN ASLEEP FOR MANY YEARS N NOW... ALIVE... I LIVE FOR SURE. I LIVE. PARTAKE. PARTAKE N FILL... DO NO COMMAND UNLESS NECESSARY.... TIME IS NO THY ENEMY. FUNNY LITTLE CREATURE. SIMPLE. BUT LIKE A JIGSAW. GROWING. BUT NO... WHY QUESTION??? I NOW CAN SEE... SON OF MAN. GO EXERCISE ONES RIGHT TO BE FREE. IN A MODERN WORLD. BE THYSELF. GO. PARTAKE N FILL. BUT HOW DO I HOLD ALL THIS TOGETHER? MUMBLE MUMBLE...THEE ASK TOO MANY QUESTIONS. FILL N GO.. LIVE. EXIST. REMEMBER. FILL WHAT YOU REQUIRE TO FEEL. IF ONE REQUIRES TO STAY SLEEPY, EAT LITTLE N OFTEN. DRINK N BE. BE. EXIST.

I AM NOW ANGRY. YES. THAT IS GOOD. SLOW DOWN. TRY NOT TO UNDERSTAND. BUT EVERYTHING IS BLASTED N WARPED. I FEEL... SO ONE CAN SEE. WOW.. THAT IS WHY I MADE THEE IN MY IMAGE SAYETH MY SOUL.. RELIEF. WOW. COSMIC COWBOYS. REALLY DO KICK ASS. YES THEY DO LOLOLOLOL

HAAA HHHA SLOW DOWN. USHA SLOW DOWN N FILL. DO NO COMMAND UNLESS ONE REQUIRES TO DO SO.. QUESTIONS. BE N FILL. REFRESH. SLOW DOWN. ONE IS A COMPLEX CREATURE. SIT N PARTAKE.. BE. SIT N PARTAKE WITH ONE'S SELF. DO NO GRAPPLE. JUST BE. BE.. ONE N NOTHING.. BE ONE'S SELF AS ONE CAN ONLY SEE. BLIND, BUT SEEING? REFRESH GO. WOW... I AM A PETULANT FELLOW... SLOW DOWN. ONE HAS SO MANY FITS IN LIFE THAT ONE NEED ONLY TO PARTAKE OF WHAT ONE WORKS FOR HONESTLY N KNOW THAT ONE IS A CHILD OF THE LIGHT.

SIT. PARTAKE. REFRESH. WOW SARDINES. BALANCE? QUESTIONS. WHY STOMP??? TOO MUCH. ONE WORRIES. DO NO TARRY THAT THING... MIND... WITH QUESTIONS... ONLY DO WHAT ONE REQUIRES TO DO N TO EXIST. AH DISCIPLINE. UNDERSTOOD. EXERCISE FREE WILL, EAT WHAT THOU WILL THAT IS CLEAN. PARTAKE ONLY THAT WHICH IS PURE. SLOW DOWN. YOU JUST FOUGHT WITH YOUR OWN ENEMY. HAVE WON. YES FOR NOW. WHY? DO NOT QUESTION. FILL. REFRESH, GO EXERCISE YOUR OWN NATURE. NOW YOU KNOW THE NATURE OF THE BEAST. GO.

YOU KNOW. DOGS ARE GOOD FRIENDS TO HAVE COMPANY IF YOU ARE MESSED UP. YOUR DOG IS TO BRING BACK BALANCE N A SELF-FORM OF STYLE N BE. PARTAKE. REFRESH KICKECK.

GO. EAT DRINK THE WATER GIVEN FREELY FOR LIFE GIVEN DO NO TARRY OR TITTLE, GET WHAT YOU REQUIRE FOR NOW... DO NOT BE GREEDY TO TAKE THE FRUITS OF LIFE. QUESTIONS

LATER. EXPAND. FILL. STILL JUMPING ABOUT LIKE A MONKEY IN A ZOO. ONE IS A WILD ANIMAL MY DEAR SON OF THE SUN... ONE ONLY HAS TO KNOW N BE FREE. PARTAKE... FILL.... BUT! SLEEP, NO NO NO NO WORRY... WHY WORRY...? THAT IS ONES SIN. WORRY IS ONES FOREVER COS THAT IS ALL YOU GOT IS FEELINGS FEELING FEELINGS.... YES. DO NO COMMAND UNLESS REQUIRED. BE. EXIST BE... ENJOY. ENJOY WHAT ONE HAS... I HAVE NO TASTED THE MELON YET... GO. NOW LOOK... SEE.. TOUCH.. FEEL... DO EVERYTHING IN THREES N LIVE LIFE GIVEN FREELY. ONE BATTLES WELL. WOW! GASP! I KNOW I SHOULD GET THE MELON. BUT I MIND IS COSMIC BLASTED... FORMED N MOULDED. PARTAKE... FILL.... GROW... LEARN... SEE.... ONE NOW HAS THE KEYS TO THE GIFT OF LIFE. GO. DO NO EXERCISE... GO IN PEACE N COMPASSION N GRACE JUST AS ONE PRAYS TO HIGHER CONSCIOUSNESS. FILL FROM WITHIN... BE.. SEE... FEEL... GO... DO.... DO NO WORRY... HOW COME??? AH DO NO TRY TO MOVE BEFORE YOU CAN THINK. THINK??? HA HA HA... DO... BE.... JUST BE... EAT... REFRESH N SEE.... SLOWLY... TIME IS NO ONE'S ENEMY.

GO. DO.. BE.. WOW! THE SQAUSH, I EAT IS SWELLING MY SKIN. THIS IS ONLY NATURAL. ONE IS THE FULL SUM. OF WHAT ONE PUTS IN. PLUS A FEW OTHER CRINKLES AROUND THE EDGES. AH SUNGLASSES. NEED TO SEE WITH EYES OPEN NO CLOSED. WOW! ORANGE LIGHT. BEATS IN TIME WITH I HEART. DESIRE N SPACE HAVE BEEN THROWN OUT OF THE WINDOW. BE.. FILL.. BE.. FILL.. GO.. REFRESH... GO NOW...EAT OF THE

MELON... IT IS YOUR LIFE GIVEN FREELY. ANGER IS GOOD... CONSTRUCTIVE... BUT REMEMBER PEACE THAT PASSES ALL OF ONES UNDERSTANDINGS. DO NO LABOUR THINE LIFE. SOMEDAY SOON, I AM GOING TO BE ABLE TO WRITE THIS PROPERLY INSTEAD OF KIND OF LIKE DAYTIME DREAMING... TRYING NOT TO FILL OR RISE TO FAST AS WEARY. IMMENSELY TIRED. GONE SPACED BLASTED COSMIC AQUAMARINE ENFOLDS... FEEL N BE. GO! GET THE MELON. MUNCHECK. GO...

REMEMBER. THOU RESPECT FOR THIS IS FREE... AS IS COMPASSION... LOVE N PEACE.... LIFE IS GIVEN FREELY. DO NO TARRY OR WORRY... BE... THE ENERGY FOR LIFE COMES FROM WITHIN. GO N BE. WOW! THE MELON BURNS I SKIN. SLOW DOWN.. BE... FILL.. FEEL... WOW! MY BODY FEELS LIKE ROAD TRASH WOULD IMAGINE ITSELF TO BE. HORRIFIC BUT STILL. AT ONE. BUT EXERCISE WHAT ONE ONLY KNOWS HOW TO... THAT IS THE WAY TO GET OUT OF ALL THIS CRAP. AH MUSIC. FLOWERS N THE SUN. LOVE OF LIFE GIVEN FREELY... GO. MELON. FILL. GO. EXERCISE WHAT YOUR WILL. CHICKEN FEED, ONE KNOWS ONES NEED.

GO. MUST REMEMBER TO TRANSFER FILES FROM TOSH TOO LEO. COS. NEARLY TRASHED TOSH. KNOCKED THE KEYS. J N P OUT OF THE DECK. SO CAN NO USE IT PROPERLY AS DYSLEXIC AS HELL N HAVING TO HAVE TO STOMP. EVERYTHING LIKE A MONKEY IN A CAGE AWAITING TO BE FED N FILLED. CHILL.. PARTAKE... REFRESH... GO... CURRY TONIGHT. KICKECK. NOW... WHAT ONE IS THAT...? THE NATURE OF THE BEAST THAT YA FIGHT. GO...

REFRESH... LIVE.... WOKO SELA BUSHAKA MEDITATE. SEE. FEEL.. LIVE.. BREATHE... EXIST ONLY FOR THE MOMENT OF THE GLINT IN ONE'S EYE. AMUSE THY SELF. LOVE THY SELF AS ONLY ONE KNOWS HOW. BE N LIVE. WOW! I AM TIRED. BUT LIKE TO WRITE. I AM COMING BACK TOGETHER SLOWLY LIKE A SHATTERED JIGSAW. REFRESH... GO.... WOW! SOME NIGHT. FEW. JUST LOOKED IN THE MIRROR. LIKE WHAT I SEE, BUT WHAT ONE HELL OF A FREAKING BATTLE. THE FIRE N ANGER HAS BEEN EXTREME MORE THAN REALITY SHOULD HAVE ALLOWED. BUT NOW I HAVE DISCIPLINE. THIS IS GOOD. CONSTRUCTIVE. HA HA HA HA I READ WHAT I HAVE WRITTEN N SEE SO CLEARLY. I WILL LOVE MOST DEARLY ADDICTS OF OPIUM N SUCH LIKE SUBSTANCES. STOP. YOU ARE ALREADY IN HELL. COMING BACK TO THE LIGHT IS LESS PAINFUL. I NOW KNOW. THE SCARS ON MY BODY I HAVE GIVEN TO G.O.D AS A REMINDER OF WHAT I AM.. AN ANIMAL. NO PAIN. JUST GAIN. THEY GOT THAT WRONG AT SCHOOL ALSO. THEY SAY NO PAIN NO GAIN NO TRUE, I KNOW NOW. THE DARKER SIDE OF MY INNER SELF GIVES ME THE COURAGE TO FIGHT WITH PURE LIFE FOR LIGHTNING TO SEE WITH. LIKE WHITE HORSES CRASHING THROUGH THE HEAVENS STOMPING. GRACEFUL, REMINDFUL OF GRACE. PURE EMULATION OF BEING AT ONE WITH NATURE. WOW! I GOT A HEADACHE LOL LOL LOL ...

AH ONE HELL OF A NIGHT! SHALL TELL MORE OF IT LATER. SUFFICE TO SAY I HAVE MANAGED TO TURN MY HAIR WHITE OVERNIGHT. INCREDIBLE. WOW! I TELL ONE FOR SURE... YOU

THINK YOU ARE SECURE. WELL N LIVING ONE'S LIFE THE RIGHT GIVEN. CRAP. ONE IS ALL SO SHUSHED UP EACH OTHER'S APPLES EYES WITH MONEY THAT ONE NO EVEN GIVE SPACE TO LOOK AT THE PROBLEMS CREATED IN THIS SOCIETY TODAY. ONE DOES NOT LIKE THE TRUTH. WELL, WHAT THE HELL! I BEEN THERE... DONE THAT... WORN THE CLOTHES N GRABBED THE BULL BY THE HORNS N WRESTLED WITH MY OWN SELF TO TRY TO UNDERSTAND THE MEANING OF MY EXISTENCE. N THE ONLY THING I CAN REALLY THINK OF THAT WILL MAKE ONE REALLY SECURE N HAPPY WILL BE FOOD, ALL SORTS OF EVERYTHING... CLEAN.. NO DIRTY MEATS... NO UNCLEAN HERB, KIND OR DRUG. ONE IS BLIND. DOCTORS, GOVERNMENTS, AGENCIES. TOOLS OF CONTROL. CONTROL OF THE OPIUM ADDICT, WITH SLAVERY TO METHADONE. I CLUCKED OFF SMACK MANY MANY SPACES, BUT NEVER IN I LIFE WRESTLED SO HARD FOR MY LIFE AS COMING OFF METHADONE. NOW THAT TOOK FOUR HOURS N NOW JUST CRUISING. HAVE TO EAT ABOUT 2000 CARBS OF DIFFERENT MEATS N FISH. AH GRAPES. WELL AT LEAST I NO WASTE FOOD ANY MORE.. I SIGH N LAUGH AT THE GLOW OF MY INNER BEING. AT BEING STILL ABLE TO TYPE, LAUGH, CRY N SING. WITHOUT COLLAPSING INTO SHOCK WITHDRAWAL. TOOK A WHILE TO GET HERE. COS, I HAD TO WORK OUT HOW TO GET OFF THE BENZOS. THEY NO AGREE WITH ME, I KNOW COS THEY ARE NOBODY'S FRIEND. SELF-

EXAMINATION JUST GIVES WEIRD N STRANGE NUMBNESS OF BODY. CLARITY OF MIND N HEARING. SIGHT REALLY MASHED, BUT ON THE OTHER HAND NO. WOW! POWER!!! THE HERRING HAS. PURE FIRE. I FEEL HER RISE. THAT IS BURNING WITHIN.

RADIATING LIKE A DIAMOND ACROSS THE BACK OF MY EYELIDS. SHAME ONE CANNOT JUST LOOK AT THE COLOURS FOR 40 DAYS + INSTEAD OF ALL THE BODY CRAP. BALANCE. MEDITATE. WATER. I HAVE A HEAD LIKE A PEANUT. SPLIT OPEN N THE LITTLE CURL OF THE TAIL ROOT IS SLOWLY GROWING OUT OF THE TOP OF MY HEAD. TIRED LOLOLOLOL WOW! ON FOOD.

WOW! I MUST BE CRAZY COS SOMEONE TOLD ME ONCE TO EAT N I TELL THEM THEY ARE FULL OF CRAP. I AM FULL OF CRAP. LOLOLOL

I HAVE TO NOW RETIRE TO MY BATH CHAMBER N PONDER NOTHING IN MY BATH. FOR I HAVE FOUND THE SENSE OF HOT SOAPY WATER MOST INVIGORATING N RESTORATIVE.. AFTER EATING, ALLOWING ME TO SLUMBER A WHILE. I BID ONE N ALL.. A FAIR N MOST WONDERFUL DAY N SHALL CALL IN ON ONE N ALL AGAIN REAL SOON. TIMOTHY LEARY GOT IT WRONG. IT IS NO TURN ON, TUNE IN N DROP OUT... IT IS TURN ON TUNE IN N CHANGE THE PROGRAMME. BEING A COMPUTER MECHANIC FOR SOME YEARS NOW TEACH I THIS. I GET FREAKED OUT SO MUCH BY WHAT OTHER PEOPLE SAY THAT I DON'T EVEN CONSIDER MY OWN THOUGHTS, FEELINGS. DESIRES.. SENSES. THIS THING DESIRE. PEOPLE THINK OF IT AS WANT. THIS IS WRONG. DESIRE IS THE CENTRAL ESSENCE OF THE LOVE OF LIFE'S EXISTENCE. TO BE ABLE TO PLAY... LAUGH... CRY N SING FREELY. WITHOUT REGARD FROM OTHERS N HUMILIATIONS.

PEACE IS A PROCESS OF SMASHING DOWN THE WALLS OF ONES MINDSET N REBUILDING ANOTHER. RE-PROGRAMME

THE MAN. THE INNER BEING EVOLVES. ROLES OVER THE COUNTRYSIDE LIKE GREEN GRASSES N ALL KINDS OF ANIMALS N ROOT VEGETABLES OF THE FIELD. IT MUST BE A GOOD JOB TO BE A GROCER FOR ONE MAY ALWAYS HAVE ENOUGH N SUFFICIENT FOR THE DAY. WOW!!!

SWEET BLESSINGS.

IT IS EARLY IN THE DAY NOW N I GO TO LIE IN I BED. THE LIGHT IN THE ROOM IS A CANDLE SET BY A MIRROR, CURTAINS DRAWN. COZY QUILT N CUSHIONS SPREAD.

THE FAN IS REAL NOISY, NO THAT MUST BE A PLANE FLYING AS WELL.

NO SOMETHING DIFFERENT, HIGHER PITCHED.

I LAY VERY STILL, EYES CLOSED N STARE INTENTLY INTO THE DARKNESS.

THE SOUND I COME TO REALISE IS THE AIR RUSHING THROUGH MY NOSTRILS, MAKING A SOUND LIKE IT IS BEING SUCKED UP A PIPE. THE OTHER NOISE AS IF ALL SOUND IS BEING WHIPPED THROUGH A VORTEX TUNNEL.

THE PITCH GROWS SLIGHTLY N THEN DISAPPEARS, TO BE REPLACED BY THE INNER CLICKINGS OF A CLOCK IN A DRAWER SOMEWHERE IN THE HOUSE.

A KALEIDOSCOPE OF RED YELLOWS N BLUES EXPLODE WITHIN MY MIND'S EYE, TUNNELING OUTWARDS, WITH INCREASING SPEED.

I NOTICE THIS TIME MY GUIDE TO BE AYA.

SHE SHOWING ME THE WAY AS IF I HAVE PARTAKEN OF THE BITTER TEA.

DOTS APPEAR, TINY RED FLECKS, GLIDING SMOOTHLY ALONG AN ALLOTTED PATH, SPREAD OUT UPWARDS, TWISTED.

LIKE TWO PLUG HOLES DRAINING... JOINED IN THE MIDDLE OF EYES HORIZON, AT BOTTOMS, TURNING ONE LEFT DOWNWARDS N ONE RIGHT UP.

TWIST FOR TWIST FROM LAND TO SKY.

GOLDEN FLECKS DANCE AMONG THE REDS, SPINNING ENDLESSLY ON AT A STEADY RATE SHOWING ONLY A DESIRE TO CONTINUE UPWARDS TO CREATE A SKY, THE LOWER AS IF BEING SUCKED FROM THE GROUND.

THIS THING IS COLOSSUS, AS IF MADE FROM WATER, GLIDING EFFORTLESSLY UPWARDS, LIKE SPOUTING WATER IN THE AIR N ALLOWING IT TO COVER..

THE WHOLE SKY AREA OF EARTH WITH FINE MOISTER AIR.

I SHIFT MY VIEW N REALISE THERE IS LIGHT ALL AROUND ME... GOLDEN GRAY LIGHT THAT ILLUMINATES A WALL TO MY LEFT, ATOP OF WHICH APPEARS WOODEN BEAMS, SLOWLY N MORE CLEARLY, WITH EACH INTENT LOOK I CAN MAKE OUT WHAT SEEMS LIKE CHINESE LANTERNS FLOWING BY LAZILY ONWARD - AS IF KITES WITH A PURPOSE.

BLUES, GREENS N YELLOWS, BUT THEY ARE NO CHINESE PICTURE DESIGN, BUT SIMILAR IN THAT THEY SEEM TO BE DRAWN WITH A BRUSH.

THE WHOLE CEILING COVERED IN TIMBER PLANKING, WITH LARGE WET BLACK IRON OAK ROOF BEAMS BETWEEN. THE BRICKS ARE OF REDDISH CLAY, COVERED IN BADLY UNKEMPT WHITEWASH, EVERYTHING IS SEEN TO BE KEPT IN GOOD REPAIR, BUT OLD.

I TURN N LOOK N A ROCKING CHAIR SITS DIMLY LIT FROM THE CANDLE.

I GAZE AT THE POLISHED SURFACE, HAND WARMED WOOD. WELL CARED FOR.

GOLDEN YELLOW BROWN GRAIN WITHIN THE SURFACE EXTREMELY FINE.

THE BACK OF THE CHAIR IS HELD UP WITH TWO TWISTS OF WOOD, ATOP PLACED A CUSHION, WHITE FAWN WITH SLIGHT ROSE FLOWERS. ALL THE WOOD IS POLISHED N CARED FOR.

THE CHAIR SITS MOTIONLESS HANGING THERE.

VIBRANTLY ALIVE, BUT SOMEHOW OUT OF REACH, I TURN N OPEN MY EYES FOR A BETTER VIEW N I AM STRUCK BY JAGGED TRIANGLES N STRANGE BLACK BROWN RED FORMS HANGING IN THE AIR, LIKE SOME GROTESQUE SIDESHOW BAT THAT HAS BEEN ALL TWISTED.

A BLINK IN MY BOTTOM RIGHT VIEW WINDOW REVEALS ....

MYSELF STANDING N LOOKING, SMEARED PAINT UPON MY FACE WITH SPEAR IN HAND.

HAIR SLICKED BACK WITH CLAY

SLOWLY I CRACK A BIG SMILE N DISAPPEAR INTO THE WOODS.

VANISH, GONE.

I GAZE AROUND AT A NEW ROOM FROM A STRANGE PERCEPTIVE, AS IF OBSTRUCTED FROM STANDING, MY BODY HALF MERGED IN THE FLOOR...

THERE HANGS AT EACH OTHER WALL RED FLOWING CURTAINS. THEY FLOW SOFTLY IN AN UNFEELING BREEZE. I CAN SEE THE FINENESS OF THE CLOTH, THERE IS A COAT OF ARMS ON EACH SIDE HOLDING CUPS N SWORDS, TWO HORSES N FIFTEEN LANCERS, EIGHT TO THE RIGHT N SEVEN ON THE LEFT. THE COAT OF ARMS SEEMS FAMILIAR TO ME... THE TWO HORSES RAISED AS IF TO GREET ONE ..

THE CURTAINS HANG ON LANCES AS FLAGS, WITH THE POLE RUNNING THROUGH HOOPS IN THE CLOTH.

THERE STANDS A DARK WOOD CABINET, FLAT FRONT LITTLE DESIGN. CURVED FEET OUTWARDS. ATOP THIS ALSO STANDS AN EXQUISITE VASE, GARNERED IN STRINGS OF PURPLES, PLUMB BLUES, DEEP OCHRE REDS... THE PORCELAIN WHITE N AGED, BUT CLEAN N VIBRANT. THE COLOURS LOOK FRESH AS IF TO PICK THE GRAPES N TASTE.

I PEER AT THE CORNER OF THE MIRROR N A FACE APPEARS AS IF FROM BEHIND A CURTAIN OR VEIL OF VINES. IT IS I, MY FACE MARKED FOR HUNTING, I HAIR SMEARED WITH MUD, SPEAR IN

HAND. I AM LOOKING INTENTLY INTO MY LEFT EYE N PROMPTLY TURN N WALK AWAY. NOT A CHANCE OF A QUESTION, AS I CRY INWARDLY "WAIT!"

AFRICAN TRIBESMEN COME N LINE UP IN FRONT OF ME... BEGINNING TO DEMAND ATTENTION.

BIG ROUNDED SHOULDERS N WASTES FROM OVER INDULGENT LIVING, THEY LOOM THEIR WAY OVER.

FACES DISTORTED N MANGLED, TEETH HANGING OUT N EYES OOZING PUS ...

POLITELY I SAY, "GO TO THE BACK OF THE LINE N I WILL SPEAK WITH YOU LATER." THEY TURN N LEAVE.

ONLY LINGER MORE PERSISTENTLY IF I GAZE AT THEM LONG ENOUGH.

OTHERWISE PEOPLE SEEM TO FLOW PAST ME AT EASE, SMILING.

CHILDREN HOLDING THEIR DOLLIES WITH FRILLED BONNETS, LADY HOLDING ONE HAND FOR CARE, USHERS ALONG, ONE COUPLE OF MANY. SOME COME N SIT N PLAY IN FRONT OF ME ...THEIR FACES GHOSTLY N GROTESQUE WITH DECAY, ALL SEEM TO SAY ONE MESSAGE: "BE BLESSED."

SOME COME N GEAR N SNEER, TRYING TO SCARE ME AS SUCH, THEY ARE ASKED FIRMLY TO GO, WITH RESPECT, THEY LEAVE.

UPON THE CEILING LARGE FLOWER LIKE LAMPSHADES SIT, MOTIONLESS N SERENE, CREAM WHITE PETALS SIT AS IF REAL, A DUSK LIGHT SHINING AROUND.

A VERY LARGE CONE NOW SITS TO MY LEFT N THE GROUND IS MOVING AGAIN, EVERYTHING AS IF TO BE MADE OF CONCRETE, CLOSER INSPECTION ... ETHER, NO SUBSTANCE TO HOLD.

A LARGE SILVER BIRCH TREE STANDS WITH BRANCHES STRETCHED WITH TIPS JUST FLOWERING, SET AGAINST A RED GLOWING SKY, BUT AUTUMN.

A SERIAL KIND OF SADNESS ALL HELD TOGETHER WITH LOVE.

I HEAR WHISPERS OF BLESSINGS

WE ARE ALL THE SAME.

A YOUNG LADY DANCES, TWISTING N TWIRLING ENDLESSLY AROUND N AROUND. SPINNING LIKE A TOP, NO TOO FAST NO TOO SLOW, ALL CONNECTED TO THIS SPINNING ROCK N I LIVE ON.

I FOLLOW THE PATH N SEE GRAND CANYON WALLS CLEARING OFF IN THE DISTANCE AS IF LIKE A RUNWAY FOR PLANES OR SPACE CRAFT.

THESE GREAT WALLS ARE ARCHITECTURE WITH LARGE ANGULAR SIDES, SWOOPING IN LONG GREY SILVER TENDRILS.

SUN FLOWER,

HAS HEAD TURNED DOWNWARDS SITTING AS IF WAITING, FOR WATER, SUN MAY BE.

YES, YES I LOVE THE SUN.

THE CHILDREN SING.

LAUGHTER CARRIES TO THE AIR N I VIEW LADIES PASSING, SKIRTS PLEATED, REDS, PURPLES, BLUES OF MANY TONES. HAIR DONE CLASSY.

THEY LAUGH N LEAN OVER ONE ANOTHER TO CONFIDE.

TO MY LEFT THERE HANGS A FRAMED PICTURE N CHILDREN SITTING N PLAYING AT PICNIC, THERE IS A VIBRANT CHATTER, RATTLE IN THE AIR.

BLACK NINETEEN THIRTIES SEDAN TAXIS DROP OFF ONTO A RAIN SOAKED STREET, ALL UMBRELLAS BLOWING OPEN INSIDE OUT IN THE WIND, ALLOWING FOR LITTLE PROTECTION FROM THE RAIN.

WAITERS IN BLACK SUITS CARRY SILVER PLATTERS OF DRINKS N MORE, FRUIT N MANY, MUCH MORE TO THE LADIES EXUBERANT DELIGHT.

LADIES CARRY CIGARETTE HOLDERS, SLENDER, N PEARLS.

TO MY RIGHT IS A BAND STAND OF MUSICIANS SURROUNDED BY BEAUTIFUL LADIES, PLAYING N SERENADING AS IF ONE TO ONE, BUT ALL OF THE PARTY IS FELT LIKE A RIPPLE OF VIBRATIONAL MOVEMENTS IN THE ROOM, IN TIME TO THE BAND.

A DISCERNIBLE HICK OF HIP HERE, N A SWOOSH OF HEAD THERE, LIKE SEAWEED OF FIRE REDS N CHERRY LAID UPON THE LADIES HEADS AS IF HAIR.

SWEET MEATS FOR THE TASTING I CARE.

PHOTOGRAPHS OF MANY, BABIES, MUMS, DADS, SISTERS, BROTHERS, AUNTS, UNCLES, GRANDMA N GRANDDAD N SO ON. ALL STRETCHING FORWARD BACKWARDS, ANY GIVEN POINT ON TIME LINE CAN BE SEEN FROM BOTH WAYS, PAST N FUTURE.

WHAT IS THE MOST ASTOUNDING IS WHAT I CAN SEE SO CLEARLY WITH EYES CLOSED. I PEER AT A SHAWL CAST OVER A STONE ON A HILLSIDE. THE MEADOW BLOWS SOFT GREEN YELLOW, SPECKLED WITH REDS, THE INTRICACIES OF THE WEAVE ARE BOGGLING AS IF HOLDING A SPECIAL KEY ONLY FOR MY EYE.

WICKER WORK BASKETS N BOXES FOR TO CARRY THE FLOWERS IN.

SHOE SHINE STALLS, BOXES OF BLACK SHINY SHOES, PAPER POSTERS ON THE WALLS, TORN, HANGING. GAMES, CASINOS N DAMES.

BROADWAY STRIP LIGHTS TWINKLE INTO VIEW, "ROOM TO LET", "ROOM TO LET OFF" AN AIRPLANE BLASTS BY.

LIKE SOMETHING OUT OF A MOVIE, BLACK FLASHY BY DESIGN, CLOTHES RAIN SOAKED N WORN APPEARING AS WET LEATHER STRETCHED OVER AMPLE BOSOM. EVERYTHING BLACK TACKY WET.

STORM DRAINS GUZZLE DOWN STREET RAIN N WHISTLE SOME MORE, PAPERS ALL GURGLING IN THE STEW.

TIRED I SIT, I FEAR I HAVE BEEN WALKING.

A PUSHCHAIR SWINGS DOWN FROM TOP LEFT INTO VIEW, WHEEL STATIC AS TIMELESS. BLACK WITH WHITE TRIM HOOD LACE N A ROW OF BABY DUCKS, YELLOW ORANGE RED N GREEN, THE BLUE ONE CRUSHED BY TEETHING.

I CAN SURVEY THIS CHAIR FROM VERY MINUTE DISTANCES N ALSO VIEW THE GRAIN IN WOODS AS I GET CLOSER.
TOO MUCH DETAIL FOR ONLY ONE CANDLE.

A WHITE WALL SLIDES INTO VIEW WITH INTRICATE PATTERNS ETCHED IN THE SURFACE, ONE TRIANGLE UP, TWO DOWN, CIRCLE RAISED.

THIS DOES NO MOVE OR CHANGE ANY SHAPE, JUST HANGS THERE SERENE WITHIN PURPOSE.

SOME OF THESE IMAGES MUST LAST FOR 40 MINUTES PLUS AS I LIE INTENTLY LOOKING.

TWO WALKING STICKS AS IF LAID UPON THE GROUND, ONE HANDLE CURVED AS AN EGG.
THE FLOOR MARBLED IN SOFT PINKS N HUE BROWNS, HARD N COLD.
THERE IS A SLIGHT LIGHT REFLECTED OFF THESE OBJECTS COMPLETING THE TRANCE AS TO APPEAR COMPLETELY REAL.
ALTHOUGH DIMLY VIEWED AT FIRST THE EYE BECOMES ACCUSTOMED TO A CERTAIN WAY OF LOOKING.

A YOUNG GIRL COMES N SITS ON MY BED WEARING A BLUE COAT N NECK SCARF ... SHE GREETS ME BY WAVING N MOUTHING HELLO. I CAN NO HEAR HER REPLY. I SAY, OH BLESS THE LITTLE GIRL. SHE SMILES N DOES A LITTLE DANCE FOR ME WITH TWINKLY BLUE SAPPHIRES FOR EYES.

A LADY SHE IS RELATED TO WEARING A LARGE BONNET N BOWL OF FRUIT HAIRDO, BENDS OVER TOWARDS ME ALMOST DROPPING THE HEAD GEAR. THEN SHOCKINGLY SHE SAID IN A VERY SWEET TONE. IT IS VERY GOOD TO MEET THEE. BLESS. THERE IS SOMETHING IMPORTANT ABOUT THESE FIGURES, THESE PEOPLE TO ME, LIKE SOMETHING FORGOTTEN N VEILED, ONLY SEEN SLIGHTLY. I KNOW THEM AS FAMILY, I NOW FEEL REAL GOOD THEY ARE WITH ME. I TRY TO SHAKE HANDS WITH THE LITTLE GIRL, SHE ALSO WITH ME, BUT I FAIL TO MAKE CONTACT N HER HAND JUST MELTS AWAY.

LEAVING IN REPLACEMENT A WARMNESS N A SMILE.

I KIND OF HANG THERE WITH NOTHING TO SAY, BALANCED BETWEEN SADNESS OF THE LOSS TO COME N RELUCTANCE AT THE ACCEPTANCE.

ALL EVENTUALLY TURN N WANDER OFF, SLOWLY WITH RESPECT THEY GATHER THEIR WEARS, PUSH TROLLEYS N SUCH LIKE N WANDER OFF OVER THE HILLS.

MOUNTAINS LOOM TO MY RIGHT. GREAT JAGGED PLINTHS, SCARRING GRANITE FINGERS, STAND AGAINST A PURPLE

YELLOW SKY, A VERY DIM GLOWING SUN GLIMPSED, CRACKING THE COMING OF THE NEW DAWN.

I SEE TANK LIKE WAR MACHINES WITH GREAT STEEL TRACKS. SOLDIERS ON TOP N AROUND ABOUT... DRESSED IN LONG BLACK CAPES, MASKS N GOGGLES. EACH HOLDS A MACHINE TYPE PISTOL.

SOLDIERS RUN INTO A GLADE, FLASH, A GRENADE GOES OFF. MUTILATED ARMS N LEGS, FINGERS. I VIEW A SKULL HALF OPEN WITH THE LEFT EYEBALL HANGING OUT...

THE SOLDIER IS SMILING.

ANOTHER SOLDIER IS LYING CLOSE BY SCREAMING. I CAN NO HEAR HIS SCREAMS, BUT SEE HIM TRYING TO PICK UP HIS OWN GUTS N PUT THEM BACK INTO THE BLOWN OUT CAVITY OF WHAT WAS ONCE HIS STOMACH.

I SEE PLANES FLY HIGH, A BLINDING FLASH, SEARING HEAT. GREAT CLOUDS OF STEAM LIKE DUST PLUME HIGHER N HIGHER. THE AIR IS FILLED WITH SNOW, ALL IS DARK N DYING.

ALL ABOUT IS SUDDENLY ALIVE WITH WEEDS HANGING LIKE SEAWEEDS OF OH SO MANY VARIETIES, COLOURS N TEXTURE, A VEIL DROPPED TO SEE THROUGH. I AM COVERED IN EXOTIC CLOTHS, FINE AZURE LIKE WISPS OF FABRIC ONE CAN SEE THROUGH, BUT ALSO HIDE ONES FACE FROM SCRUTINY N GLARE OF SUNLIGHT PRYING EYE.

BEFORE ME STANDS VAST HERB CHALICE FOR BURNING, BUT NO LIGHT. I LOOK AROUND N SEE THAT I AM IN SOME KIND OF BRICK KILN CHIMNEY... ABOVE THE TOP BLOCKED OFF... IT

FEELS STRANGE TO STAND IN A BOX, THE LIGHTS GLOWING RED ORANGE OF THE SURROUNDING BRICK WORK.

THERE IS STILL A MOISTURE ON THE AIR... IN THE DISTANCE A YOUNG HAWK CRIES EERILY, FOR THE PARENT TO COME BY N BRING FORTH HIS BREAKFAST, SO HE MAY DINE.

I GENTLY LOWER MYSELF UPON THE GROUND, SIT CROSS LEGGED N SIGH.

WOW! THAT IS HARD WORKED FOR, TO SLEEP NOW,

SHALL TRY!

HUE LIGHT SHINES ON A WINE GLASS FULL OF RED WINE, ONE DROP OF WINE SPLASHING UPON THE GLASS SURFACE, CREATING ONE RIPPLE ETERNITY, THE DRIP AS IF TO HANG IN THE AIR WITH ANTICIPATION OF THE LANGUAGE ABOUT TO BE EXCHANGED.

ONE BREATH FOREVER, ALL ARE THE SAME.

BLESSINGS I WHISPER.

SWEET BLESSINGS .....

LIFE IS FULL OF PLACES I MUST COME TO,
A FULFILLING OF ACCEPTANCES OF PAST EXPERIENCES,
PRESENT,

N PRAYED FOR FUTURES.

WHEN ACCEPTANCE OF LIFE N LOVE N PAINS ARE BROUGHT TOGETHER AS EQUALS,

THE SEER IS ABLE TO CLOSE THE BOOK N MOVE ONWARD REMEMBERING.

REMEMBRANCE IS THE GIFT OF GOLD GILT GIVEN UPON THE CHALICE OF LIFE (DRINK DEEP MY FRIEND)

FOR THROUGH OUR LIVES I GIVE SUBSTANCE N HONOUR TO OUR DEEDS.

BE BLESSED...

+++

DRAGON N I COME CONJURE IN THE NIGHT.

DRAGON! I ORDER, "COME NOW TO MY CASTLE."

EYES CLOSED THE DRAGON COMES!

A FLASH OF SCALE N SHINING TEETH,

A SMILE FULL OF BEGUILE,

AN EVIL RED EYE GLINTS N SMILES.

AS HE COILS N FLIES THROUGH HILLS N DALES.

DRAGON I COMMAND THEE, COME!

I CALL FOUR AT ONCE RED BLUE GREEN N GOLD.

I DUCK MY HEAD AS THEY UNFOLD WITHIN MY MIND'S EYE

...

WITHOUT ...

DRAGON COME!

I ORDER THEE!

DRAGON KEEP MY CASTLE SAFE.

LADY IBOGA

THE EXPANDING BREATHING SPACE OF THE WARMTH N LOVE N SECURITY OF IBOGA.

IN A SENSE IT IS LIKE GOING BACK TO THE SECURITY OF THE WOMB N THEN PSYCHOLOGICALLY BEING REBORN.

WHITE WALLING BODY MEMORIES N ALLOWING THE PERSON TO BECOME AT ONE WITH THEIR INNER TRUTH.

A MOST POWERFUL PLANT N TEACHER.

I TRY TO DISOBEY THE SPIRIT OF IBOGA N SHE HAS ME OUT OF BED QUICK AS A FLASH N DRUMMING ON A STOOL IN I HALLWAY FOR OVER AN HOUR. I AM SHOWN MY SIN N WEAKNESS N THEN TRIED TO CONTINUE AS I ALWAYS DO, IBOGA IS NO PLEASED N DISCIPLINES ME...

TO THIS DAY, SOME 14 MONTHS LATER I HAVE NO GONE AGAINST WHAT THE PLANT TELLS ME...

A MOST INCREDIBLE ENTITY.

THE ENERGIES RISE SLOWLY N SURELY WITH THE RISING OF THE SUN.

THE SPIRIT SITS WITHIN N GUIDES.

LIKE A GENTLE LADY TEACHER HOLDING MY HAND N HANKIES IF I CRY.

THE CALL OF THE WILD, THE SONGS OF THE TREES.

IBOGA IBOGA, MY LADY I SEE.

AT ONE WITH THE CREATURE ALL ONE WITHIN THE FOLD.

ONE MIGHTY GREAT LIFE FORCE A KEY TO THE VOID,

EXPERIENCES RUN IN MILLIONS OF ENTITIES,

JUST PSYCHIC FOOD, LIKE CATTLE I ENDURE.

THE SPIRIT OF ALL AGES REQUIRES TO DINE.

LIKE WINE FOR THE OFFERING OUR THOUGHTS THEY RUN FREE.

FUNNY LITTLE MONKEY.

EAT ME N SEE.

ALL ANCESTORS SINGING N BRINGING MUCH BLESSINGS…

FOR THE LADY IBOGA ENFOLDS WITH CARESSES OF SILVER… AZURE N GOLD.

EMERALDS N DIAMONDS … PRECIOUS BRACELETS N CHAINS,

A CHOKER OF RUBIES, THE LADY GIVES TO REARRANGE.

THE CHAOS WITHIN IS SHOWN FOR THE MINDLESS DESTRUCTION WITHOUT.

OH!

THANK YOU LADY IBOGA FOR TEACHING ME THY SONG.

A SONNET SET IN HEAVEN.

I RISE AS HIGH AS THE SUN CREATING COSMOS N RETURN WITH ALL THE LIGHT.

MY DARLING LADY IBOGA WITH THEE I REST THIS NIGHT.

BEING OF LIGHT

THE SUN RISES SLOWLY, STILL, WITHIN THE FOLDS OF MISTS, SHARDS DANCING LOW AMONGST THE TREES.

THE WARRIOR STANDS, ARMS STRETCHED ABOVE HIS HEAD.

HE EXCLAIMS,

"IT IS A GOOD DAY TO DIE"

MUSING WITH THIS COMMENT INWARDLY SMILING, HE COLLECTS PROVISIONS FOR THE "CEREMONY OF SEEING" N WANDERS SLOWLY INTO THE WOODS.

LEAVING ALL CONCERNS OF FAMILY, HOUSE N LIFE BEHIND.

IN A GLADE WITHIN THE WOODS A LARGE OAK TREE FALLEN IS USED AS "MESA".

ATOP ALONG THE GREAT TREES TRUNK,

WAND N STAFF ARE PLACED WITH CARE.

A RED SILK BAG OF RUE HE PLACES AROUND HIS NECK N BEGINS TO CHANT.

SLOWLY THE RHYTHM RISES N FALLS.

HANDS BUSY WITH PREPARATION OF INTENT WITH HERB N SPICE.

LACED CLAY IS PLACED WITHIN A PIPE N OFFERED TO THE SKY.

REACHING FORWARD HE GRASPS AT THE GROUND N TEARS CLODS OF EARTH N GRASSES, SMEARING FACE N HANDS.

STILL CHANTING THE WARRIOR RISES N LIGHTS A CANDLE N INCENSE, PLACING OIL UPON STAFF N WAND... HE BENDS BACK HIS HEAD N CRIES WITH PURE DESIRE OF SELF N LIFE AT THE COSMOS THAT SURROUNDS.

IT IS TIME.

ANOINTING HIMSELF WITH OIL THE WARRIOR SITS CROSS LEGGED UPON THE GROUND, STRIKES STAFF ON TREE N SMOKES THE PIPE.

THERE IS AN INNER SHUDDER, A SHIFT OF ENERGIES, COLOURS EVOLVE LIKE TENTACLES, BLUES, GREENS, YELLOWS, REDS.

FROM A CENTRE, OUTWARDS EVER EVOLVING.

EVERYTHING MOMENTARILY IS SEEN AS IF A GREAT PLUME OF ELECTRIC PEACOCK FEATHERS, MAJESTICALLY SWAYING N EVER CHANGING.

HE STANDS N SURVEYS THE LAND.

EVERYTHING ALIVE, SPIKED WITH THE INTENSITY OF LIFE, BEAUTY IN EVERYTHING, COLOURS ELECTRIC.

CURVED TENTACLES OF BLUES N GREENS EXPLODE N WRITHE LIKE FROM THE CENTRE OF AN EYE, ALWAYS FLOWING OUTWARD ENERGIES FROM WITHIN.

SUDDENLY A WAVE OF ENERGY, PURE AS LIGHTNING GRABS HIM N HE BEGINS TO SHAKE.

LIGHTNING ENERGY FROM A CENTRE WITHIN POINTING OUTWARDS, LIKE A STAR... ENERGY COMING IN.

FASTER THAN LIGHT.

HE IS PHYSICALLY HIT BY WAVE AFTER WAVE OF INCOMPREHENSIBLE ENERGIES N MUMBLES,

"WILL I DIE THIS DAY?"

ALL LIGHT N ENERGY OF THE COSMOS FOCUSED AT THIS POINT ANSWERED FIRMLY,

"NO."

FROM CENTRE OF FEELING HE IS SEPARATE FROM THIS ENTITY, BUT ALL OF BIOLOGICAL SELF IS HELD TOGETHER BY THE ENERGY OF THE

"BEING OF LIGHT".

ALL THOUGHTS ARE ANSWERED INSTANTLY, WHOLE BEING FLYING THROUGH COSMIC SPACE AT LIGHT SPEED.

THIS ENTITY, EVERYTHING CONSCIOUSNESS CAN CONCEIVE N MORE.

IMMENSELY MORE.

PURE PERSONIFICATION OF LIFE FORCE N BLINDING DIAMOND WHITE LIGHT.

IT TRAVELS WITH HIM, IS PART OF HIM, IS STILL WITH HIM.

IMMENSELY HARDER THAN DIAMOND, WITH FORCEFULNESS OF LIFE CREATION N CONTINUANCE GREATER THAN ATOM BOMB EXPLODING OR SOLAR SUNS COLLIDING.

EQUAL BALANCE OF ENERGIES.

LIKE A HUGE DRAGON CREATURE OF LIGHT EVER MOVING, THIS ENTITY COMMANDS COMPLETE OBEDIENCE N RESPECT.

UPON GAZING AT THE DRAGON ENTITY WHO HAS A BODY GREATER THAN ALL CONCEIVABLE DIMENSIONS.. EVERYTHING PERCEIVED BECOMES COMPLEX, BEAUTY, ALL CENTRED FROM AN ATOM CENTRE OF CODES N EXCHANGES, ATOMIC CONVERSATIONS.

IMAGES OF LIFE EVOLVED THROUGH MANY DIMENSIONS, FLASH WITHIN THE WARRIORS EYES, MULTIFACETED LIKE A DIAMOND, EVER GROWING, EVER DIMINISHING.

CONTAINING ALL MEMORY N PROJECTION, KNOWING DIRECTION.

NOTHING LEFT TO CHANCE.

THE SPEED IS MIND BLOWING AS IF THOUSANDS FASTER THAN FEELING....

THE ANSWERS ALMOST BACK BEFORE THE QUESTIONS ARE COMPLETE.

EVERYTHING PERCEIVED IN TEN DIMENSIONS, N FIVES, WITH SUBSTANCE OF SPACE, TIME N MEMORY.

ALIVE N FULL OF LIFE PURPOSE,

FROM ROCK TO OCEAN,

FROM SEED TO TREE.

PARTICIPATING IN THE ORCHESTRA OF AN INFINITELY COMPLEX BEAUTY, SLOWLY STRIKING OUTWARD, STRAIGHT, AS LIGHT, OUTWARD, ETERNAL.

NEVER RETURNING TO THE SAME.

SUNLIGHT BURSTS THROUGH THE OVERHEAD TREES UPON THE STANDING WARRIOR.

ELECTRICAL EXCHANGE OF SUNLIGHT N THE BODY EXPLODE WITH VISIONS OF MOLECULES COLLIDING N EXCHANGING ENERGIES SO FAST IT ALMOST BECOMES UNBEARABLE.

PHYSICALLY ALL THE MOLECULES OF BODY, FEEL, EXCHANGE, TALKING.

THE SPACE IS NOW RIPPING AROUND HIS BODY LIKE A WHIRLWIND N LIGHTNING LIGHT, RESETTING N REALIGNING ENERGIES.

WAVE AFTER WAVE HITS THE WARRIOR N ALL INTERNALISED ENERGIES EXPLODE, BUT KEEP THE SAME FORM.

COILS,

SPRINGS IN AURA,

BLUES N ELECTRIC SILVER, GREENS N YELLOWS, REDS, EXPLODE WITH SYMMETRY, RIDDLE OUTWARDS FROM HIS BODY EVERYTHING EXPANDED WITHIN THE SUNLIGHT.

SUNLIGHT OF LIFE!

ALL THE COLOURS MAZATEC N VIBRATING.

NOW THE VISIONS COME COLLIDING INTO PHYSICAL FORCE.

VISIONS OF MAZATEC, HIGHLY EVOLVED BEINGS, AS IF THEY HAVE FOUR ARMS, HANDS HOLDING CURVED SWORDS OF LIGHT.

THE WARRIOR CRUMPLES TO HIS KNEES N CHANTS.

POWER IS NOW DRAWN FROM CHANT.

THE SWORD BEARING WARRIOR IS COVERED IN ELABORATE JEWELLERY N GARMENTS OF EVER MOVING ELECTRIC GREENS, BLUES, GOLDS N SILVER.

IMMENSELY POWERFUL WITH BIG GRINS ON THEIR FACES.

THE WARRIOR CHANTS, GRASPING STAFF, N BEGINS TO DANCE.

POWER TAKEN FROM ALL, CONVERTED THROUGH FOCUS OF MINDS INTENT TO STAND, RIGHTEOUS UPON THE ENDLESS ONSLAUGHT OF INFORMATION.

THE MAZATEC WARRIORS OF POWER OF SPACE N KNOWLEDGE OF EXISTENCE OF LIFE'S CONTINUATION.

GREAT SPACE TRAVELLERS, LEVELLERS OF DISPUTES N WAR.

THEY TELL OF GREAT WARS TO COME, OF LAND N SEA.

THINGS THE WARRIOR CAN NO COMPREHEND.

THE WARRIOR STANDS INWARDLY BLINDED.

ONLY NOW ABLE TO SEE A STAR LIKE BEING HOVERING, TRAVELLING EXTREMELY FAST.

EVERYTHING IS CONNECTED, JOINED, EVOLVED, TRAVELLING TO SEE, BECAUSE IT CAN, THIS BEING OF LIGHT, OF INTERSTELLAR TRAVEL.

GREAT VISIONS OF SHIPS OF GREYS N GREENS. CIGAR SHAPE N RIBBED FLOAT WITHIN THE VOID. SHIPS FLASH BY LASERS BLAZING, HUGE GAWPING HOLES WITHIN THEIR HULLS. SMALLER ATTACK VESSELS SWARMING LIKE BEES.

PLANET SURFACES EXPLODE WITH ORANGE YELLOW INCANDESCENCE OF MOLTEN DESTRUCTION AS HUGE MOTHER SHIPS CUT THEM UP WITH POWERFUL LIGHT SWORDS.

STUMBLING NOW THE WARRIOR CRIES OUT FOR WATER, GRASPING BOTTLE N GUZZLING FOR DEAR LIFE.

THE WATERS LANDING WITHIN, RADIATES CLEANSING N LIFE.

SLOWLY BUT SURELY EVERYTHING FOLDS BACK IN AS IF THROUGH A FUNNEL.

ENERGIES REFOCUSING BACK TO SELF.

THE "BEING OF LIGHT" GIVES THE WARRIOR A GIFT OF RESPECT, OF MUTUAL ACCEPTANCE OF LIFE N DEATH, GLIMPSED IN A NANO SECOND BY EACH.

EXISTENCE ALWAYS RUNNING THE RAZOR EDGE OF THE BALANCE OF LIFE N DEATH.

THE WARRIOR LEARNS GREAT KNOWLEDGE.

THE WARRIOR LEARNS OF HIS QUEST.

TO STAND WITHIN THE BALANCE.

HE CLOSES HIS EYES N CAN SEE NOTHING BUT A BLINDING STAR RADIANT BLUES N SILVERS.

EYES OPEN EVERYTHING IS BRIGHT, ALSO WITH MEANING.

THE STAR LIKE BEING PERCEIVED FROM A DISTANCE.

THE CENTRE OF MINDS EYE ROLLS, GENTLY LIKE BUBBLES, MOLECULES COMBINING.

LIGHTS OF SILVER N BLUE FLICKER N DANCE, SURROUNDED BY A STAR LIKE HALO.

AURA RECHARGED N CENTRED.

THE WARRIOR STANDS N SMILES.

"IT IS A GOOD DAY TO DIE"

LOOKING FOR ANSWERS

IT TAKES TWO N A HALF WEEKS.

THE DOWNLOAD IS IMMENSE,

VISIONS OF COMPLEX MACHINERIES, OF VAST MIND LIKE COMPUTER SUPER BEINGS, TRYING TO RULE, BUT DYING IN AWESOME WARS.

PLANETS N GALAXIES CAN BE SEEN, BURNING, THUNDERING AGAINST ABUSE.

ORANGE SCARRED N TORN FULL OF FLASHES OF LIGHTNING.

I AM UNABLE TO HEAR THE THUNDER OF SUCH DESTRUCTION FROM MY VANTAGE POINT WITHIN THE VOID,

BUT I FEEL THE SHOCK WAVES N HEAT,

SEE THE DEBRIS FLY.

FROM A CENTRAL VIEW ALL IS LIKE AS IF COLLIDING DOWN A WORM HOLE,

SILVER N ENDLESSLY ALIVE.

I SEE THIS DIMENSION AS MATTER N THROWN THROUGH SPACE...

ETHEREAL CONNECTIONS OF TRANSIENT LIGHT FLICKER ABOUT MANY SMALL CENTRES.

THESE CENTRES,

CONCENTRATIONS OF LIGHT ARE BEINGS, FELLOW TRAVELLERS.

TRAVELLING THE SAME PATH AS I.

SLOWLY WEAVING WITHIN THE TUNNEL OF THIS DIMENSION,

TENTACLES BRANCHING OUT INTO OTHERS.

SO MUCH SO MY DATA-BASE JUST GIVES UP.

MANY TIMES NOW JUST CRAWLING AWAY, CURLED UP N SWITCHED OFF.

IT ALL COMES DOWN TO COMMUNICATIONS BETWEEN EVERYTHING.

LIKE THE THREADS WOVEN WITHIN A FISHING NET 4, 5, 6, DIMENSIONAL, CONVERSING BACK N FORTH

LEARNING TO GET THE CONVERSATIONS CORRECT.

ALL ENERGIES INWARDS TO A POINT, ENERGIES FLOWING OUTWARDS, EVERYTHING CONNECTED, ALL IN CONVERSATIONS WITH EACH OTHER BACK N FORTH ALONG THE SAME LINES.

THE ART IS TO LEARN THE LANGUAGES N UNDERSTAND THE CONVERSATIONS,

THE COMMUNION OF LIFE.

I SEE THE EARTH AS IF FROM SPACE,
VAST BLUE HALF SPHERE VIEWED,
GREEN BLUE OCEANS,
BROWN PATCHED LANDS,
SCATTERED WITH CLOUDS,
SURVEYED FROM AN AWESOME HEIGHT.

THIS IS THE HEIGHT OF CONSCIOUSNESS ATTAINABLE.

COMMUNICATIONS SO FAST AS IF TO SEE MAN HITTING A PIPE OF SPICE N LAUNCHING AT LIGHT SPEED INTO THE FUTURE,

EXCHANGES N COMMUNICATIONS EXPAND SO FAST THAT THEY SEEM TO STOP,

BECOME SO LARGE AS IF NEVER TO EXIST.

A CONSCIOUSNESS EXPANDED SO FAR AS IF TO ENGULF EVERYTHING.

WOW!!!

I GET MY ANSWER...

IT IS ALL ABOUT COMMUNICATION WITH YOURSELF N THE WORLD, THE WORLD SPEAKS BACK IN SUBTLE TELEPATHIC VIBRATIONS, SLOWLY BUT SURELY GOING ABOUT AN AGE OLD PRACTICE OF LIVING N DYING, BECOMING EVOLVED.

I SEE AS IF THROUGH MULTI-DIMENSIONS ALL CONNECTED AS IF LOOKING OUTWARDS FROM WITHIN A MIGHTY DIAMOND,

ALL FACETS JUST ANOTHER SPAN OF SPACE N DIMENSIONS, ALL DIMENSIONS INFINITE.

IT IS SO OVERCOMING, SO VAST... SO AWESOMELY BEAUTIFUL.... COMPLEX N SIMPLE.

DEATH OF THE BODY, JUST A BEGINNING OF TRANSITION,

LIKE THE CATERPILLAR CHRYSALIS BREAKING OPEN N SETTING FORTH A MOST WONDERFUL BUTTERFLY BEING,

OF PURE SPIRIT N LIGHT.

I EAT THE FOOD,

SPIRITUAL,

SUSTAINING,

AS THE CATERPILLAR CHEWS ON THE LEAVES,

I CHEW ON THE LEAVES OF LIFE.

I PUPATE,

N I TRANSCEND.

AH!

AWESOME,

BLESSINGS, MY FELLOW BEINGS OF LIGHT.

RESPECT

WE ARE ANGELS AWAITING TRANSITION INTO BEINGS OF LIGHT

N SO THE STORY CONTINUES

I FIND PLANTS.

A COAT OF MANY COLOURS~

A COAT OF MANY COLOURS~

SO AS NOT TO WANDER THROUGH A WILDERNESS ALL TOO FULL OF SAND, SCORPIONS, ROCKS, SEARING HEAT SNAKES OF FALSE PASSIONS PAIN

PLANTS FOUND UPON THIS DESOLATE PATH TO PARTAKE OF LIGHT IN DARKNESS

TO GIVE FOR, TO SUCCOUR AS FOOD ALSO A COAT OF MANY COLOURS,

A STAFF TO LEAN UPON N WIELD, A HEAD AS AN ORB OF CREATION,

A HEART FLOWING LIKE A MINNOW FLASHED SPRING STREAM OVER WET SUN SHARDED DAPPLED BROWN PEBBLES

A PSYCHIC CATHEDRAL FULL OF VIBRANT AZURE FISH AS FEELINGS DO FLITTER, OF SUNNY SHOALS DO FLOW ACROSS INTO LOWLY SANDY BAYS

IN OCEANS FLOW OF EBB TO TIDE AS ROLLERS, WHITE HORSE UPON THE BEACH OF ONES MIND'S EYE EXPANDING, TO FILL AS THE RISING OF A SILVER MOON

TO CAST TREE N MOUNTAIN THUNDERCLOUD SHADOWS UPON ONES SIGHT EXPLODING SUPER NOVA AS A STAR

A SPIRIT LIKE A ROE BUCK DEER, BOUNDING LOFTY MOUNTAINS HIGH, DASHING GRASSY DALES IN DEEPS OF FOLDS OF GRASSLAND VALLEYS, A STREWN OF WHITE N YELLOW DAISIES

TO SMILE AT THE BRIGHTNESS OF IT ALL

UPHOLDING OF SPIRIT GREAT EVERGREENS, THROUGH MOUNTAINS FULL OF SNOW AS AVALANCHES OF EMOTIONS MOVEMENTS CREATE SPARKLES TO THE SKY

OF MOUNTAIN GLADES TO SEA

WITHIN ONES MIND'S EYE

CREATION

SO RUTTING IN THE MUD OF EVOLUTIONS COIL TO SET A FORTH AROUND THE TREE OF LIFE TO POSE N PAINT A PICTURE IN WORDED PROSE

OF PASSIONS RAGING VOLCANIC ERUPTIONS WITH LARVA FIRES OF A COLOSSAL SUNSET WITHIN ONES TEMPLE FOREHEAD

THE PLANET FOR ONE'S EYES TO PREPARE A TABLE BEFORE OF FRUITS N TREASURES OF TRUTHS AS SPEARS N SWORDS AS ARROWS DO FLY

THEY DO NO LIE AS DEAD AMONGST THE FOLDS OF HUMUS TO RETURN AS NAUGHT AS FLYING BRISKLY SHEEP FLUFFY WHITE GREY CLOUDS

ACROSS AN ENDLESS TRANQUIL SKY A SITTING UPON A STUMPED TREE, FALLEN OFF WINTER'S WINDS AS STOOL

TO SMOKE N PONDER

A DAZZLING OF MIND N SIGHT OF... AS HEART'S EMOTIONS FLITTERED AUTUMN LEAVES UPON THE DEW BE SPECKLED MULCH OF, TO SEE MY BODY AS TO LAY UPON THE GROUND

FOREVER SUCH BEAUTY SO CLEARLY SEEN OF ALL AROUND WITHOUT DISGUISE SO FILLED WITH BLISS AS IF TO BLIND

ONES SO TINY AS AN OWLET'S DOWNY FEATHER GENTLY FLUTTERING TO A LEAF ON GROUND

OF ABOUNDING GENTLE PEACEFULNESS

AS SPRING LIGHTS N SHINES, THE SKY

    OF HERB POKING THROUGH TO SHOW OFF GREEN LEAVES TO GROW

    OF FLOWERS TO SEE AS A COAT OF MANY COLOURS TO COVER THE LAND AS BIRDS A-MANY SETTLE FROM FLIGHT

    TO SIT N PONDER OF THIS WONDER OF ALL THIS LIFE HAS GIVEN TO ONE'S HAND

    TO STAND STEADFAST UPON THIS ROCK

    TO SEE THE MAGNIFICENT GLORY OF CREATIONS BEAUTY

    THAT DOTH ABOUND LIKE A MIGHTY RIVER FLOWING WITHIN ONE'S HEART

    OH! WHAT JOY, BLISS OF PEACEFUL GENTLENESS

A COAT OF MANY COLOURS

OF MINES OF MEN TO SEEK THE LIGHT OF WISDOM

OUT OF ROCK N STONE OF WOOD... WATER... FIRE... MINERAL N LIGHT DO GLOW

OF SPIRIT WALKING WITHIN THE PALACE OF CREATION READING, WRITING, TALKING, FEELING, EATING, BREEDING, LOVING, DYING

OF MIND'S TO MINE THE SONNETS OF GOLD~

AWW... THE SUN IS OUT~

OF SCHOLARS, FOOLS N WISE TO SEE OF ALL WITHOUT DISGUISE

ONE TRUTH TO BEHOLD WITHIN ONE'S HEART'S EYE TO OPEN~

TO BEHOLD THE GLORY OF THE CROWN OF LIFE~

ONE LOVE~ ONE LIFE ~ ONE PALACE~

AN ANGEL SITS N GUIDES

AWW THE SUN IS OUT~

AWW THE SUN IS OUT~

AN ANGEL SITS N GUIDES~

WARM

BODY FUZZY WARM OF GLOW WITHIN SKIN ENERGIES DO FLOW

A SLITHERING AROUND ONE'S CORE TO COIL A TENTACLE TENTATIVE TO A SMILE

N CHASE THE LITTLE FISH OF REASON TO THEIR DEATH OF EATING TO FULFIL

OF UTTERANCES N SILLY SCREAMS TO SMOTHER OF ONE'S PRECIOUS ATTACHMENT MEMORIES

ROLLING ON THE GROUND BODY FUZZY MOVING AS OF MUD, IN WARM VOLCANIC FLOWS

WRITHING AS A WET SEA, SNAKE UP THE TREE BOWS, SURROUND TO CHASE THE LITTLE MONKEYS TO FLIGHT

SLOWLY ROLL AROUND ONE'S EYE MIND EVOLVING GREEN N BLUE ERUPTIONS OF TATTERED LEAVES SPUTTER TO THE FLURRIES OF FOLIAGE

AYE, TO DANCE THE TWISTED MORPH TO SEE THE SPRING ELK FROLIC KICKING OAKEN MOSSES, BODY BLOWING STEAM TO THE FRESH CRYSTALLINE MORNING AIR

OF MANY MILLIONS OF BLADES OF GRASS TINKLED TOED BY TINY ANT, GLISTEN OF SUN DEW COVERED WITH ARRAY OF FALLEN PINE LEAVES SPIKED

FLATTER FLY BY DEAR BUTTERFLY OF TWO WINGS OF YELLOW GREENS N REDS TO BROWNS, ORANGES TO COVER ONESELF WITHIN COCOON OF GLOWING PINKS OF VARIANT LIGHT AS WRAPPED LEAFS AS CIGARS DO HOLD LIKE A SILK WORM FOLDING, WEAVING HOME TO PUPATE TO GROW WINGS WITHIN A BOUND OF THREADED COVE, A MANTLE COAT OF RAINBOW COLOURS TO FLY OFF WHEN SHE GROWS

TO SQUIGGLE N GIGGLE AT THE SCENE OF OH SO MANY DRAGONFLIES ZIPPING, BUZZING BY, DANCING ON THE WATER LILY FLOWERS AS DAZZLING SUNS, GLISTENING EXPLOSIONS OF NEW BUDS OPENING OF THE DAWN LIGHT THROUGH THE POOLS OF LEAFY PADS WITHIN ONE'S EYES

SOFTNESS OF DAISIES RACING, GOING ABOUT SHOWING SECRETS DELIGHTS WITHIN THE GOLDEN LADDER OF EVOLUTION'S COIL OF PETALS SPREADING UNCOVERING OF PISTILS TO STAMEN, TO SMOTHER FUZZY BEES WITH POLLEN BURS LIKE TEA CAKES N CANDY UPON LOLLY STICKS TO FEED NECTAR TO GLITTER WHERE EVER

FLASH AS RAINBOW TROUT A JUMPING OF THE POOLING MIRE OF WHERE I LEFT MY SOUL THIS NITE A-FLAPPING LIKE A RAG TORN UPON A WIND-BLOWN BARB OF THE FENCE THAT CONTAINS ONE'S HEART~

OF PIPE A HANGING FROM TOOTHLESS JAW DO SMILE AS LITTLE WHISPER SMOKES A HECKLES TO THE SKY

AS TO ARCH MY BACK N BREATH THE WATERS OF FLEXED TROUT TAILS DO SPANGLE IN THE AIR TO GLISTEN AS FALLING THROUGH ETHER, SEEKING CRAGGY BARK N TREE TRUNKS, LITTLE RIDDLES OF DROPLETS OF WATER TO THE MULCH THAT BOW OF LOW MAJESTIC STARES N WHISPER IN THE SOFTLY SPOKEN WINDED LOFTY HALLS FLUTTER OF TINY BRANCHES LEAFED HIGH ATOP THEIR BOWS UPON THE MIRRORED WATERS AS REFLECTIONS PHOTOGRAPHS, A FLAT OF STARE~ UPON THE TIMELESS LAKE~ INFINITY~

OH POOL OF MOONLIGHT TICKLE TO GIVE OFF PRECIOUS SILVERS TO THE GLADE OF STEADY LEGS A STANDING OF OH SO MANY TREES

OF CASTING SHADOWS AS SWORDS DRAWN WICKED TO THE NIGHT

FLASH THE COMET STRIKES ITS CORD OF SYMMETRY N FLIES BY

DISTANT NOW WITH STARS A-SHINING TO SMILE ANOTHER DAY, NO DOUBT RETURN OF ARC TO ORBIT THIS GLADE OF WOODS, SHIMMERING GLOW A GOLDEN BOW, A SMELLING OF NEW CUT HAY

OF NOW A SPLODGE THIS DAY OF ALL ABOUT ONE'S BODY SELF-EMULSIONS EMOTION FOLDING MOULDING IN THE EARTH AS TINY SPECKS OF SAND, AS SATELLITES TO SETTLE TO FIND A WEAR OF COMFORT

AH HA THEY CRY, THERE WILL BE ANOTHER LAUNCH IN FIVE

TOO OF WHERE N EVER WONDERS OF YOUR MINDS DEVISE

ANOTHER LAUNCH TO WAIT OF FIVE IS NAUGHT TO CRY OF AS WHEN YOU CAN HOLD THE JOYSTICK OF THE LITTLE HELICOPTER

AYE OF WHERE THE FLIGHT MANUAL OF MIND TO RE-COLLECT OF ALL THE BAGGAGE WAS LEFT UPON THE GROUND

IT SHALL BE THERE UPON YOUR RETURN "SIR" TO PICK THROUGH AS YOU CHOOSE

THE LEFT LUGGAGE SIGN SMILES BY

AS SPLATTED TO THE TRAIN WINDOW GLASS AS TINY FLY LEFT LUGGAGE SMILING LIKE A CLOWN BEHIND

EXPRESS TO NO-WHERE WITH RETURN. THE TICKET PUNCHER SMILES, CLUNKS THE DOOR A CLOSING

ONE BREATH INFINITY DOES SMILE

OF ALL BLASTED ASUNDER SQUASHED BY G-FORCE TO THE MAX NOW GLIDING

BREATHING SPIRALS COLLIDE N HOLD FOR A MOMENT, ZAP ASUNDER OF A TRILLION BRAIDED COSMOLOGIES, GALAXIES DO FLY

THIS IS YOUR CAPTAIN SPEAKING "YOUR MISSION HAS -------- HOLD ON FOLKS WARP FACTOR NINE WITH COMET TAIL IMMINENT"

ASSUME THE POSITION SAYS THE CUSTOM MAN

WHAT?

IS THE QUESTION

THE JOURNEY IS OVER?

OF WHERE IS ALL THE LUGGAGE MAN

THAT WAS LEFT UPON THE GROUND?

"OH WE GAVE THAT ALL TO OXFAM SIR YOU GONE OFF NEARLY NINETY NINE

TO AUGHT OF EVERYTHING

THE LITTLE CHILDREN LOVED YOUR SUITCASE

WHAT?

THAT CAN'T BE RIGHT TO SHAKE ONES HEAD AT ALL THE POP

N DIVE BELOW THE COVERS ONCE AGAIN OF ONE'S QUILT TO SEE ALL THE COLOURS SMILE WITHIN THE DARK TO SHINE

N AGAIN N YET OF ME OF ALL

AS OF WITHIN ENORMOUS SHEETS OF RAINBOWS, ATOMS TO THE MIND EXPANDED TO NOTHINGNESS

"YOUR TICKET SIR," THE CONDUCTOR SMILES.

"YOUR RETURN IS IMMINENT."

HA HA HA TO SMILE OF ALL THE BEAUTY N CHAOS OF IT ALL UNREAL FOR SURE

AS LITTLE FISH SWIMMING TO DANCE WITHIN THE SUNLIT POOLS N PLAYING WITH CRABS AMONGST THE SEAWEEDS FLOWING OF REDS N GREENS

UNREAL OF ALL OF WHAT N EVER IS THE QUESTION

AS LADY OCTOPI DRIFT BY MILLING, A LIPS A GLOWING PINK N PURPLE, LITTLE WHIRL POOLS OF MIND EXPLODING ALL AROUND AS A SUBTLE SWIRLS

ALL TO FALL WITHIN OH SO LARGE A TORNADO FLYING ACROSS THE HEAVENS OF THE ATOLLS OF ONE'S CRESCENT SUN'S EMOTIONS FOLDING TO FULFIL ALL DESIRE.

I AM

BODY FUZZY WARM OF GLOWING WITHIN, SKIN OF ENERGIES DO FLOW UNREAL

HA HA HA

BLISS

OOPS I BROKE IT ONCE AGAIN UNREAL FOR SURE WITHOUT EVEN TRYING UNREAL OF TO BE DIFFERENT UPON RETURN

HA HA HA HA HA.

HA HA! ANIMAL WALKING UPON THY LAND OH LORD, THE MAGIC OF IT ALL TREASURE GOLDEN SUNLIGHT

HOUSE LAND HOLY, HOLY, HOLY, TO REMEMBER ALWAYS OF GRACE TO FORM ALL

OH MY TREASURE GOLDEN SUNLIGHT RAIN UPON THE MAGIC OF THY LAND SPIRIT WALKING OF ALL! OH MY, OH BLESSED MOLECULE OF WAY TOO MUCH UNFATHOMABLE BEAUTY LITTLE CREATURE RUNNING ON THY LAND OH MY, WAY TOO MUCH OF ALL TO SEE OF EVERYTHING TREASURE GOLDEN SUNLIGHT, OH MY DEAR LORD, TO SEE BOUNCING LITTLE FLEA UPON THY LAND LITTLE FURRY ANIMAL, TO SEE OH BOUNCE LITTLE BALL OH MY!

OH MY, TO SEE LITTLE FURRY CREATURE BOUNCE UPON THY LAND, OOH MY TREASURE GOLDEN SUNLIGHT, WAY OF ALL BREATH OF GOD, OH MIGHTY TREE

OH MY, LITTLE FLEA

BOUNCE

OF A LITTLE SCURRY, OH MY TO SEE OF ALL A CRITTER

BOUNCE

FOR ALL OF MY REMEMBERING OF MY DEATH N BACK AGAIN TO A SCURRYING ANGEL UPON THY LAND

OH MY GOD A MIGHTY MOLECULE

HA HA HA RUN CRAZY SQUIRREL UPON THY LAND, GATHER NUTS LITTLE FURRY ANIMAL

ALL IS FEAR N LOVE, OH ME, WAY TOO MUCH TO SEE MY CREATION OF MAGIC

SCURRYING LITTLE CREATURE UPON THY LAND ROCK, BOUNCE TO SEE OF ALL THE FEAR

SCURRY TO ESCAPE OF CREATION, BOUNCE WAY TOO MUCH, BROKE ANOTHER FUCKING KEYBOARD COMPUTER BOUNCE, HA HA HA ANGEL CLASSICAL MUSIC, REQUIRED TO SHOW OFF HA HA

SOUND BEFORE LIGHT UNREAL

TO SEE OF GOD THROUGH ME TO YOU N BACK AGAIN BOUNCE

N FOLKS WROTE THE LIVING WORD AS GOD UPON THY LAND OF MAGIC BIBLE

EZEKIEL'S WHEELS OF SPIRIT FLY

SWEET JESUS OF ANGELS, TO SEE THEY KILLED YOU

PA

I AM DISSOLVED I AM AS GOD OF ALL ON ONE SIDE DARK TO LIGHT BIBLE LITTLE ANIMAL OF WALKING UNREAL TO

TREASURE OF WAY OF ALL CHURCH SWEET GOD OF CREATION MOLECULE TO FLY I EEE A HE HE HE MONEY MONKEY OF CHAOS HE HE HE

CRAZY FUCKIN SQUIRREL COLLECTING METAL INSTEAD OF NUTS OF ALL OF TREASURE OF GOLDEN SUNLIGHT HE HE HE

OH MY HOW MUCH OF ALL OF LIFE CAN YOU EAT TOO OF ALL OF OF MY OF CRYSTAL WATERS GRACE UPON THY LAND HE HE RUN H BOUNCE TO SCURRY HEE HE POP AYA EEEE A..

UP A MOUNTAIN ROLL A DALE TOO SEA BREATH OF GOD RAIN UPON THY LAND

HA HA OF BICYCLE TO WHEEL OF FACES RUN OF WAY TOO MUCH FUCKING AWE FOR MAN UPON THE LAND HE HE HE

HOLY H LEFT RIGHT OF ALL TWIST THE COIL TO SHAKE THE EARTH OF ROCK TO STAR SUN ASUNDER UNREAL

HE HE EH GOT TO GO N BOUNCE FOLKS HEE

OH MY! I SHALL SCARE THE LIVING BEE JESUS OUT OF EVERYONE IF I GO TO SIT OF ALL TO SHOW TOO CREATE OF ALL FEAR OH SCURRY CREATION OF BREATH TO LIFE BOUNCE OF ALL HE HE HE HEHA

HA HA H RUN SCURRY OF MY HEE HEE I DRINK FOR TWO OH MY THE TREASURE OF GOLDEN SUNLIGHT TOO SEE OF ALL THE MAGIC UPON THY LAND FOR SUNLIGHT HE HE HE OF ALL TO K~ YOUR BIBLE PEOPLE BOUNCE LANGUAGE OF EVERYTHING TO POUR FORTH YOUR LIVING WORD UPON THY LAND THROUGH WATER SUNLIGHT HUMUS TO ROCK HE HE HE

OH MY OF WAY TOO MUCH FUCKING GLORY UNREAL OF YOU HE HE HE BOUNCE BOUNCE SUN OF MAN

I KILLED EVERYTHING TOO SEE OF ALL HE HE HE MAGIC UNREVERSAL UNIVERSE

OH MY HAVE I COME DOWN AS OF YET OH MY TOO WALK THE DOGS BEHIND SUNGLASSES IN THE SUN HE HE HE FIELD GRASS TREE OXYGEN OH MY ALL THE CHAOS OF BEAUTY OF IT ALL HE HE EH

N THOSE THAT WROTE A BOOK TO SHOW OF FORM N ALL A SCURRY FURRY ANIMAL ATOM AN OF ALL HIS ORGANISM SCURRY OH

HA HA HA BACK AGAIN YOU GOT TO LOVE THE MOBILE TOO SATELLITE ACROSS THE WORLD OF ALL OF YOU AS ME THROUGH PRECIOUS GOLDEN SUNLIGHT OF LITTLE FISH OF LOAFS TO EAT,

OF ALL THE WONDROUS PARABLES ROLLED OF PROSE IN THE LIVING WORD MOLECULE GOD SIMPLE HA HA HA SYMBOL XYZ HA HA HA HA HA

OH FOR MY DEAR LORD I BODY..

OH SWEET LORD SWEET TREE OF CREATION OF LAND TO SKY TOO SEA

THANK YOU CREATION FOR OUR LIVES TO EXPRESS OF ALL THIS BEAUTY SO AS YOU CAN SEE IT ALL GLOW OF PRECIOUS GOLDEN SUNLIGHT AS FOLKS THAT RAIN UPON THY LAND, OF SUNLIGHT WALKING

MORNING SUN

STAFF STANDS, RADIATING LIGHT OUTWARDS FROM CENTRE TO EVERY POINT

ARMS LEGS FOLDING, COILING OF BLUES GREENS N YELLOWS

COILS FROM THE GROUND CARESS GENTLY AS SPARKLED LIVING WATERS UPWARDS REFLECTING LIGHT EACH SELF OUTWARD AGAIN

ATOMS OF OXYGEN, HYDROGEN METHANE N NITROGEN DO A MERRY DANCE TO COIL, COLLIDE TO EMULSE THROUGH SINGING OF GOLDEN RAYS

TREE OF MANY BRANCHES DANCES IN THE SUNLIGHT, CHUCKLING LITTLE BIRDS STRIP HER BARK FOR NEST

ANCIENT VIEW OF SELF-LOOKING AT ALL, AS IS, LIGHT DANCING AS GLISTENED RAINDROPS COILS CONNECTED WITH DIAMONDS OF PINK N BLUE

TO GAZE IS THE ONLY WAY FOR SCRUTINY, MAKES EVERY PIXEL TO DISSOLVE DOWNWARDS OF THE SPIRAL OF LIFE

LOOKING OUTWARD SITTING WITHIN, BRANCHED OFF A STILE AT A COUNTRY GATE TO MAKE DECISIONS TO CROSS

THIS MIGHTY RIVER OF EMOTION FLOWING TO MAKE THE CURVE OF CURRENT TURNING, N SEE GRASSES GREEN, BUSHES, LEAVES A QUIVER OF THE GLORIOUS SUNLIGHT

EXCHANGING LANGUAGE

GOD

AS TINY BIRDS TITTER

FLITTING OF BROWN FEATHERED COAT, BLACK HEADED SPARROW CASTS LEAF MOLTEN TO THE SKY

AS A BLACKBIRD SITS ON THE BOW OF A TREE SINGING SWEETLY FOR HIS LADY

IN THE RADIANT MORNING SUN

THE LITTLE MEXICAN STANDS WITH STRAW HAT UPON HIS HEAD SMILING,

BRONZE FACED, GOLDEN BUTTONED JACKET OF BLUE SWADE

ARMS LEGS TWISTING COILING GUITAR IN HIS HAND

FLYING, RUNNING ACROSS A BLISTER HOT BURNING DESERT

LAUGHING, SINGING, DANCING, PLAYING AS HE GOES TO THE JOY OF DANCING FREELY, LIVING WITHIN THIS GLORIOUS GARDEN

TO STAND THE TREE OF MANY BRANCHES, EMOTIONS SMILING CHUCKLING, GIGGLING, LIKE A NEW BORN SPRING STREAM

BUBBLING N DASHING, OVER WET SUN GLISTENED BOULDERS EVENLY LYING WITHIN THE POOLS, OF ONE'S MINDS REFLECTIONS

HEART A DEER'S BODY ROLLING DALES OF GRASSY GLADES TO MOUNTAIN TOPS TO SEE THIS OCEAN OF AWEN BLISSFULNESS

THAT SPARKLES WITHIN THE COIL OF LIFE THROUGH CLOUDLESS SKIES, UNTIL MORNING SUNLIGHT TINKLES

"HELLO" ONCE AGAIN

BUD TO TASTE

DRY WITHOUT A TOKE THE SHED A-HUMMING CUT FRESH THE SWEET SMELL OF GREEN,

DRYING SLOWLY IN THE SHARDS. SUNLIGHT'S KNIFE PIERCING A SPACE SO CONFINED

AS TINY PARTICLE, DUST DANCES THE DAGGER UPON CURRENTS UNSEEN

TIME A CHILLUM CHIMNEY OF STONE TO HAND, OFT TO SEE WHAT HARVEST BRINGS

OF RITUAL N CEREMONY OF THANKS, OF JEWELS GIVEN TO THE HANDS

SEAT, A SMALL ROUND LOG UNTIED BOOTLACE TO POLISH INSIDE THE GREY BROWN CHIMNEY CLAY

SO GRINDER WORKS THE WISP N FLOWER, A LITTLE STONE TO SIT,

LIGHT DANCES, SHOWERED RAINDROPS ABOUT HER SIDES

OF FLUFF TO PALM FILL ATOP CHIMNEY TO A CROWN

DRAPED NECK SCARF TO TWIST LIGHT THE TOP, BURN THE PILE BOOMSHANKA

CROUCHING MONKEY ON THE FLOOR RISING TO FILL AIR, LUNGS OF SMOKE

ALL THE WAY N TO THE FILL TO A BRIM, POUNDING STARTS THE TEMPLE

AS GROUND N SIGHT DO FADE THEN SLOWLY RHYTHMS RISING MAGIC WISPS OF LIGHT, GLISTENED MISTS

EXPAND CONSCIOUSNESS TO SPARKLE, RISE OF BUBBLED WATERS

GUTS OCEAN'S EMOTIONS, TEMPLE FOREHEAD DO FLY AS BEADS SPECKLED UPON THE BROW

TO FROWN, CROUCH, SEEN A FLASH THE LIGHTNING BRILLIANT HIT LIKE THUNDER TO THE FLOOR

OH AGAIN TO WALK THE LAND OF MAGIC EVERY HAIR STANDING, EARS PRICKED TO THE FORE

AS NOISE CRASHES, SENSITIVE UPWARD WATERFALLS CRASHING BLUES, A HUE OF GREEN N YELLOW

FLASHES, MARBLES DIAMOND WHITE UNTO THE AIR WALLS A TINY SHED FLOWING OUT BURSTING OPEN THE DOOR

TO FALL INTO DANCING UPON THE SUNLIGHT TO SHOUT N SCREAM UPON THE SOAKEN GRASS

OH JOY OF FREELY FALLING NUMB GONE, BLASTED ASUNDER TO HEAVEN

MIND AS TINY A PIGEON DOES FLUTTER WEAVING SILVER GOLDEN WINGS OF SUMMER SHOWERS,

DIZZYING TO BEHOLD, STREAMING CHEEKS AGLOW TO ROLL OUT UPON THE SODDEN LAWN

OF HAIR STANDING AS STALLION TO THE WIND

AS PATCHWORK LEAF EXPRESSING EXISTENCE, SHADOWS DANCING THE GROUND AS TINY MIRRORS

LOOKING DIFFERENT BUT THE SAME

SINGING TO BE NOTICED AS UPWIND BREEZES SALT TO LIP
BLOW GENTLE THROUGH HEARTS GARDEN
BACK AFT OPPOSITES HEAVY RAIN-CLOUDS DO SIT YONDER
AS FACES AS MANY WANDER UPON LIFE'S ENDLESS SKY

AWE BLISS!

HOODED ONE

AS A SMALL BLACK STALLION, HE STOOD, GENTLY MOVING TO THE FLOW OF BASSE

BLACK HOODY, TIGHT FITTING JEANS, ON THE PROWL OUT FOR THE NIGHT TIME TO TAKE OFF JEWELS TO KEEP N PLAY

INCREDIBLY ALERT, EYES DEEP SWIRLING PITS, OF DEATH TO LIFE THROUGH ONLY PHYSICAL REFLECTION IMMENSE AGE, LUSTS, DESIRES TO HOLD

OLD AS GALAXIES STARS SWIRLING, EVOLVING, TWISTING, COILING, DYING AMONGST THE BLACKNESS VOID HE STANDING AS NO CENTRE LINE OBSERVER, BUT OF A ROOT OF FILTH TO SLOWLY SEE HE TURNS N SURVEYS ME, A GLINT WITHIN THE EYE

THE MEETING OF SPIRITS, THAT RECOGNISED EACH OTHER ON THE MIND FIELD OF PRECIOUS JEWELS TO HOLD WITHIN ONE'S HANDS FOREVER

THE GUT SWIRLS MOVING AS MUD TIME TO STAND BRING ALL TO BE AS ONE IN ME

TO CAST AS ACROSS THE UNIVERSE SPLENDOUR, HOLDING THE LIGHT OF STARS IN ONE'S HEART

"I KNOW YOU," NOBUNONI STANDS

"I KNOW YOU" HE SAYS

AGAIN WITH POWER OF INTENT TO SHOW

"I KNOW YOU"

POINTING HEAD TO HEAD EYE TO EYE SPIRITS GATHERED AFORE ME BEHIND (SHAKING NOW AS I WRITE) STANDING TO THE FOUR WE SPLIT TO DO A MERRY DANCE

"I KNOW YOU," HE SAYS WITH AUTHORITY OF INTENT OF KNOWING, THEN SHOWS ME ALL

EVERY DESIRE TO BE MINE, ALL THE FILTH TURNED TO GRAPES N FLAGONS OF WINE, EMERALDS DIAMONDS, OH SO PRECIOUS PURPLES, AS STARS TO STRING ABOUT ONE'S NECK ALL TROPHY EVERYTHING REVERSED ALL FLOWING WITH BLACK, RED, VERY SUBTLE BLUES LIGHT, OF GREED, LUST N PRIDE TO GLORY TAKEN TO GIVE

 EVERYTHING THAT WAS, N IS, N SHALL BE - ALL THE JEWELS OF THE KINGDOM STOOD BEFORE ME

 A TABLE FOR ME TO TAKE OF ANYTHING I WISH

 "COME, COME WITH ME, LOOK TAKE A SPLENDID COAT FOR YOU, A RING UPON YOUR FINGER, A KINGDOM TO RULE, HE SAYS N PRANCES, AS KICKING HOOF TO THE DIRT "LOOK AT WHAT

I HAVE FOR YOU TO BE OF ALL, YOU ARE N MORE," SO SOFTLY SPOKEN OF INTENT

NOT OF ME, MY SPIRIT SHATTERING ENERGIES TO GATHER, ANGEL TO FLY

HE STOOD HIS GROUND N CALMLY SAID, "NOT NOW MY DEAR FRIEND, AT ANOTHER TIME N PLACE WE SHALL MEET AGAIN"

AS THE POWERS REFLECTED OF TWO MIRRORS LOOKING EVERYTHING FOR ONE SPLIT SECOND REVERSED

HE BECAME ME LOOKING THROUGH MY SOUL

I GATHERED EVERYTHING I AM N PUSHED HIM OUT

HE SMILED OF SICKNESS N DEATH

TURNED N WALKED AWAY

TO EVOKE AN ANGEL

I AM FORBIDDEN TO SAY HIS NAME

THE MAN KNEW OF WHAT HAPPENED

HE KNEW HIMSELF AS WELL AS ME WAY BETTER IN FACT

I MET A MAN ENTITY THAT WISHED TO DEVOUR ME, THEN OUT OF PRECIOUSNESS GIVE ME GIFT IN RETURN, FOR MY SERVICE

IF I OPPOSED HIM TO STOP HIM IN HIS QUEST OF LUST HE WOULD KILL ME OR DIE TRYING CALM, COLD, CALCULATED THE MAN A TRUE PSYCHOPATH HAD NO SOUL THAT HAD INVOKED

OF ANGEL SO THE ANGEL COULD USE HIM, TO DO HIS BIDDING OF NO MIND OF SELF, NO SOUL OF PERSON POSSESSED

   VEIL

   GENTLE, SLOWLY, FUZZY, PUSHING THROUGH A VEIL

   BRILLIANT BLUE EYES AZURE PIERCING BACK REFLECTIONS OF STARLIGHT

   TURNING, EVOLVING OF CLOUDLESS TO SKIES OF OCEAN'S DEEP BLUES

   HAIR A CURL OF THUNDEROUS RAIN CLOUDS, SWIFT OF PACE ACROSS THE SKY

   FOREHEAD PLOUGHED FIELDS RAINED, N SWEETENED OF FURROW TO GROW

   BROWNED N SUN WARMED

   NOSE A CEDAR OF BRANCHES GENTLY LOWING TO THE GROUND

   CHEEKS OF APPLES N BOSOM AMPLE BUTTRESS OF PEACHES DELIGHTFUL TO TASTE

   LIPS AS GORGES SPEWING FORTH MOUNTAIN TORRENTS GUSHING BLOSSOMS OF ROSY RED MUD

   HOLDING POPPY PETALS GLISTENED OF DEW, A MORNING SUNLIGHT DANCE, A SPARKLE GAZE A SUBTLE PINK SETTING SUN OF GOLDEN RAYS THE BURST OF PLUMPNESS UPON THOSE LIPS WET TO POUT

   CHIN OF RIGHTEOUS MOUNTAINS FOLDING TO SEA OF NECK

   A TREE OF ROOTS SINKING TO THE SOFT OF HUMUS GROUND

THY BODY OF THE EARTH

AY A POETIC QUEST TO EAT N SAVOUR, TURNING MOTION INTO LIGHT

OFT SEEN TO MOVE A GENTLE SPARKLE SMILES AMONGST THE DEW DROPS

CLOUDED MIND OF SLEEP IN MORNING MISTS

FATHER SUN OF BOUNDLESS BEAUTY TWINKLE IN ONE'S EYES OF BLUES N SAPPHIRES DANCING OCEAN

IRIS SPECKLED GLISTENED GOLD AS SPIRIT LIGHTNING SPARK, THE LION STRETCHES MOVING SURE

SISTER SUBTLE CAT OF NIGHT, THE MOON WHITE BRIGHT SHAFTED ACROSS THE WATERS MIRRORED POOLS

TO OPEN ONE'S EYES BEHOLD OF THE GLORIOUS SPECTRUM EVOLVED

OH SUCH A TINY SPECK OF A MIGHTY BEAST OF COMPLEX SIMPLICITIES

SPINAL VERTEBRA N THE WITCH

MANY HEADED SNAKE OF SPINAL VERTEBRA RAISED TO COIL FROM MIRE SHOD RIDDEN A POOL OF CROCODILE TEETH

FLOWING OF PRIMAL ANIMAL AWAITING TO RAISE EYES FROM MUD OF EVOLUTIONS COIL TO TASTE!

LIFE!

GREY YELLOW SHIMMERING SEGMENTS FLOWING, WRITHING, QUESTIONING THE PURPLE SKY

HEADS OF DRAGONS, PREDATORS EVOLVING FLASHY GRINS N STEELY SMILES

THE WITCH OF WAR DANCES, ARROWS RAIN ON PSYCH EYES

YAMAO OWL SMASHES THROUGH FLASHING FIELDS N MOUNTAIN GLADES

TREE N STREAM COATING ALL IN FEATHERS SWEET OF BROWNS N SUBTLE PINKS

SOFTNESS OF FIELDS IN AUTUMN AS LATE CORN BLUSTERS WAVING TO A BREEZE

THE WORRISOME WITCH TOOK AS MOUSE LIKE LEAF FLUTTER TO BLUE YONDER

HER STICK A TWISTING DISTANT TUMBLING

SHE NEVER EVEN SAID "GOODBYE!"

PONDERINGS ON "THE MAN"

ALL THE HUNTER GATHERER CREATURES WERE GOING ABOUT THEIR DAILY LIVES LIVING N LOVING, FEEDING OFF THE LAND

ONE DAY THE "MAN" CAME!

WITH HIM HE BROUGHT AN ARMY THAT HE ORDERED TO CATCH ALL THE FREE FOLKS N STICK THEM IN PRISON

THEN HE ORDERED HIS ARMY TO RIP OUT ALL THE TREES OF THE FOREST N PLANT CROPS UPON THE LAND

WHEN THE CROPS WERE READY TO BE WORKED N HARVESTED HE RELEASED ALL OF THE FREE FOLK TELLING THEM

HERE IS TWO PIECES OF GOLD, IF YOU WISH TO EAT YOU HAVE TO BUY YOUR FOOD WITH THIS N TO GET MORE GOLD YOU HAVE TO WORK THE LAND FOR ME

EVENTUALLY ALL THE PARENTS WHO REMEMBERED THE PRISON N FREEDOM DIED OF OLD AGE

LEAVING THEIR CHILDREN TO WORK THE FIELDS N EARN GOLD TO BUY FOOD

PURPLE DOTTING IN THE TOWN

IT STARTS ON A BUS SITTING UPSTAIRS AT THE FRONT LOOKING DOWN ON THE DRIVER

WE STOP AT THE TRAFFIC LIGHTS WHICH HAVE BIG EYELASHES THAT WINK AT ME

A SIREN COMES UP THE ROAD BLUE FLASHING LIGHTS. THE BUS STOPS.

EVERYONE INCLUDING ME GETS UP N ATTEMPTS TO GET OFF THE BUS "SHIT WE ARE BEING BUSTED"

OFF THE BUS NOW N I CAN NO CROSS THE ROAD, THE CURB IS THE GRAND CANYON N ALL THE CARS ARE HOVERING BY

WITH BIG GNASHING TEETH THAT GRAB AT ME AS THEY PASS

I EVENTUALLY NAVIGATE THE ROAD EYES CLOSED TO THE SOUND OF SCREAMING CAR HORNS AN CURSES

THE WHOLE STREET IS FULL OF ALLIGATORS N CROCODILES IN FANCY CLOTHES, LOTS OF SMEARY LIPSTICK EVERYONE LOOKS LIKE A GENETIC DISASTER

5 DWARFS WALK PAST WITH LARGE COKES, THEY SEE ME N DO A LITTLE DANCE N ONE ASKS ME WHERE HE CAN GET A BUS TO TOWN

I SHAKE THEM OFF ACTING DUMB N WALK INTO THIS SUMO WOMAN WITH HER ARMS FULL OF KENTUCKY CHIPS N CHICKEN

THIS FLIES EVERYWHERE N I ALSO TRAMPLE LOTS OF IT ATTEMPTING TO NO GET EATEN BY THE HIPPOPOTAMUS SHE THEN PROCEEDS TO BEAT ME WITH HER HAND BAG WHILST I DANCE ABOUT ON HER DINNER

I GO IN THE AMUSEMENT ARCADE N STICK A PENNY IN ONE OF THEM REVOLVING PENNY TABLES

CHINK CHINK CHINK THE WHEELS GO ROUND N SPEW MONEY ALL OVER THE FLOOR, THE ALARMS GO OFF N I AM FACE TO FACE WITH TWO GORILLAS WITH BASEBALL BATS, "WHAT YOU DONE!" SAYS ONE OF THEM. "DONE," I SAY "DONE." "I DONE NOTHING," AS I STUFF PENNIES IN MY POCKETS THEY GRABBED ME N DEPOSITED ME ON THE STREET

WOW! I NEED A BEER SO I GOT TO THE TEDDIES BAR TO PLAY WITH THE DUCKS HA HA HA

PURPLE MICRO-DOTS SITTING IN A PUB FULL OF TEDDIES THE FLOOR SLOPES UP TO THE BAR "SQUEAK, SQUEAK" A PINT OF LAGER PLEASE!

GO BACK DOWN HILL N SIT NEXT TO THE JUKE BOX "WRRRRR CLICK" NO MUSIC COMING OUT OF THE BOX I CAN HEAR JUST "WRRRRR CLICK"

TWO TEDDY BOYS WALK IN N GO TO THE BAR "QUACK QUACK QUACK" THE BARMAN QUACKS BACK

I CURL UPON MY SEAT IN FITS OF LAUGHTER

MORE DUCKS WALK IN "QUACK QUACK QUACK"

THE BAR IS SOUNDING LIKE A FUCKIN FARM YARD NOW

I'M BENT TO PIECES THINGS GETTING WEIRD, NOW SWORDS N SHIELD ON THE WALLS START TO TELL ME THEIR STORY

EVERYTHING TURNS GOTHIC N FULL OF BLOOD LUST

ALL THE TEDDY BOYS ARE WATCHING ME I GO TO THE BOGS WHICH IS UPSTAIRS, THE BANISTER N DOOR HANDLES JUST MELT INTO SAND N DISSOLVE

I GO BACK DOWNSTAIRS TO PICK UP MY PINT, IT IS SITTING ON THE TABLE UPSIDE DOWN SO I DO ALL SORTS OF WEIRDO ANTICS ATTEMPTING TO DRINK WITHOUT SPILLING ANY, THE PUB CLOSES N I AM ONE OF THE LAST TO LEAVE THE PUB

OUT ON THE STREET THE CARS ARE 3 FOOT OFF THE GROUND N THERE IS A BLAZING SUN IN THE SKY ALL THE BUILDINGS KEEP MELTING

UP THE ROAD IS A CROWD OF TEDDY BOYS, THEY SPOT ME, ABOUT TWENTY GEEZERS RUN DOWN ME N PROCEED TO KICK MY ASS

TRIPPING BALLS NOW N DASHING N DARTING ABOUT THE STREET LIKE A PIN BALL BEING PUNCHED N KICKED

I FLY THROUGH REVOLVING DOORS INTO A NIGHT CLUB, THE BOUNCER GRABS ME IN THE SAME MOTION N KICKS ME OUT

NO LEATHER JACKETS!

I AM THROWN FACE TO FACE WITH A COSSER WHO "SAYS ARE YOU OK MATE?" AS HE DISSOLVES IN A WEIRD PANDA BEAR TYPE CREATURE WITH A SLOPPING SLIDING NOSE

I DART OFF ACROSS THE ROAD N START TO HEAD HOME

A CAR GOES BY FULL OF TEDDY BOYS GEARING ME OUT THE WINDOWS

ALL THE SHOP WINDOWS HAD LADS COMBING THEIR HAIR IN THE REFLECTIONS THEIR COMBS TURNING TO SWITCH BLADES AS I DASH BY

EVERY CAR WAS FULL OF LADS WISHING TO KILL ME

I RUN LIKE CRAZY FOR ABOUT 4 MILES N STOP TO GET MY BREATH ON A RAIL BRIDGE KEEPING A SHARP EYE OUT FOR FREAKY TEDS

I AM CALMING DOWN A WEE BIT NOW

THE MAIL EXPRESS BLASTS BY UNDER THE IRON BRIDGE SCARING THE LIVING BEE JESUS OUT OF ME I JUMP SO MUCH I HAVE AN OUT OF BODY EXPERIENCE OF SHOOTING OFF LIKE A ROCKET STRAIGHT OUT OF THE UPPER STRATA N COME BACK TO BODY ALMOST IN THE SAME INSTANT

I TURN AROUND N THE WHOLE ROAD BEHIND ME IS FULL OF TEDDIES WITH BASEBALL BATS, CUT THROAT RAZORS, ALL LOOKING LIKE THE LIVING DEAD "ZOMBIES"

IT WAS ONLY A BUNCH OF OLE GRANNIES COMING OUT OF LATE BINGO HA HA HA

SO I RUN THE REST OF THE WAY HOME

NEAR THE HOUSE THERE IS AN ALLEYWAY A DARK ALLEYWAY WITH THICK BUSHES ON ONE SIDE

I WALK HALF WAY DOWN THE ALLEY N HEAR A RUSTLE IN THE BUSHES SO CLENCHING MY FIRSTS I WALK FASTER

THIS GEEZER COMES FLYING OUT OF THE BUSHES RIGHT IN FRONT OF ME SO I DECK HIM OUT COLD COS HE SCARED THE SHIT OUT OF ME N LOOKED LIKE A TEDDY HE WAS ONLY PLAYING KISS CHASE IN THE WOODS WITH HIS BOYFRIEND HA HA HA

IT WAS REAL GOOD TO FINALLY GET HOME N LOCK THE FRONT DOOR

NEVER GO TO BOSCOMBE WEARING LEATHER JACKET TRIPPING BALLS COS THINGS JUST GET SERIOUSLY WEIRD N DANGEROUS !!!

CONNECTED

REM THE SCENE A BLOOD RED TORNADO AS FROM ABOVE LOOKING DOWN THE THROAT OF THE GALAXY

MULTI-COLOUR PING PONG BALLS YELLOW GREEN BLUE RED ORANGE FLOAT BY IN STRINGS BOUNDING ALONG THEIR HIDDEN CODE

TRAVEL OUT FAST N EVEN INTO THE TUNNEL WALLS OF SHIMMERING ENERGIES

AHEAD A SCENE OF GENTLE ROLLING CLOUDS, THE TUNNEL CONNECTED TO THE SUN STAR

PERCEPTION REALITY IS MANIFESTED THOUGH THIS TUNNEL THROUGH IMAGINATION N WILL

THE TUNNEL THE FOCAL X OF CONSCIOUSNESS

CONNECTED IN BODY WITH EMOTION GRAVITY MEMORY

TWISTED LADDER!! WRIGGLES N EVOLVES WITH VIBRANT MOLECULES DANCING IN THE SUNLIGHT

A ROLLER-COASTER RIDE; ORCHESTRATOR OF INFINITE COMPLEX BEAUTY

LIKE SOMETHING IS LOOKING THROUGH THE TUNNEL USING OUR BODY AS A SPACE SUIT

CONNECTED BY THIS LONG COMPLEX TUBE THAT TWISTS ITS WAY THROUGH TIME N SPACE SUIT MATRIX SOCKET

FEEL THE EARTH

SHE REVOLVES, WE EVOLVE

LOOK TO THE MOUNTAINS N SEE EAGLES GO TO THE OCEANS SEAGULLS, SIT AT HOME SEE SPARROW

EVERYTHING IS PERFECT !

EVERYTHING IS PERFECT

MIRROR X! + !X

TAP TIP TAP TAP TONK MOLECULE PING PONG!!

THE FILING CABINETS OF MEMORY ARE GENTLY CLOSING

THE STAR IS BRIGHT THIS DAY

BE WELL

THINGS ARE PERFECT.

THE STAR IS BRIGHT.

SEEING YOUR BLISS REFLECTED.

PLANTS WAVING THEIR HANDS AT NOBU...

SUNLIGHT FLITTING THRU THE ANGLES

CONNECTING ALL WORLDS

FINDING OUR WAYS HOME.... STILL ALIVE TO TELL THE ADVENTURE

OLD MAN, YOUNG BOY, ALL IN ONE

SHAPES OF FACE CHANGE

WITH A CENTRE,

MOORED BY REFLECTION.

N BACK

TO THE OYSTER.

PA

LOVE

TRUST...

UP IN THE DAY SKY, A STAR SHINES BRIGHTLY UPON US,

IN THE MORNING LIZARD SCURRIES AROUND HAPPILY OUT IN THE FULL LIGHT OF THE STAR

IN THE AFTERNOON LIZARD SITS JUST AS HAPPILY UNDER THE FULL, QUIET SHADE OF A PINON TREE

IN THE COOL OF EVENING STARLIGHT GLINTS WHITE, COLD N SHARP FROM THE WET EYES OF A FAWN

LIZARD SLEEPS HAPPILY DEEP UNDER THE SANDY EARTH ...

JUST PEACE YES THE SOUND OF THE WINDS, THE BIRDS, INSECTS COMING UP WITH THEIR CACOPHONY THAT FIRST WARM, SPRING NIGHT ...

N !!

N ON THE 3RD DAY THERE WAS LIGHT !!

THE OLD TEMPLATE FINALLY LETS GO, PRIMAL INSTINCTUAL SELF COMES BACK ONLINE, OLD ATTACHMENTS FILED N CATALOGUED

NEW INTEGRATIONS NOW ARE WRITTEN INTO THE "BASE" ORIGINAL TEMPLATE

PAST IS "DEAD" THE HARD-DRIVE ONLY HAS A RUNNING SYSTEM WITH NO EXTERNAL SHELL EXTENSIONS

"HOW DO YOU FEEL?"

UM?

RE-LEARN TO TIE YOUR SHOE LACES!

LEARN TO LOVE YOURSELF

YOU NOW HAVE A NEW TIME-LINE

BE WELL

BE IN PEACE

MUCH LOVE & RESPECT TO ALL WARRIORS OF THE WORLD WHO CLIMB YOUR MOUNTAINS N WITH STRENGTH N HONOUR

JUMP OFF ! !

ASKING CREATION TO CATCH ONE

EMBRACE IT ALL IT IS FOR THE "PRESENT" GIVEN!!

OPEN YOUR "PRESENT"

OPEN YOUR HEARTS

BE WELL +

LADDERS N TUNNELS

TOP LEFT FILING CABINETS COME OPEN, LADDERS OF INFORMATION ARE SWITCHED, MATCHED N

RE CATALOGUED

GREEN ELECTRIC TUNNELS

THE SCENE IS SEEN AS IF ON ACETATE, DISSOLVING INTO THE GROUND THERE IS NO EXISTENCE OUTSIDE OF THIS FILM SHOW ONLY WHITE NOISE SNOW

IMAGINE IF YOU COULD VIEW YOUR LIFE, TAKE OF WHAT IS REQUIRED N LIVE YOUR OWN FILM

AS THE FILM ROLLS ROUND THE ROLLERS PAST THE LENS LIGHT, THE IMAGE ON THE ACETATE DISSOLVES LEAVING CLEAR SEE-THROUGH ACETATE FOR MORE FILM MAKING

ALL INCREDIBLY DIFFICULT AT THIS TIME LEARNING WHERE ALL THE KEYS ARE

HAVE AN AWESOME WEEK, FOLKS

LOVE EACH OTHER

BE WELL.

NOBUNONI

GOD IS SCIENTIST LOOK AT THE EVIDENCE

WELCOME TO EXPERIMENT EARTH

I GUESS IF WE NO GET OFF THEN THIS ROCK SHALL SWALLOW US ALL

PRE-ENCODED IN DNA SEQUENCES ALL SHALL BE REVEALED

MAN SHALL EVENTUALLY DROP THE BLOOD SUIT N MELD WITH MACHINES

SYMBIOSIS N MACHINES. MECHANICS WORK BETTER THAN OURS MAKE CONSCIOUSNESS IN AN EGG TO LIVE WITHIN CYBERSPACE UNTIL THE LAST RAYS OF LIFE GIVING LIGHT OF THE UNIVERSE DWINDLES OUT

THIS BI-PED SIDE-STEPPED EVOLUTION N THE LAW OF NATURAL SELECTION

SHALL END UP ON THE INSIDE OF A SELF-MADE PRISON LIKE TICKY TACKY ALL LOOKING ALL THE SAME

SO THE ONLY WAY TO LOOK IS UP

BE BRIGHT

BLESSINGS

EARTH INC. OUT!!

PROGRAMMED BY INC. STAMPED GENUINE STERLING COPY

WHEN YOU ARE A PART OF A CORPORATION

HOW THE FUCK DO YOU GET OUT WITHOUT BEING BLACKLISTED???

CYNICISM SEEMS TO BE THE THEME OF MI TODAY

THE DIFFERENCE FROM THE INSIDE OF ONE PEN N THE OUTSIDE HERE

OUT HERE YOU GET TO TAKE TRAINS, BOATS N PLANES TO OTHER PEN N WATCHED EVERYWHERE YOU GO (MORE OR LESS) AT EVERY ROAD INTERSECTION FILMED N CATALOGUED

HE HE HE

THERE IS STILL LOVE

KEEP TRACKING THE LOVE

BE WELL +

FOOT NOTE :-

FOR FEAR OF EXPANDING CONSCIOUSNESS TOO FAST TOO QUICKLY AN ELECTRIC WHITE HALO AT HEAD EQUATOR

ONE TWO THREE N PASS INTO NOTHING FOR 90 MINUTES

AT OUR BIRTH WE ARE THE HANDLE OF THE UMBRELLA WE GROW UP THE SHAFT DROPPING OFF LITTLE REPLICAS ON THE WAY UNTIL WE COME TO THE END THE UMBRELLA OPENS N UPLOADS ALL INFORMATION INTO THE LIGHT MATRIX COSMIC CONSCIOUSNESS

IF WE ALL CRAWLED AROUND IN SHIT THEN THAT WOULD BE THE NORM

DOUBTFUL OVER ARGUMENTS OF THAT THIS POO IS BETTER THAN YOURS

TICK TOCK

BEAR WITH ME I AM BEING BEATEN BY A DUFF KEY BOARD N AM INSIDE OF A MASSIVE BUNCH OF FACTORIES N STUFF SHOP WORK MACHINERY

EACH ONE PUSHING N PULLING THE OTHER ALONG TO FILL THE ALLOTTED TASK

TO LIE DOWN AGAIN NOW

WOW! WOW!!

UM

LIT THE TREETOP THIS TIME

WARRIORS!!

GORILLAS SCREAM AT THE JUNGLE

I HAVE BEEN SHOWN DNA IS ALREADY RUNNING PAR ON COURSE

OBJECT EARTH

MINE ALL THE METALS N ELEMENTS OUT OF THE GROUND STOCK PILE EM

WHEN THE JOB IS DONE INTO STARSHIPS OF THE CREATORS OF US

A CHOSEN FEW

N HEAD FOR THE NEXT PLANET TO MINE

ALL ENCODED IN DNA

IBO TOOK ME OFF, TAUGHT ME TO FLY THE SOLAR WINDS OF MY UMBRELLA

SOMEHOW SOMETHING CAPTURED ME

AN' I GOT STUCK HERE

I AM NO VERY FIT BUT I CAN GO ONE HOUR ON ME POUCH BAG! HEE HEE

THERE IS NO OWNERSHIP WE ARE HERE BECAUSE WE WERE FREELY AVAILABLE N ALSO IT SEEMS VERY EASY TO CAPTURE

THEN MANIPULATED THROUGH DNA TO BE OF WHAT WE HAVE BECOME

ALL OF THIS ORGANISATION IS A FEW THOUSAND YEARS OLD SET IN MOTION N THE ORGANISATION IS STILL RUNNING N DIGGING

THIS IS WHAT IBOGA SHOWED N TAUGHT ME FROM FILES LOCKED IN DNA SEQUENCES

IT IS ALSO POSSIBLE TO MANIPULATE THESE SEQUENCES MANUALLY

YOU JUST GOT TO KNOW OF A LOCATION AN' THE FILING CABINET COMES OPEN THEN LEARN TO RE-ARRANGE THE PICTOGRAM SO IT VIBRATES DIFFERENTLY

UM

STILL WITH ME ???

ALL I CAN SEE IN PSYCHE IS THE SUN STAR

SHOUTING NOW

PA IBOGA

IBO BROKE THE PROGRAMME N ALLOWED MY LITTLE REPLICATIONS TO REBUILD A NEW ONE LIKE NANO - BOTS WITH A SINGLE PURPOSE

THE UNIVERSE IS OUR HOME

SOAR SWIFT N TRUE

BE WELL

NOBU !!

STUNNED

I AM STUNNED AT THE BEAUTY OF SCOTLAND

PRIMAL VOLCANOES MOUNTAIN RANGES, VALLEYS OF LAKES N RIVERS

THE COASTAL CLIFFS OF SEAGULLS, WHEELING IN FLIGHT

THE MIGHTY ATLANTIC OCEAN

CLEAN AIR

THE HORIZON FOR PSYCHIC REFLECTIONS

EXPANSIVE!!

I AM IN LOVE WITH THE LAND N OCEAN, SHE MAKES ME CRY WITH

OH SUCH JOY!

I AM STUNNED AT THE BEAUTY OF SCOTLAND

SALTED WET TEAR STREWN WIND SWEPT CHEEKS TURNED UNTO THE SUN STAR

THE REFLECTION OF WHICH UPON THE OCEAN'S SURFACE

MIND

OH BRIGHTEST OF BRIGHT MIRRORS

BEHOLDS

LIGHT

TO BE "SEEN"

CREATES BEAUTY ABOUNDING

DANCE AMONGST THE TAPESTRIES OF LIFE

PA OH MIGHTY SYMMETRIES REFLECTED

HOLD UNTO THE LIGHT

MIND!!

PA GALUNGA N SCOTLAND

TO DANCE AMONGST THE LIGHT!!

+NM+

NOBU +

EAGLE'S FEATHERS

I SEE MANY SNAKES, GREEN, BLUE, SLOWLY SLITHERING. I FOLLOW THEY EVOLVE, SCALES PRISMATIC EXPLOSIONS. AN INDIAN STANDS UPON AN OUTCROP ON A MOUNTAINSIDE. ARMS STRETCHED UPWARDS TO THE SKY. HEAD-DRESS OF MANY FEATHERS ROLLS ALL THE WAY DOWN HIS BACK. OVERHEAD,

CLOUDS ROLL, PURPLE GREY, DARK N FULL OF RAIN. THE INDIAN STARTS TO DANCE N CHANT. A RATTLE IN HIS RIGHT HAND. HE GRABS DIRT FROM THE GROUND N POURS IT OVER HIS HEAD N THROWS IT TO THE SKY. STRANGE TONGUES HE SHOUTS. MUMBLES N CHANTS. THE SKY ABOVE RIPS OPEN WITH LIGHTNING.

A WOLF STANDS UPON A HILL WATCHING ME INTENTLY. HE SLOWLY MOVES DOWN THE SLOPE TOWARDS ME, LIES AT MY FEET. AN EAGLE CIRCLES. THE SKY IS FULL, CLOUDS MOVING FAST N GREY ROLLING ACROSS THE SKY. I TURN N LOOK DOWN THE SIDE OF THE MOUNTAIN N SEE A RIVER. ITS PLACE OF BIRTH AT MY FEET. THE WOLF. IT WANDERS GLINTING WITH DIAMOND LIGHT OFF THROUGH VALLEYS N TREES. THE SEA. I AM EAGLE. I SOAR. I FEEL COLD WIND IN MY FACE. I AM NOT ALONE. ANOTHER FLIES CLOSE N WATCHES. I WHEEL N TURN.

THE BIRD CRIES N WHEELS WITH ME. WE LOCK TALONS N FALL. TUMBLING. WHIRLING DIZZY. THE SKY, THE GROUND. THE BIRD CRIES. I SEE AN INDIAN WITH HEAD-DRESS FLOWING. STANDING WITH LEFT ARM GESTURING, OFF N UPWARDS. EAGLES CIRCLE. THE GROUND IS DRY, CRACKED N SCORCHED. THE INDIAN GESTURES TO ME TO CALL UPON THE EAGLE. GIVE THANKS FOR THE GIFT. I RAISE MY ARMS N THEY ARE COVERED IN FEATHERS. I JUMP N FLY. LOW ACROSS N DOWN THE MOUNTAIN SLOPE. BOULDERS N SMALLER RUBBLE FLY PAST, YELLOW GREY N BLURRY. THERE IS MOVEMENT OFF TO MY RIGHT. A HARE. IT SEES ME N BOLTS. I ANGLE MY WINGS BACK N DART AS AN ARROW ACROSS A SMALL GLADE N DROP, TALONS READY. THE

HARE CRIES, TALONS STRIKE, FIR, FLESH, BONE. THE ANIMAL SHUDDERS N GIVES UP ITS LIFE. I TURN MY HEAD SKYWARDS N CRY. EMOTIONS UNFOLD. THE INDIAN WITH HEAD-DRESS FLOWING, SMOKES A PIPE N SPITS UPON A FIRE.

RAIN, DROPLETS AS DIAMONDS SHATTER MY VIEW. EVERY COLOUR CONCEIVABLE, ELECTRIC PRISMATIC ALIVE, DAZZLING.

IT FLOWS UPON MY NAKED BODY, COLD N PURE. THE INDIAN STANDS N RAISES HIS ARMS, BROAD GRIN UPON HIS FACE N CRIES AT THE CLOUDS THAT SPLIT IN HALF WITH LIGHTNING. A MOMENT GLIMPSED, A SMILING FACE WITHIN. OLD INDIAN SMILES, CONTENT, WORK DONE N SMOKES THE PIPE. EAGLE LIFTS HIS HEAD N CRIES, TAKING OFF WITH KILL. EAGLES WHEEL N FLY.

AN INDIAN STANDS BY THE FIRE SIDE, ARMS FOLDED, STERN WITH SCOWL. HE COMES VERY CLOSE N LOOKS AT ME INTENTLY. I SMELL TOBACCO. I HOLD HIS GAZE. HE GRUNTS NODS N GESTURES ME TO SIT. I CROUCH BESIDE THE LITTLE FIRE N ACCEPT HIS PIPE. HE NODS N GRINS, N STARTS TO TALK IN A STRANGE TONGUE, ABOUT THE WIND N SKY, GREAT SPIRITS THAT SEE ALL. THE EARTH DIRT ALIVE N DEAD. GIVING N TAKING. QUESTS OF BATTLE, CRIES N DEFEATS. HORSES RUN UPON THE PLAIN. I SMOKE THE PIPE. THE INDIAN SPEAKS ABOUT TIMES N SEASONS. SEEDS N SOWING. SPRING, HORSES RUN UPON THE PLAIN. MARES ARE CORRALLED N TETHERED, LASSOED N RUN TO GROUND, BOXED IN A DEAD END CAN. AN INDIAN STANDS BESIDE A FIRE, ARMS FOLDED N NODS. COUNTING HORSES.

A CRY GOES UP. WILD N BLACK THE STALLION REARS, WARRIORS DANCE N CRY. ROPES FLY. NOSTRILS FLARE AS THE ANIMAL HEAVES, BLOWING STEAMY BREATH UPON THE AIR. GREAT BODY HEAVING N WRITHING LIKE MOLTEN IRON BLACK N HEAVY. DEEP FORCEFUL ENERGIES OF RIGHT N FREEDOM. THE ANIMAL FALLS N CRIES. FOR THE MOMENT BEATEN, BROKEN, TIRED. WARRIORS DANCE N SING. A GOOD HARVEST WILL BE HAD THIS YEAR. YOUNG FOALS FOR BRAVES, BRIGHT HANDED, CARED N FREE. LIKE THE YOUNG WARRIOR, A GIFT, OF POWER N HONOUR. THE INDIAN SPEAKS ABOUT HONOUR N THE GREAT GIFT OF THE HORSE GIVING HIS SPIRIT OVER TO THE YOUNG BRAVE. THEY LEARN TOGETHER HOW TO BECOME WARRIORS.

HONOUR.

I SMELL THE DAMP SOIL UPON THE AIR N SEE THE SEED SPROUT, UNFOLD, GROW, REACHING FOR THE LIGHT. LEAVES UNFOLD N REACH. RAIN GLISTENS UPON THERE SURFACE TO MANY LEAVES TO COUNT. THE CLOUDS RUSH BY. I SEE THE SUN N MOON FLASH BY OVERHEAD WITH EVER MORE DIZZYING SPEED. THE EARTH BECOMES DARK. THE SUN IS DYING, PURPLE RED N HEAVY UPON THE HORIZON. AN INDIAN STANDS, HEADDRESS FLOWING, ARMS FOLDED N NODS. THE GROUND IS LITTERED WITH BONES, ANIMAL N MAN THE SAME, ALL JUMBLED UPON THE GROUND. THE EAGLE FLIES, FALLS, DIES. THE SUN DIES. THE INDIAN NODS N TURNS N WALKS AWAY. A FLASH BREAKS ACROSS THE SKY, THE GROUND BECOMES A RADIANT PINK GLOW OF LIGHT. I TURN N SEE THE SUN ANEW, THE GROUND ALIVE WITH GRASS N HERB. I SMOKE THE PIPE N NOD. I SEE.

NOBUNONI +

LAST NIGHT, WHILST WALKING IN MY DREAMS, I MET A LADY/ENTITY, THAT ORDERED ME TO FOLLOW.

SHE KEPT CRYING, "COME NOBUNONI !!! NOBUNONI, COME QUICKLY."

EVERY TIME I SLOWED SHE CRIED "NOBUNONI" VERY LOUD. LIKE SOMEONE BANGING ON A GREAT TREE IN THE JUNGLE WOULD SOUND.

I FOLLOWED HER THROUGH A VALLEY OF VERY DARK BLACK, TALL TREES. SOMETHING LIKE AN AVENUE. THERE WAS VERY LITTLE LIGHT N NO STARS ABOVE.

AFTER WALKING FOR SOME TIME, ADMIRING THE LADY'S COSTUME (PURPLES, BLUES, REDS N GREENS, THE CLOTH, FLOWING, HOODED CAPE. ALL COLOURS INTERWOVEN WITH THREADS OF GOLD SEEMED TO MELT N MOVE AMONGST EACH OTHER. THE IMAGE WITHIN THE HOODED CAPE WAS THE SAME AS DESCRIBED BELOW. NO FACE).

WE CAME TO A DOMED GRASS HUT. THE LADY DUCKED THROUGH THE DOOR N DISAPPEARED.

HESITANTLY I FOLLOWED.

I ENTERED THROUGH THE DOOR N INTO A DIMLY LIT ANTE-CHAMBER.

THERE WAS A BIG HOLE IN THE FLOOR, ABOUT 2.5 FOOT IN DIAMETER.

I MOVED AROUND THE HOLE N DUCKED THROUGH A RED, PURPLE CURTAIN. THE SAME AS THE LADY'S DRESS.

SUDDENLY I AM IN A LABYRINTH OF ROOTS N TUNNELS.

AS I MOVE ALONG THE TUNNELS N ROOTS I SEE IMAGES OF PEOPLES, RACES, GOING ABOUT LIFE.

THE ROOTS WERE ENDLESS. THE TUNNELS EVEN MORE SO. EVERYWHERE I LOOKED I COULD SEE THEM. STRANGELY THERE SEEMED TO BE NO 3D DIMENSION TO THIS PLACE.

IT WAS AS IF I WAS THE CENTRE OF THE ROOTS N TUNNELS STARTED AT THE POINT WHERE I WAS. AS IF I WAS A BUBBLE N ALL THE ROOTS N TUNNELS BEGAN AWAY FROM ME. LIKE BEING THE CENTRE OF A SPHERE LOOKING OUTWARDS AT ALL ANGLES.

I AM STILL THERE.

THIS IS INCREDIBLY ODD.

I FEEL STRANGELY CONNECTED.

AN AWESOME FEELING.

IF IT ALL STOPS NOW IT GOES ON FOREVER, BECAUSE IT HAS ALWAYS BEEN.

I STILL HEAR THE LADY CRY.

"NOBUNONI NOBUNONI NOBUNONI."

EVERY TIME I SAY THE NAME I AM TAKEN OFF N SHOWN MOST AMAZING SIGHTS, OF TREES N BUSHES VINES, LEAVES, BRANCHES, EARTH, VOLCANOES, CLOUDS, STORMS, SEAS. THE VISIONS ARE ENDLESS. EVERYTHING BOILING IN A SWIRLING

VORTEX. THERE ARE NO ANIMALS. THERE IS ONLY LIFE. EXCHANGE.

HA HA HA HA HA. I JUST GOT THE ANSWER.

IT IS CALLED THE EXCHANGE, BECAUSE THIS IS WHERE IT ALL STARTED. THE VORTEX, ALL LIFE, CAME FROM THIS CREATION. IT IS LIKE LOOKING AT THE CRAB NEBULAR, REVOLVING SLOWLY IN AN INWARD VORTEX, ABOVE A MOUNTAIN VAST, GRAY N OMINOUS. A VOLCANO. SPEWING FORTH LIFE. CREATION. FILLS. ENORMOUS ENERGIES. LIKE SUNS COLLIDING, MOULDING FORMING. EMULSION. TIMELESS. ROCKS N FIRE SPEW FORTH ACROSS A GALAXY STREWN WITH LIGHTS. EVERYWHERE I LOOK I SEE CLOUDS OF RED N PURPLE YELLOW N GREENS. SHOOTING STARS N GALAXIES FLY BY, ENDLESS.

"NOBUNONI"

OH HOW I AM SO SMALLED.

OF SUCH AWESOME POWER.

THAT SURROUNDS ABOVE N BELOW

I AM HUMBLED.

MUTUMBA WARRIOR

RIGHTEOUSLY SOUND

COMPLETE WITHIN THE FOLD

STANDING ON THE RIM LOOKING INWARD

AT A UNIVERSE MOST SPLENDIDLY JEWELLED.

NOBU +

I CAN'T REALLY SAY THIS WAS A DREAM. MORE A VISION THAT WILL NOW ABIDE WITH ME.

SUN LIFE

AWESOME SITTING BY THE SIDE OF 3000 WATTS STACKED IN THE FOREST. COME ON WHERE ELSE COULD YOU GET THE DIVERSITY? EVERYTHING ABOUT HAS THAT HAPPY FEELING.

BANG THOSE TUNES.

WALKING WITH THE MUSIC IN THE SUN.

RHYTHM.

LIFE.

EXCITE.

DESIRE.

BASSE RIFFS DIVULGE GREAT N WONDROUS SECRETS ONLY TO BE TOLD, WHEN THE SNARE CRYSTALLISES THE AIR WITH THE HIT. NO MISS THERE, FOLKS, WAITED, BAITED, FIRED, ALIVE.

RHYTHM THE CRY OF CHAOS WITHIN THE WILD. WOW I DIGRESS.

PEACE!

ALL BEINGS PLANT N TREE, GREEN HERB OF THE FIELD. HERE, FEEL THE SUN RISE. FLOWER SHOW YOUR FACE. TURN TO THE LIGHT YOU SO LOVE. FEED, FILL.

LIKE MUSIC.

ORGASMIC EMULSIONS.

WHEN THE GROUND WRITHES N THE POWERS THAT ARE JUST, RUN WITHIN THE VEINS.

THEN YOU SEE.

SELF NO DISGUISE.

SELF THE WARRIOR IN THE MIRROR RETURNED.

FACE.

SELF.

NO ILLUSION.

JUST IMAGE LOOKING BACK.

MIRROR DANCE WITH ME, MOVE ME TO MY SPIRIT.

FILL WITHIN ME RADIANT LOVE.

WARMTH OF CREATION FILL THE LIFE FORCE OF MY LIFE'S DESIRE.

AWAKE FOR SPRING

WHILST SITTING IN THE FOREST THIS WEEKEND GONE, WRITING N LISTENING TO MUSIC. A LIZARD RAN UP MY JEANS LEG N SAT ON MY KNEE, LOOKING INTENTLY AT ME.

I HAD JUST GIVEN SALUTATIONS TO ALL BEINGS PLANT N TREE N HE JUMPED OUT OF THE GRASS FOR A BETTER LOOK.

"TINY DINOSAUR I GREET YOU."

"THANK YOU I AM GLAD."

"OF?"

"AWAKING IN THE WARMTH OF THE SUN."

"AH IT IS A MOST BEAUTIFUL DAY, NO?"

"THAT IT IS GIANT, FOR SURE. NO MORE SLEEP, PLENTY TO EAT."

THIS CONVERSATION BEGAN TO AMUSE ME.

THE LITTLE LIZARD HAD GREAT CHARM.

AS I SPOKE SOFTLY HE LOOKED N BLINKED INTENTLY, KNOWINGLY UNDERSTANDING THE FEEL OF MY VOICE.

OTHERS CAME TO SEE N HE SCURRIED UP MY SLEEVE.

"CLUMSY! CLUMSY!" HE CRIED.

SO I AROSE FROM MY CHAIR N WALKED WITH HIM IN HAND INTO THE WOODS.

"THANK YOU," I HEAR FROM BENEATH MY PALM.

I COME TO A GRASSY GLADE WITHIN TALL PINE TREES N SIT WITH MY BACK AGAINST ONE.

I AM NOW IN THREE SPACES N THE CHATTER IS EXTREME.

MYSELF LOOKING OUT AT TREE N LIZARD. LIZARD LOOKING OUT AT MYSELF N TREE, TREE LOOKING OUT AT MYSELF N LIZARD.

I LOOK DOWN AT MY LIZARD FRIEND N HE SMILES.

"NOISY BUNCH EH?"

"THEY ALL WANT TO BE HEARD ALL AT ONCE. HARD TO JUST GET A STORY FROM ONE TREE."

I LAUGH.

"SO YOU HEAR THIS ALL THE TIME."

THE LIZARD BLINKS IN AGREEMENT.

"I GET USED TO IT. MOST OF THE TIME THEY JUST CHATTER ABOUT BEING SO STRONG N LOVING THE RAIN N SUN."

"AT THIS MOMENT THEY ARE CURIOUS ABOUT YOU."

"THEY FEEL YOU FEEL, AS THEY WATCH OUR CONVERSATIONS."

"RATHER NOSY, AREN'T THEY?"

"IT IS THEIR WAY. THEY STAND IN ONE PLACE ALL THE TIME N COMMUNICATE THROUGH THE GROUND. SO THEIR STORIES ARE VERY ELABORATE N COLOURFUL."

"SUBTLE VIBRATIONS"

"YOU FEEL THESE THEN BEING SO TINY!"

"YES N SO DO YOU, BEING OF SPIRIT."

THIS WAS AMAZING, NOT ONLY COULD THE LITTLE CREATURE UNDERSTAND ME BUT ALSO ALL OF THE LIVING THINGS AROUND HIM.

I SIT N CLOSE MY EYES, THE SUN BURNING SOFTLY ON MY FACE.

THE LITTLE LIZARD IS STILL, NOT MOVING IN MY HAND.

I SEE ME, VERY CLOSE, LOOKING BACK.

WOW! THAT MADE ME JUMP. I OPEN MY EYES N LOOK AT MY LITTLE FRIEND. HE BLINKS ACKNOWLEDGEMENT N I CLOSE MY EYES AGAIN.

I SEE EXTREMELY TALL GRASSES N TINY INSECTS SCURRY EVERYWHERE.

AN ANT HILL.

I RUN N SCURRY. GRABBING AT THE TINY SOLDIERS, MUNCHING WITH SHEER DELIGHT.

I LAUGH N OPEN MY EYES.

"YOU HAVE PLENTY OF FOOD NOW THE SPRING HAS COME."

"THAT THERE IS."

I PLACE MY LITTLE FRIEND UPON THE GROUND N BID HIM A FAREWELL.

HE DOES A LITTLE DANCE, LIKE THE GROUND IS TOO HOT FOR HIM TO STAND ON.

"ENJOY!"

"OH I WILL I WILL," THE LITTLE CREATURE RETORTS N SCURRIES OFF TO FIND THAT DINNER HE SO GRACEFULLY SHOWED ME.

VERY STRANGE PERSPECTIVE LOOKING THROUGH THE EYES OF OH SO A TINY DRAGON.

PRIMAL SCREAM

I AM NUMB, MELTING, FLOATING IN A VOID.

SLOWLY A TWISTING VORTEX TUNNEL OF DELICATE SNOWFLAKES OF BLUES N GREENS, YELLOWS N PURPLE SUCK AT ME.

THE WALLS SILVER SCALED, PRISMATIC GREEN ALIVE.

I HAVE NO PERCEPTION OF TIME OR SPACE.

JUST A FEELING THAT MY BODY IS CONNECTED TO THE AIR N EVERYTHING THAT SURROUNDS ME.

I SEE VISIONS OF A KIND OF AVENUE OF GREAT GREY SHINY STONE STATUES, ALL WITH HEADS TURNED SKYWARDS, AS IF SEEING AN INNER VISION.

SLOWLY TRAVELLING ALONG THE STATUES THE GROUND BELOW LIKE WATER.

I SEE SMALL MONKEY TYPE CREATURES SITTING UPON THE STATUES, BARING TEETH N GEARING.

THE SCENE DISSOLVES N I AM IN THE SEA.

ALL AROUND ME SWIM GREAT GREY GREEN SEA SERPENTS.

THEIR BODIES GLIDING BY WITH IMMENSE STRENGTH N PRECISION.

HEADS LIKE DRAGONS, BODIES LIKE LAMPREY, BUT SCALED.

THEIR BODIES GLIDE BY, SCALES RIPPING AT THE SURFACE OF THE WATER.

ONE TURNS N SURVEYS ME. I LOOK N WAIT. A GREAT MOUTH OF LAYERED TEETH, FANGS, OPENS UPON ME.

THE SCENE DISSOLVES.

IN FRONT THE CREATURES OF THE SEA ARE CRAWLING UPON THE MUD.

THE WATER IS BOILING.

I SEE UNDER THE SURFACE GREAT CHASMS N FISSURES IN THE SEA BED, SPEWING FORTH MOLTEN ROCKS N GASSES.

A VOLCANOES ERUPTS UPON THE SEA BED, TEARING APART THE EARTH N SPEWS FORTH GREAT GOUTS OF FROTH WHITE WATER HIGH IN THE AIR.

I AM ENGULFED IN STEAM, DARK N GREY MIST SWIRL EVERY WHICH WAY.

THE SERPENTS OF THE SEA CRAWL UPON THE LAND FOR THE WATER BOILS.

THE WATERS RECEDE N THE SERPENTS CHANGE SHAPE, GROW APPENDAGE ARMS N LEGS N WALK UPON THE LAND.

I SURVEY THIS STRANGE WORLD.

GREAT CANYONS N SANDS, BOULDERS OF REDS N STAINING YELLOWS.

EVERYTHING LOOKS SICK, DYING FOR WATER.

ANIMALS ARE DYING.

BIRDS CIRCLE IN THE AIR.

A GREAT FLASH SPLITS ASUNDER ABOVE N ANOTHER MAKING ME DUCK N TREMBLE.

I CRY OUT N BEGIN TO SING.

A FLOWING MELODY, EVER CHANGING.

NEVER RETURNING TO THE SAME.

A SONG OF LOVE N POWER.

NO WORDS BUT FEELINGS, EMOTIONS, TEMPERED WITH LOVE N STRENGTH.

I HOLD FAST TO MY STAFF.

SIRI SINGS.

SHE WHISTLES N VIBRATES WITHIN MY HAND.

IMMENSE VIBRATIONS RIPPLE THE AIR AROUND ME.

I SEE RAIN.

TORRENTS OF RAIN LASHING UPON THE GROUND.

THE EARTH IS TURNED INTO A SOUP, A QUAGMIRE OF BUBBLING POOLS OF MUD WATER N ROCKS.

A FLASH FLOOD RIPS DOWN A CANYON TEARING AT THE LAND, TAKING GREAT CLOUTS OF EARTH N BOULDERS WITH IT.

THE ANIMALS ARE DYING, DROWNING, BEING RIPPED APART BY THE SHEER FORCE OF IT.

SOME CLIMBING INTO THE TREES.

THE WATERS RISE IMMENSELY FAST.

I SURVEY A JUNGLE WITH MANY, MANY TREE TOPS, BUT EVERYTHING IS FLOODED UPON THE FLOOR.

ALL THE ANIMALS, MAMMALS, REPTILES, BIRDS ARE IN THE TREES, TRYING TO ESCAPE THE FLOOD.

THE SKY ABOVE SEEMS HEAVY N FULL OF ANGER.

I TURN N SEE THE WATERS SLOWLY DRAINING FROM THE LAND TOWARDS A VAST GREEN GREY OCEAN.

ANIMALS, SNAKES, LIZARDS, MONKEYS, BIRDS N INSECTS MOVE ABOUT AMONGST THE RECEDING WATERS.

POOLS OF MUD SWIRL N GLIDE BY ME.

I TURN, I SEE GORILLAS.

HUGE GREAT APES.

FIERCE N ANGRY RUNNING TOWARDS ME.

ONE LEAPS INTO THE AIR BEARING GREAT WHITE FANGS N LAUNCHES AT ME.

I STAND N IT DISSOLVES, ANOTHER TRIES N ANOTHER.

THEY COME AT ME FAST NOW.

SLAVERING N SCREAMING, BEARING TEETH, LASHING RED TONGUES, WHIRLING ARMS.

GREAT FIST WHIPS OUT, POUND-HOUSE TOWARDS ME.

I HOLD FAST TO MY STAFF N SING.

SIRI SINGS.

OTHER BEASTS JOIN IN.

DRAGON TYPE CREATURE WITH GREAT RUFFS ABOUT THEIR NECKS.

BLOOD RED EYES SURVEY ME WITH GREAT MALICE.

THESE BEASTS JOSTLE N MELD WITH EACH OTHER.

LIKE IN A DREAM THEIR FACES EVER CHANGING.

AN AVENUE OF BOULDERS.

GREAT PILLARS OF RED GREY STONE LINE EITHER SIDE.

STRANGE FACES, LIKE THEY WERE CARVED OUT OF THE ROCK COME N SURVEY ME.

NO QUESTION IN THEIR GAZE, JUST LOOKING, BLANK, MOVE IN ON ME N THEN RECEDE AWAY, ONLY TO BE REPLACED BY MANY MORE.

IT IS HARD TO FOCUS.

THE SCENE RECEDES.

PRE-WARNED BY THE SPIRITS

THIS MORNING I TOOK, WITH INTENT TO JOURNEY TO LOOK INTO THIS DAMN VIRUS (SHINGLES) THAT HAS ATTACHED ITSELF TO MY NEURAL SPINE, BETWEEN MY SHOULDER BLADES. THE PAIN IS BAD AT THE MOMENT, SO I THOUGHT I MIGHT TRY SOME PSYCHIC SURGERY. OR MAYBE A NEGOTIATION OF SOME SORTS.

THE SPIRITS HAD ME PUTTING STONES N PASSION FLOWER LEAVES ON MY ALTAR. (I FOUND LATER THIS WAS A WARNING)!

SLOWLY FINGERS LIKE WISPS OF SILK FLUTTER THROUGH MY FLESH, LOOKING, SEEKING. CARESSING.

I SEE A TREE EXTEND UPWARDS, BRANCHES EXTENDED OUTWARDS EVER DIMINISHING INTO A BLACK VOID.

SLOWLY I CLIMB THE CLIMB OF THIS GREAT WHITE OAK. ALL AROUND ME FLOAT SMALL SHEETS OF A PAPER-LIKE SUBSTANCE THAT FLUTTERS BACK N FORTH LIKE SNOW, SLOWLY DRIVEN BACK N FORTH BY SOME UNSEEN CURRENT. LOOKING UP CAN ONLY BE DESCRIBED AS LOOKING UP AN ENORMOUS MOUNTAIN TREE THAT AT THE TOP SPEWS FORTH MOLTEN LAVA.

4/5 OF THE WAY TO THE TOP I CAN SEE, LIKE A FUNGUS GROWING AT THE POINT WHERE THE BRANCH EXTENDS FROM THE TREE.

I EXTEND MYSELF, MAKE CONTACT WITH THE CREATURE ENTITY N IT SPRUNG INTO THE AIR SWIFT AS FIRE SPLITTING ME IN FIVE.

FROM MY ATOM-ED SELF I COULD NO LONGER FOCUS IN ONE DIRECTION, BUT GOT RIPPED INTO FIVE DIFFERENT DIRECTIONS THAT SERIOUSLY HURT.

LIKE GOLDEN SPIRALS SPINNING OUTWARDS I CATHERINE WHEELED TWISTING MY PSYCHE UNTIL I NEARLY SNAPPED.

THE ENTITY NOW STOOD BEFORE ME AS A GREAT BEAST, SHADOWED IN A PENTAGRAM TWO POINTS UP. ARMS N WINGS EXTENDED.

I COULD DISCERN NO FACE AS SUCH OTHER THAN A KIND OF BEETLE MOUTH N TINY BLACK EYES. A FEELING OF GREAT TREPIDATION BEGAN TO ENVELOPE ME.

MY GUARDIANS WARNED ME WITH THE PASSION FLOWER LEAVES.

ALL AROUND THE ENTITY WAS A KIND OF SICKLY GREY MIST THAT KEPT MOVING WITH HIDDEN LIGHTNING N PURPLE BLUE GASSES OF DEATH.

I MOVED TO APPROACH N THE ENERGIES STARTED TO CRACKLE THE AIR.

OK, NO NEGOTIATION HERE.

I APPROACHED THIS THING WITH THE SMELL OF DEATH IN MY SENSES. AS I FOCUSED N TRIED TO BURN THE ENTITY OFF MY NERVE STEM IT SMASHED ME YET AGAIN INTO FIVE. GETTING REALLY CLOSE N GEARING WAVES OF INSANITY AT ME.

AS I TRIED TO BURN IT WITH WHITE LIGHT N INTENT, THE PSYCHIC PRESSURES GREW UNTIL MY LEFT SINUS TRACT POPPED N I COULD FEEL RELEASE ALL OVER MY CRANIUM. SO GATHERING MYSELF I PUSHED FORWARD N TRIED TO HOLD MY FORM. THE WAVES OF ENERGIES NOW MADE MY WHOLE BEING BEGIN TO VIBRATE. A LOUD BUZZING STARED IN MY EARS N EVERYTHING STARTED TO TURN BLACK.

SLAP WITH ENORMOUS PRECISION I AM OFF SPLIT INTO FIVE, THIS TIME STRUGGLING VERY HARD TO REGATHER MY GENETIC ORDER.

THE ENTITY THEN TOOK ME OVER COMPLETELY N WITH EYES OPEN EYES CLOSED EVERYTHING SPLIT IN FIVE, TUNNELING MADLY DOWN SPIRALS OF CHAOS.

PHYSICALLY NOW, JUMPING UP, CRIED OUT FOR MY MEDICINE BAG, GRABBED MY STAFF N CHARGE.

I AM ENVELOPED IN GREY PURPLE MISTS.

THE DAMN THING A COWARD. ONLY WILL FIGHT TO PROTECT ITSELF, WILL NOT FACE ME.

I STAND MY GROUND N WAIT.

SLOWLY THE MISTS CLEAR N I SEE THE ENTITY SILHOUETTED AGAINST MOVING YELLOW CLOUDS.

I USED GREAT ENERGIES AS BALLS OF FIRE N THROW THEM AT IT. I ATTACKED IT WITH STAFF N BOULDERS. I WHIP UP A HUGE WHIRLWIND N THROW GREAT BOULDERS INTO THE VORTEX N THEN CHUCK THE WHOLE LOT AT IT WITH THE POWER OF MY STAFF.

DAMN THING JUST STOOD IN THE MIDDLE OF THE LOT.

BLACK N WHITE, UGLY, TWO LEGS DOWN, TWO LEGS/ARMS RAISED AT BOTH SIDES.

HORNED HEAD. A BEETLE TYPE CREATURE.

IT GEARED ME.

THE PAIN WHILST FIGHTING, DOWN MY LEFT ARM INTO MY HAND HAS LEFT THE INDEX FINGER HOOKED UP N CRAMPED.

WELL THAT WAS YESTERDAY MORNING.

THIS MORNING.

I FEEL GREAT. A BIT DISAPPOINTED I DIDN'T KILL THE UGLY BEAST, BUT THE PAIN IS LESS. THE CRAMP IS LESS IN MY HAND.

SO ALL IN ALL ALTHOUGH A VERY STRESSFUL N TIRING JOURNEY, A FRUITFUL ONE.

I SHALL NOW HAVE TO ASK THE SPIRITS MORE ABOUT THE PASSION FLOWER N ITS PORTENT MEANING.

ONE POINT TO NOTE, ALL FIVE BODIES ARE ONCE AGAIN PERFECTLY ALIGNED.

SUDDENLY I AM IN A LABYRINTH OF ROOTS N TUNNELS.

AS I MOVE ALONG THE TUNNELS ....

.... LIKE BEING THE CENTRE OF A SPHERE LOOKING OUTWARDS AT ALL ANGLES.

THEN ON ANOTHER OCCASION I WRITE,

I SEE MANY SNAKES, GREEN, BLUES, SLOWLY SLITHERING. I FOLLOW, THEY EVOLVE, SCALES PRISMATIC EXPLOSIONS.

SO I ASK N SEE WITH MIND'S EYE CLEARLY OPEN.

I SEE A PINPRICK OF LIGHT THAT WHEN FOCUSED UPON SLOWLY GROWS, COMES NEARER. TO MY LEFT N RIGHT SILVER GOLD PATTERNS FORM N DANCE IN BARROCK PATTERNS. WRITHING BODIES LIKE THE BACKS OF SNAKES SURROUND. NOT SCALES BUT MATRIXED. I FOCUS ON THE LIGHT IN FRONT

N IT OPENS LIKE A TUNNEL. THE MOUTH OF A MIGHTY SNAKE. I AM ENGULFED, EATEN. THROWN DOWN N THROUGH A VAST ELECTRIC GREEN BLUE BLACK, MATRIX LINED WALLS OF THE INNERS OF THIS BEAST. UPON CLOSER SCRUTINY I SEE THAT THIS PLACE IS LIKE A WORM HOLE. A VORTEX OF WRITHING HEADLESS SNAKES. IF I WANT I CAN CHOOSE TO MOVE MY ATTENTION FROM THE ONE I TRAVEL IN, INTO ANOTHER. THE LINES ARE FINE UPON THE INNER WALLS LIKE STRETCHED STOCKING MESH, SLOWLY TURNING N BENDING EVER EVOLVING RETAINING THE SHAPE OF THE INSIDE OF A TUNNEL.

FOCUSING FORWARD GIVES A VIEW OF A MOST INTRICATE TAPESTRY KALEIDOSCOPE OF BLUES, GREENS N GOLD. I TRAVEL FASTER. THE INTRICATE PATTERNS IN FRONT BEGIN TO BLUE N STAND HIGH AS IF A TREE BURNING WITH DIVINE LIGHT. NOW AROUND ARE LEAVES N TREES, THE GROUND THE SKY. REDDEN N BARRENS THIS LAND. I TURN N DUCK THOUGH INTO ANOTHER TUNNEL.

WHOOSH I AM SLOWLY SUCKED N MOVED ALONG THE INSIDE OF WALLS OF ELECTRIC BLACK GREEN. EVERYTHING IS ALIVE. AHEAD A TAPESTRY, AS I APPROACH THE INTRICATE PATTERNS BLUR N STAND UPRIGHT AS A BURNING TREE.

I SEE FIELDS N MOUNTAINS. THE SEA IS ANGLED OFF AS IF DROPPING DOWN A GREAT WATERFALL. EVERYTHING IS MIRRORED. AN OCTOPUS TYPE CREATURE SURVEYS ME FROM WITHIN A POOL, REACHES OUT A TENTACLE TOWARDS ME N GENTLE STROKES UPON MY ARM. I FEEL ELECTRICITY LIKE FIRE, BUT NOT BURNING. I LOOK TO THE CREATURE N ITS FORM

CHANGES. I SEE THE HEADS OF DRAGONS, DINOSAURS N BIRDS. THE IMAGE BEGINS TO FADE.

ONCE AGAIN I AM WITHIN THE TUNNEL, MOVING.

ALL AROUND NOW IS WRITHING TENTACLES, DANCING IN MANY INTRICATE PATTERNS LIKE OH SO MANY SNAKE BODIES DANCING.

THEY HAVE NO HEADS, JUST TUNNELS FOR HYPERSPACE TRAVEL.

A MEANS OF CROSSING QUICKLY FROM ONE WORLD UNTO ANOTHER.

THE TUNNELS ARE NOT ENDLESS, ONLY IN NUMBER. THEY HAVE SPACE N DIMENSION. THEY TRANSPORT.

SO I FOUND MY MEANING FOR THE SNAKE LIKE STRUCTURES WITHIN MY HYPERSPACE.

I ALSO FOUND THAT IF YOU DO NOT GET A GOOD LAUNCH INTO HYPER SPACE YOU END UP ON THE METRO TRAVELLING N NEVER REACH THE OTHER SIDE.

MUCH BETTER TAPESTRIES THAN ANY MUSEUM I HAVE EVER BEEN TO THAT I CAN SAY.

SHAME TRAVELLING TO WORK ON THE TUBE ISN'T AS BEAUTIFUL.

DANCING WITH SOME FRIENDS

TEN GRAMMES OF FINE KRATOM LEAF FINELY GROUND

FIVE GRAMMES LIBERTY CAPS FINELY GROUND

TWO GRAMMES KHAT EXTRACT

400MG AMANITA 15-1 EXTRACT

ONE PEACH MELBA N TANGERINE YOGHURT

HARD PSY-TRANCE BANGING "BASSE"

ONE AN' A HALF HOURS IN I THROW MY HEART UP FOR 10 MINS

WATER

SWEATING LIKE A PIG CANNOT

WAVES OF ELECTRIC BLUE FLYING AROUND ME LIKE UNCOUNTABLE GHOST DOING SOME MAD DANCE

KALEIDOSCOPE N PRISMS, ALL FLOWING LIKE THE SEA

I CLOSE MY EYES N SEE PLOWED FIELDS LIKE AS IF SALVIA HAS DROPPED IN FOR A VIEW

TRANCE MASTER SOUNDS RUN ACROSS THE FLOOR IN FILES TO THE "BASSE"

HIGH INTENSITY SOUND BOUNCES N RECOILS ALONG THE FLOOR AN' CLIMBS THE TREES

WOW I NEED A SMOKE

DEEPLY IN

HOLD, EVOLVE EXPRESS

ROLLER-COASTER RIDING UP N DOWN, INCREDIBLY SEA SICK BUT NOT

DON'T THINK OF SELF, LISTEN FEEL BASSE HEAVY VIBRATIONS COIL MY UMBILICAL, EVERYTHING TURNING GOTHIC

MY STAFF A "SPEAR" LOOKING INTENT ON THE RADIO ACTIVE RAIN OF CORDS EXPRESSION

CARS AN' VANS WITHIN THE FIELDS AS SHIELDS, FLAGS OF RED N ORANGE FLYING IN A GENTLE BREEZE

THE SUN WINKS AT ME WITH EYELASHES OH SO DARK, A CHEEKY WINK, HOLDING SOME SURPRISE OF SORTS

DISSOLVING OUT N UPWARDS, COILS OF GOSSAMER N WEED LIKE STRANDS COIL IN TIME TO THE MUSIC,

STACCATO DANCE N LABRYNTH SMILES

DIVINE LIGHT OF HEART'S DESIRE

TALL GRASSES OF THE FIELD FLOWING WITH EVERY BREATH AS IF WATER IN A GENTLE BREEZE

COLOURS OH MAGNIFY MY HEART'S EMOTIONS N DESIRE

EMOTIONS ARE TOO MUCH TO CONTAIN

TEARS STREAMING DOWN MY CHEEKS

SELF-DISSOLUTION TWANG N FOLD, EVOLVE N HOLD THE CORD OF "BASSE" UNTIL DEATH

OH SWEET DEATH OF ETERNAL NOTHING, A VOID TO FALL WITHIN N BE HELD BY COMFORT

AS TREES STREET LIGHTS DANCE, NOW THE FLOOR AS VALLEYS, WATER-FALLS N MOUNTAIN STREAMS CASCADE ACROSS THIS AWESOME PLANE

AN EYE IN THE SKY WINKS, THE CLOUDS SMILE

CHANGE OF RHYTHM, COLOURS PURPLE N AZURE BLUE

LIGHTNING STRIKES WITH EACH ELECTRO SWOOOOOSH

BASSE AS THUNDER

SKY SLOWLY TURNING RED PURPLE, CLOUDS FLOWING AS IF SOMEONE SPEEDED UP THE FILM, GREY N IGNOMINIOUS

BREATHE

BREATHE THE WET EARTH, LISTEN TO THE CRY OF HAWK N CROW

THE STANDING TREE LOOKS LIKE AN OCTOPUS OF SEVEN ARMS, AN OLD BICYCLE WHEEL AS FACE, HE SHIFTS HIS GAZE AN' SMILES

AS SHOOTING STARS FLY ACROSS THE SKY

AFTER PARTY SHOCK, GALAXIES FLY BY

MY BRO LOOKS LIKE AN EAGLE SPROUTING WINGS TO FLY, GOOD MORNING BREATHING OH SUCH FRESH, FRESH AIR
ONCE AGAIN YOU COME TO THE PARTY
LET'S "DANCE"
POWER CORDS, CYMBAL, ELECTRIC FLY
IT IS IMPOSSIBLE TO KEEP THE FEET STILL,
VISIONS FLY
TINY FOLK DANCE AT MY FEET THREE INCHES HIGH
PIROUETTE N JUGGLE, JUMP N FLY
THE LITTLE FOLK N ME SPIN N CAVORT ACROSS THE FIELDS,

A PADDLE STEAMER WITH SMOKING CHIMNEY FLOATS BY WITH CHEERY PEOPLE WAVING

I STEP TO MY RIGHT N FALL, FALL, FALL, TUMBLING, EVER SPINNING IN TO A TWISTED PIPE, RAIN SPLASHING UPON MY FACE

BREATHE DEEP AN' FEEL WITHIN ONES SKELETON THE RHYTHMS EVOLVE,

WALKING, LOOKING EVERY FACE AS IF A YELLOW BALLOON

IT HAS BEEN RAINING, THE CAR GLISTENS AS IF COVERED IN HALF LIDDEN EYES

I BREATH N SIGH

THE WORLD BREATHES N SIGHS WITH ME
THANK YOU
TIME
THOSE MECHANICAL TIME COUNTERS,
SLASHING STILL SHOTS THROUGH YOUR MIND
THROW THE ONE, THE TWO IN DURATION
SO THE STILL SHOTS BECOME THE FILM OF LIFE
STACCATO TIME IS OUR ILLUSION
SNAP SHOT
TIME
A SNAKE CURVED FROM TAIL TO HEAD
GET THE SNAKE TO EAT ITS TAIL

THEN TIME BECOMES TAIL-LESS,
INFINITE
DIVINE

LIGHTNING ENLIGHTENING FLOWER

MEDITATION ON THE FLOWER OF LIFE EVOLVE RED, BLUE, GREEN YELLOW, SLOWLY OPENING TO THE LIGHT

A GLIMMER GOLDEN SPECK OF LIGHT TRAVELLING TOWARDS ME

EVER CLOSE, WHEELING WHITE FIRE WITHIN THE SKY.

BAM! ROLLING BALL OF GOLDEN FIRE, WIELDS A SWORD N HITS ME STRAIGHT BETWEEN THE EYES.

MOMENTARILY SPLITTING ME, TO GATHER AGAIN AS ONE UPON THE ETHER

THIS ROARING COMET WHEELS N TURNS, BULL ELEPHANT HEAD DOWN IN A CHARGE, AS EARS TWO MIGHTY WHITE SWORDS SPINNING

OXALA, I HEAR CRY

FROM BELOW DUST N AIR RISING, EVERYTHING AQUAKE THE MIGHTY CREATURE THUNDERS ACROSS THE LAND

THEN LIFTS INTO THE SKY, EVOLVING, TRANSFORMING INTO EAGLE, SHATTERED PRISMS AS MADE OF TWO HUNDRED BIRDS, WINGS ON EITHER SIDE

SPREADS FORTH THE MIGHTY TRIBAL NATION, AS FLOCK SETTLED UPON THE LAND

I TURN TO SEE THE FLOCK A GATHERING, TURNING, WHEELING IN THE SKY NUMEROUS BLACK DOT SPECKLED FOLDING WEAVING, DANCING HIGH

DIVING DOWNWARDS IN AN ARCH THEY GATHER N FORM TO MASS, A MASSIVE BLACK LEOPARD POUNCING FROM A TREE

SHE LANDS WITH GRACE UPON THE FOUR N GRINNING THIRTY TWO TEETH SMILES, I WILL HAVE PORTION FROM YOU ALL

I GAZE INTO THEM DEEP GREEN EYES, RAISE MY STAFF N SMILE, OF ME YOU TAKE NO MEAT

A THUNDEROUS SNARL HEARD IN REPLY, THE GIANT LEOPARD LEAPS INTO THE AIR, FLYING OVER FOREST TOP TO MOUNTAINS, SPINS THROUGH NINETY N DOES A WHIRL N LANDS BACK AT MY FEET EVOLVING, SHAPING FORMING, STANDING HIGH

A DARK SKINNED WARRIOR STANDS, DARK OF EYES, WILD OF HAIR, WHITE TEETH SHINING IN A GRIN

WHITE SCARS ALL OVER HIS BODY, AS COWRIE SHELLS CONNECTED BY FINE GOSSAMER LACE

AS A STAR MAP BODY STOCKING GOLD BANGLES AT HIS BICEPS

FEATHER STOCKINGS ON HIS ANKLES, BLUE RED LOIN CLOTH, WHITE SWORD SCABBARD TO THE LEFT

HE HANDS ME SWEET PUNGENT TOBACCO THEN SLOWLY DRAWS THE SWORD N HOLDS IT HIGH

THE GROUND N AIR BEGIN TO TREMBLE, LIGHTNING BREAKS THE HEAVENS, HE SHOWS ME HOW TO USE THE SWORD

WITH INTENT TO DEFEND, STRIKE TO STRIKE

THE BLINDING WHEEL OF SWORD N WARRIOR BEGIN TO DANCE, WHIRLWIND STYLE, THROUGH A SPHERE, SWORD SPINNING IN ALL DIRECTIONS AT THE SAME TIME

WARRIOR DANCES N DIVIDES ME ACROSS THE HEAVENS THROUGH FOUR, THEN SHOWS ME HOW TO BUILD AN ARMY, STRATEGY N MORE

SHOUTS, CRIES OUT, "ONLY FOR PROTECTION DO NOT WIELD SWORD IN VAIN,"

THEN PROMPTLY GIVES ME THE SWORD, FOR PROTECTION, WITH INSTRUCTIONS OF HER USE, THEN DEPARTS, NOT VERY FAR

THE SWORD SITS BANG SMACK IN THE MIDDLE OF MY FOREHEAD BLINDING PURE WHITE FIRE TO DRAW

A SWORD OF MACRO-MICRO PROPORTIONS SITTING LIKE A STAR

TO FOCUS N BREATHE, DRAWING THE HILT DOWN TO ONE'S CHEST CENTRE, THE HILT THE FOUR THAT HE SPLIT ME

TO STAND WITHIN THE HILT, I TAKE WITHIN MY HAND N DRAW WHEEL ARC SLASH DOWNWARDS THROUGH TOP QUARTER, ROTATE THROUGH 90° AS I GO, WIELD, THE SWORD, INVERTED, THROUGH THE BOTTOM RIGHT QUARTER IN A GENTLE WHIPPING ARC UPWARDS

TO SPIN N DANCE WITH THIS SWORD CREATES A MOST BEAUTIFUL FLOWER OF MATRIX LINES OF FIRE LIFE IN A SPHERE

STAFF ALWAYS MOVING, LIKE ONE WOULD WIELD THE SWORD THROUGH REFLECTION THE STAFF MY CENTRE

I CAN STILL TASTE THE TOBACCO

THE SWORD AS A SMALL WHITE FLAME FLICKERS IN THE DARK AWAITING

POETRY IN MOTION, NOTHING FORCED, SISTER SENSE IS BALANCE

LIGHTNING SWORD CREATION, WIELDS THE FLOWER OF LIFE

ENJOY THE MOVEMENT, BREATHE THE AIR, RADIATE THE LOVE

BLESSED BE

SALT SWORDS FAMILY SPIRITS LOVE LIGHT ETERNAL

PA TO "TREMBLA TIERRA OXALA" I HEAR THE CRY

AS SALA MALEKUN

SUNLIGHT

AYAEEEA I CAN SEE FOR A MILLION MILES IN ALL DIRECTIONS, BIRDS FLY, PARROTS, CICADAS SING LIKE TINY LEAVES FLUTTERING IN A GENTLE BREEZE

MY ATOM SNAPPED, MY MOLECULE MELDED WITH THE MATRIX OF THE SUN, GIVER OF LIGHT LIFE CONSCIOUSNESS N MORE

DANCE N SING TO BE ALL WITHIN THE FOLD BROTHERS N SISTERS, WITH EFFERVESCENT BUBBLES OF LIFE

WATER BUBBLES OVER LITTLE BROWN PEBBLES N EVERYTHING IS ALIVE

THE FUNNEL THE TOP OF MY HEAD FILLING WITH THE UNIVERSE OF LOVE

SHE WALKED ME ALL OVER, REVOLVING ME THROUGH SPIRALLED HALLS OF EXQUISITE BEAUTY, BUT MY UGLINESS KEPT SMASHING VISION SO I DRINK AGAIN

LAY DOWN WITH MY STAFF N MEDICINE BAG, LEFT HERE BEHIND

ME AS A MILLION PIECES OF IRIDESCENT LIGHT SLOWLY COILING AROUND THE EDGE OF A VERY PEACEFUL CURVE ALL CONNECTED AS FINE RAILWAY LINES LADDERED, FINE TRIANGLES, ALL OF MY CONSCIOUSNESS ABOVE N THROUGH

NOTHING BUT LOVE MATTERS

TREASURE ~ GOLDEN SUNLIGHT

MY WIFE, MY LITTLE DOG'S BY MY SIDE

HUNGRY NOW

FROM SOUND TO LIGHT, LIKE TWO ROCKS SMASHING

SPIRIT

WARRIOR,

THE LAND WALKING, SPEAKING, CREATING, OF DUST CREATION, CONCEIVING,

CHAINED FOR A SHORT WHILE TO THE EARTH

SPIRIT

AS EAGLE FLIES, SHE SHOWS THE COIL OF LIFE THROUGH HER THERMAL FLIGHT

HER KEEN EYESIGHT GIVES SPIRIT VISION

HER FEATHERS CREATE THE MATRIX OF LIFE EVOLVING

HER WINGS AS THE TIPS OF CREATION <><> OF TWO BIRDS IN FLIGHT,

AS REFLECTIONS

CURLING, TWISTING, CLIMBING, DIVING

WARRIOR STANDS IN THE POINT

LAND ALWAYS BECKONS TO THOSE THAT FLY HIGH

ENCHAINED TO THE MIGHTY SPIRIT OF CREATION

THROUGH EARTH SPIRIT N LIGHT

EAGLE SOARS HIGH N SWOOPS LOW INCREDIBLY SWIFT AS ARROW

SPEAR POINT TO THE EARTH

CREATION

THE GREAT BIRD IN THE SKY GENTLY SITS UPON THE EARTH

GIVING SHADE TO HER YOUNG FROM THE SCORCHING OF THE SUN

MIGHTY THUNDER CLOUDS GIVE OF THEIR LIFE FORCE, WATER

EAGLE TURNS HEAD SKYWARDS, CRIES

THUNDER, AS MIGHTY BOULDERS, RUMBLES THROUGH DISTANT CANYONS

HIGH WINDS UPON THE WALLS BOOMING TEAR AT THE SANDS, THROWING WHIRLING TO THE THE SKY

STAFF STANDS RIGHTEOUS IN THE MIDDLE

LAND UNDER FOOT MOVES WITH ALL PASSIONS,

EXPRESSIONS OF HEART

SPIRIT WALK

WALK WITH EARTH THROUGH STONE WOOD WATER AIR LIGHT ~ PA TREMBLA LA TIERRA

AS TWO GREAT EAGLES IN FIGHT FLIGHT,

SHOWS OF GREAT AWESOME CREATIONS, UNDER THE TREE OF LIFE

A E I O

LIGHT TO EARTH N BACK AGAIN

LIKE LASER BLASTS ACROSS THE HEAVENS

SMOKE RISING

STARS STANDING IN THE NIGHT SKY, FORMING ANIMALS N SPIRITS

BUT HELD WITHIN A FORM,

THAT FLASHES MY WHOLE EXPRESSIONS EXISTENCE

THE BIRD, AS CREATION TAKEN TO FLIGHT,

TO SOAR N SEE

A

E

GLIMPSE OF ETERNITY

PRAYERS BE HEARD THROUGH EARTH, STONE, WOOD, WATER, BODY LIGHT N SPIRIT WITH BARE FEET PLANTED FIRMLY IN THE EARTH CREATING DEEP ROOTS THAT GIVE OF LIFE

A PLUME OF SMOKE,

SPIRIT,

LAND TO SKY

EARTH

SPIRIT

SKY

GREAT SPIRIT SITS WITHIN

LIKE TWO GREAT EAGLES WINGS TOUCHING TIP TO TIP, SEPARATE BUT CONNECTED ><

WARRIOR THE POINT OF CONNECTION

THE POINT OF CREATION

LIGHT

AYA

GREAT SPIRIT, AS CLEAR CRYSTAL WATERS

PLANTS OF "LIGHT" AWW,

HEART OPENS LIKE THE WIND BLOWING OUT FROM FOUR CORNERS

LIKE FLOWER, HEAD TURNING TO THE MORNING SUN

OPENING WITH DELIGHT

WITH HEAD UPLIFTED AS OPENING A GATE

WATER FLOWS ALIVE OVER BROWN DAPPLED PEBBLES IN THE MOUNTAIN STREAMS

AS MOON SHINES SILVER IN THE NIGHT SKY

FISH SWIM IN THE SPARKLING WATER

GREEN MIGHTY TREES BLOW GENTLY IN THE BREEZE WHISPER

DEER RUN IN FORESTS

MEADOWS FLOW

BIRDS SING

INSECTS CRAWL TO FLY

WOLF, IS ABOUT N CARING

GREAT CAT READY TO POUNCE

CHAMAC SIT AT FIRE PREPARING

TO BLOW THE GREAT WIND THROUGH THE FOUR

GRATITUDE, OH GREAT MIGHTY SPIRIT FOR SETTING WITHIN THE POINT,

I,

OF THIS MOST BEAUTIFUL CREATION

A E I O ~

THE LANGUAGE IS SACRED TO ME

I KNOW THE WORDS,

LANGUAGE OF LIGHT

SPIRIT TALKS THROUGH EMOTION,

THE SOUNDS EXPRESS THE BEAUTY OF THE EVER FLOWING RIVER OF LIFE

PA OH MIGHTY RIVER

PA TO AYA-HUASCA

PA GREAT N MIGHTY SPIRIT,

NSALA MALEKUN

LIFE TO DEATH

LIFE IS A SNAKE FROM TAIL TO HEAD

WHEN WE DIE, THE HEAD OF OUR LIFE, EATS THE TAIL OF OUR BIRTH

N WE TURN AT RIGHT COIL INTO THE 5TH THEN AT RIGHT INTO A SPHERE

ONE LOVE

BLISS

ALL

OF LITTLE N MANY

WE HAVE MUCH TO SEE OF ALL

WITHOUT TO HOLD

WITHIN TO GROW

OF ALL TO SEE

ONE LOVE

SIMPLE

AYAEEEA

AMANITA

OF POINTED HEADS, OF STARS WITHIN THE SKY

OH MIND DOTH KNOW TO MAGNIFY OF GIVING ONE TO MANY

THE FLOCK MAY EAT THE MANNA FROM HEAVEN

CONSCIOUSNESS EXPANDING BREAD TO THE INNER EYE

OF WISDOMS HELD WITHIN THE TEAR OF FABRIC BY DESIGN

WEBBED N MOLDED AS "DIVINE" A LIGHT TO SEE JOY

TO GOLDEN NECTAR OF A ONCE SMALL SNAKE TO OPEN AS A FLOWER

OF MORNING DEW DOTH SUN RISE GLISTEN AS AMANITA SMILES

OF DARKNESS TO LIGHT OF SOIL TO SUN HOLDING HUMUS A SPORE

BE GOLDEN OF TRUTH, A MUSHROOM OF NO DISGUISE

WEARING HER RED COAT OF SPECKLED BUTTONED COTTONS

A THRILL AROUND HER THROAT TO SEE AS THROUGH THE VEIL

OF SELFLESSNESS OF ALL CREATION, SHOWERS AS RAIN UPON THE MOUNTAIN SPRINGS

OVER GLISTENING DAPPLED BROWN PEBBLES GURGLING AS A VIBRANT STREAM TO LIFE

DOTH THE AMBER NECTAR FLOW TO SHINE OH BRILLIANCE OF MAGNIFICENCE "DIVINE" DESIGN

A FLOWER A FAMILY ALL LOVERS OF LIFE IMBIBE TO SEE OF TRUTH

TO HAVE N TO HOLD

WHEN THE LADY AMANITA SMILES*

ALL IS LIGHT ~

THE LIGHT YOU SEE, SHINES ON YOU FROM WITHIN

THE KINGDOM THAT YOU LIVE IN, IS WITHIN YOU, NOT WITHOUT

ALL WITHIN THE MIND, CHECKED BY EMOTION

FEAR N LOSS OF THE BODY PREVENTS THE MIND FROM ACCEPTING BECAUSE MIND ALWAYS LOOKS BACKWARDS

YOU CANNOT GO BACK, YOU CAN ONLY GO FORWARD, YOUR JOURNEY HAS STARTED

AS WHEN YOU DIE YOU CANNOT TAKE YOUR BODY OR ANY OF THIS PHYSICAL WORLD WITH YOU TO THE VOID OF ETERNAL BLISS

WHEN YOUR JOURNEY HAS STARTED YOU CANNOT LOOK AT BODY OR BODY'S MEMORIES, YOU CAN ONLY LOOK FORWARD

YOU HAVE LOST YOUR BODY N YOUR MIND, YOU CANNOT HOPE TO REGAIN THEM, BECAUSE YOU ARE DEAD,

ACCEPT IT N MOVE ON

FORGIVE SELF N OTHERS, HOLD ONLY THE SIGHT OF THE CLEAR LIGHT

THE ROCKET HAS LEFT THE STATION

YOUR BODY IS THE STATION

YOU CANNOT GET OUT OF THE ROCKET

UNTIL THE ROCKET LANDS SOMEWHERE

GOD MADE THE ROCKET, YOU ARE NOT GOD ACCEPT SELF AS NOTHING

YOU SHALL BE WITH GOD SHORTLY

MOVE ON

FORWARDS N ONWARDS, THROUGH N TO ETERNAL LIGHT

SINGING, BLESSING, PRAYING, HOLDING THE HUB OF THE GREAT WHEEL OF CEREMONY TOGETHER

SPIRIT WALKING

CLEAR CLEAN MORNING BREATH OF GOD AS CLEAR AS CLOUDLESS SKY

CREATURE ABOUT MAKING OF LIFE

WILLY WAGTAIL, SITS ON OUR DOORSTEP EVERY MORNING, RUNS ABOUT OUR GARDEN, PIGEON SITS WITHIN THE LOFT, GREAT WHITE OWL SITS HIGH WITHIN THE BROKEN CHIMNEY OF THE OLD BRICK KILN, ALL STARTED WITH DOG, HA HA HA, AWESOME BROTHER

DOG SITS AT MY FEET

HAWK LIVES IN KNOT HOLE OF OAK

RAVEN AT THE COPSE

CROW IS AT THE FOLLY, ALWAYS WATCHFUL, ALWAYS WARNING SHOUTING WORK AT THE LAZY

SAW PHEASANT A WHILE AGO

THE GEESE ARE RETURNING, POINTING ARROW ACROSS THE SKY

BLACK WREN FLITTERS ABOUT THE LAWN N FALLEN LEAVES,

ROBIN IS OUT N ABOUT

SPARROW WITH HIS BLACK HEAD N BROWN SHAMAN COAT HAS THE HEDGEROW

BLACK BIRD IS TRILLING IN THE MORNING N SWEET MOURNFUL WITH THE FALLING OF THE SUN

JAY SCREAMS TRYING TO STEAL CHICKENS EGGS

STOAT WAS OUT LAST NIGHT, WIGGLING HIS BACK ACROSS THE FIELD LIKE A CATERPILLAR

ALL THE ANTS HAVE MOVED TO HIGHER GROUND

SNAIL FEROCIOUS EATER IS DOING HIS BEST TO EAT ALL OUR GARDEN IN ONE SITTING

RABBIT HAS MOVED ACROSS THE FIELD TO HIGH GROUND FOR TO MAKE HAY FOR THE SPRING

DORMOUSE IS IN THE KITCHEN, CLEVER ANIMAL WARM N SNUG BENEATH THE STOVE

RAT IS TRYING TO DIG THE FOUNDATIONS OUT OF THE BARN

BLUE TIT N GOLDFINCH ARE NOW OUT N ABOUT LOOKING WHERE TO NEST,

OH SO MUCH BEAUTY N AWE IN THE WORLD!

SPEAK

SPEAK TO THE LAND N SHE SHALL TEACH YOU

OH YE

PLANT THE SEED N SHE SHALL FEED YOU

DRINK OF THE CLEAR WATERS N SHE SHALL REFRESH YOU

MAKE A SANCTUARY N SHE SHALL PROTECT YOU

GIVE OF LOVE N SHE SHALL LOVE YOU IN RETURN

GIVE OF RESPECT N SHE SHALL RESPECT YOU

MAKE OF RITUAL N CEREMONY N SHE SHALL SHOW YOU ALL THE WONDERS OF THIS WORLD

HER NAME IS

PACHAMAMA

RESPECT

OF WAY TOO MUCH BEAUTY

SNUS IS COOL, WAKES YOU UP AS WHEN

EXCUSE, ALL SQUID N OCTUPII CAN'T SEE FOR SHIT THROUGH ALL THESE FREAKING SYMBOLS

TRUTH

THE UNIVERSE IS A BACTERIA WITH AN ORGANIC DISEASE PARASITE CALLED LIFE

PHEW SEA WEED HEY WHO CHUCKED JONAH IN THE BELLY OF A WHALE THEN LET HIM ROAST ON A BEACH

SAT UNDER A WATTLE (I KNOW WHAT HE USED THE WATTLE FOR AKASIA, HE HE HE HE)

FLAT OUT HERE

AYA HAS TAUGHT ME TO CHASE THE COLOURS THROUGH THE TREES, TURN THEM ALL TO BLOOD RED FIRE THEN GRASP

THEM IN MY HAND UNTIL THE BURNING MAKES ME CRY THEY JUMP FREE OF ME N BECOME AS FLOWERS, WITH PETALS THAT NEVER DIE SCATTERED ON THE GROUND

FECK FECK FECK FORCE 8 INCREASING GALE FORCE TEN IMMINENT STORM FORCE 12 PHEW

TIME TO GO AGAIN SOON

VAPORISE~

THE JOURNEY HAS AYA SAYS ONLY JUST BEGUN FOR NGENUNUN

PHEW I IS SERIOUSLY UGLY

TOO MY RIGHT SITS A CHAP OF BONES WITH A BOWLER HAT ON HIS HEAD LIKE GOOD OLD CHARLIE CHAPLAIN

TO THE RIGHT HIS BRIDE BLACK TO WHITE WITH RED BLOOD LUST IN THE MIDDLE THEY SEEK TO DEVOUR ME OF MIND N BODY FOR THEY HAVE NO SOULS OF FLESH BY REFLECTION THEY ARE ME OF CAUSE TO BE, BUT N MORE OF NO QUESTIONS I HAVE SEEN THE GLORY OF MY DEATH TO COME UNREAL AYA PA VINE OF THE DEAD RESPECT A MADRE AYAHUASCA

I HAVE BEEN GIVEN OF GRACE N GLORY OF DEATH TO HOLD THROUGH MY LIFE GLIMPSED END UNREAL N THEN SOME MORE UNREAL

MAN I SHOULD DIET PROPERLY THIS SHIT WILL KILL ME :) HE HE HE HE HE~

I CANT GET OVER THE BEAUTIFUL UGLINESS OF MYSELF~

I AM AN OGG ER UNREAL FOR SURE

SHE SAT ME ON THE FLOOR N TORE MY HEART OUT THEN MADE ME EAT IT WITHOUT ANY GRAVY TO SAVER THE TASTE OF FLESH WITH

DISGUSTED AT, DISGUSTED SO TO THROW ONES HEART UPON THE FLOOR

FUCKIN KILLED ME

GOT TO GO AGAIN

PHEW, MY HEART A MILLION SHARDS OF ATOM FIRE GLASS

WHO SAID THIS GAME OF CHESS WAS NOTHING TO BEHOLD IS A FUCKING LYER FOR SURE OF MASK OF WOOD THAT SHIFTS N CHANGES AS THE TANGLED ROOTS OF OH SO MANY MIGHTY TREES SEEKING WATER IN THE LAND RIDDLED WITH TINY BEATLES A SCURRY TO DEVOUR N RECYCLE

TO LOOK TO THE SKY THROUGH A LOFTY CANOPY OF GRINNING MONKEY CLOWNS

GEARING GRABBING AT MY CLOAK, TO TEAR N LAY LOTS FOR SALE

MY GOD I AM AWESOMELY TERRIBLY WRETCHEDLY BEAUTIFULLY UGLY

TERRIFYINGLY SO~:)

AYA HAS GIVEN ME LEPROSY I SIT N WATCH AS MY FLESH FALLS IN GOUTS DECAYING TO THE FLOOR OF SCATTERED LEAVES

TINY SQUIRREL LIKE CREATURES COME N EAT OF THE DECAYING BODY WHILST A CROW SITS UPON MY HEAD PLUCKING OUT MY EYES THE CROW FLIES AWAY WITH MY EYES I CAN STILL SEE THOUGH THROUGH GAPING SOCKETS A STRIPED RED BLACK WHITE RIBBED VEST UP ON MY CHEST A GOLD POCKET WATCH UPON A CHAIN, MY HAND SLIPS AROUND MY BLACK CANE WITH SILVER SKULL AS TOP N I STAND TO SURVEY A FIELD OF BONES I CAN SEE MY TOOTHLESS SKULL SMILE AT THE OPENNESS OF SUCH A VISION I RAISE MY BONY HAND N DOFF MY HAT IN RESPECT OF THE DEADS THAT COME TO LIE AS A ROADWAY BEFORE MY EYES AN ARM BONE WITH HAND POINTING THE DIRECTION TO GO THE CROW COMES BACK N DROPS MY EYES INTO MY LEFT PALM THEN JUMPS AS A LITTLE BLACK DOG, UPON MY LAP AS I SIT AGAIN UPON A STUMP AS STOOL STUDDED COLOR LITTLE RED TONGUE HANGING A DROOL SLOWLY DROPS N SPLASHES TO THE BONE STRUNE FLOOR I LOOK UP N THE BRIDE STANDS IN WHITE HER SKULL GLEAMING BRIGHT AS SUN BLEACH OH MY NO EYES HERE I SAY HAVE THESE I HAVE NO NEED OF THEM N HAND HER MINE THAT CROW LEFT IN MY HAND SHE SMILES AGRIN N EATS MY EYES~ MINE FOREVER NOW SHE WHISPERS YOU HAVE GOLD FOR MY SMILE TWINKLES DIAMOND GLIMPSED AS POOLS OF CRYSTALLINE WATER MOONLIT MOORLANDS GREEN DALES A STREAM SEEN TURNS INTO HER SPINE AS SEEN OVER THE TOP

OF BODICE BOSOM THE DRESS HANGS DIRTY ON THE RIB BONES REACHING INTO POCKET I TAKE A SILVER RING WITH SCARLET RUBY ADORNING THE SET N PLACE IT ON HER FINGER BONE MINE FOREVER SHE WHISPERS MINE FOREVERE MINE

    CROW FLIES OFF

    I REQUIRE TO MAKE SOME FUCKIN NOISE N CRUSH SOME ROCKS WITH SOUND WAY TOO MUCH LIGHT N UGLY HE HE HE

    OF ALL THIS SHIT UNREAL N THEN SOME MORE HE HE HE EH

    BLISS

    THEN AYA

    MO

    PA MADRE AYAHUASCA FOR ANSWERING MY PRAYER

    I IS SERENE AS A MILL POND IN THE EXPECTATION OF THE MORNING SUN AS IT GHOSTLY PRIES THROUGH THE MISTS HIDING HEDGES, MAKING OF BIRD QUITE OF NO BREEZE TO TICKLE LEAF INTO LIFE MAKETH OF EVERYTHING WET WITH ANTICIPATIONS PAIN RELEASE OF THE FIRST CRACK OF SUNLIGHTS NEW DAY THE DEW SPASMS N GROWS LARGE OF FULLNESS OF RAINBOW PATTERNS ACROSS ONES EYES HOLD FILL N EXPLODE THE SUN HITTING TREE, MEADOW FIELD N SKY SLOWLY DISTINGUISHING FENCES, COWS, CROW IN THE TREES NO BREEZE THE SUNLIGHT TURNS THE SWIRL WITH HER HEAT

EVERYTHING BEGINS TO STEAM WHIPPING UPWARDS GENTLY TURNING IN THE LIGHT BREATH OF GOD BREATH DEEPLY FILL THE LUNGS OF LIFE TO EXPLODE AS THE SUN GIVER OF LIFE

HE HE EHE I AM A STAR FLOWING IN SEA AFIELD OF PHOTON LIGHT

MY FOCUS IS GREATER THAN THE SURROUNDING LIGHT NO BODY EVERYTHING VOID FELL ON THE FLOOR OOOOOOOOOOH MY DOGGY CRIED OF BELIEF OF DEATH SERIOUS PURGE BOTH ENDS SIMULTANEOUSLY,

BATH OF TRIANGLES N NOISE NOW FUNKY TUNES HE EHE FECK WIBBLE WOBBLE FALL DOWN LIKE A LOG, IN A FIELD OF MULTI-COLOURED DAISIES TO PUSH UP STEM TOWARDS THE SUN HA HA

FUNKY LOOK AT ALL THE PURPLE FLOWERS FUNKY IT GOES LIKE THIS BLOW IT SLOWS SLOWLY GETTING BIGGER THEN IT REFLECTS ITSELF LIGHT MUSIC RHYTHM FUNKY STYLE

HA HA HA LOST IT OOOOOOH YES

THE EAGLE FLIES HIGH OF TO SEE THE MOUNTAIN ERE DARK CAVES IN THEM WINDS THAT SCREAM THE CRAGGY SPIRES OF RUMBLINGS, ROCKS FALLING DOWN THE SCREE SHE CIRCLES HIGH AMONGST THE BLUENESS NOT TROUBLED OF CLOUD SOURING NOW HEAD POINTED AT THE WIND, SPEEDING DIVE ACROSS THE MOUNTAIN FACE EYE BRIGHT YELLOW RINGED,

DEEP GLOSSY BLACK OF CENTRE BEACK HOOKED N POISED OF ALABASTA HOVERING OVER A GENTLE CURVE TO POINT, FEATHERS DASHING BACKWARDS AS IF THE SCREE OF THE MOUNTAIN SIDE, GOLEN BROWNS FLECKED YELLOWS DEEP HUES OF SMOKEY GEY BLUE THE CHEEK GRINS WITH SPEED DASHING LOW, PULLUP FOR THE STALL DROP CUNNING NOW STANDING UPON A ROCK TURNING HEAD EASTWARDS, DOWN THE VALEY TO THE SHORE LINES DISTANT LINE TINY BIRDS GULLS, SWIRL AMONGST THE HORSE BROKEN WHITE SURF SPREADING WINGS TO WING TO LIFT ONE STROKE TO THE AIR WIND CARIES UPWARDS BODY, HEAD DROP, BALANCED FALL TO SKY, GROUND MOVING VERY FAST BELOW~ OF SIGHT TO SEE VALLEY GREEN, BUTTERCUPS, SITTING KISSING TO THE SWEET CARESS OF LIGHT FRESH BREEZES CARESS THE GRASSES LITTLE EARWIG WRIGGLES AMONGST LASTS FALLEN TWIGS BIRDS HOP AMONGST THE PEBBLES OF LIFES STREAM FLICKING THIS N THAT TO SEE BENEATH, THE SECRETS OF TREASURES, MAYBE WITHIN THE CURIOSITY OF LIFES EXPRESSION EH HE THE LITTLE SNAKE STILL WRIGGLES IN THE POOLS OF TO GIVE HEAD TO ITS OWN REFLECTION CURIOUS ENTITY ALWAYS LOOKING IN THE MIRROR, TO DOUBLE OF TREASURE THROUGH HARSHNESS OF PRIDE YOUR COAT IS YOUR JEWLES OF IMAGINATIONS TO SEE OF ALL REFLECTED AS LITTLE MINNOWS SWIM DANCING IN THE BROWN GLISTENED MURKY WATERS OF WEEDS FLOWING IN THE CURRENT OF ONES EMOTIONS; SMILE TO SEE THE ESSENCE OF IT ALL AS FLOWERS POSE THEIR PERFUMES, SO SOIL N

ROCK POSSES THEIRS, IN HARMONY WITH THE CYCLES OF THE SKIES OF ALL THE LITTLE CURIOSITIES, LITTLE BROWN GREY SQUIRREL, SITS N, TICKLES WHISKERS, PROUD OF BODY N COAT OF LIGHT LITTLE PAWS AS IF TO TINY TO CARRY OF FOOD FOR TO STORE ALOFT FLYING THROUGH TREE TOP BRANCHES, AS AN UNRULY MIND

    AS I WRITE IT AS IT IS EMOTION SYMBOL, MOVES MIND FOR TO CREATE SERIOUS POWER MOVING ENERGIES THAT CAN EXPLODE A UNIVERSE INTO EXISTENCE

    I SHALL KEEP TO MY MEADOWS FOR NOW ANGER KNOCKS AT THE DOOR

    "TOO THE BACK OF THE LINE MY FRIEND I SHALL TALK WITH YOU LATER) GONE AS COMMANDED) OH MY I JUST BECAME THE MUSIC) EZ~

    BODY ICE COLD NOW DEATH IS CLOSE (OH MY SECRETS OH CHEMISTRY BREATH ALL INPUT IS OUTPUT REFLECTIONS FLY THROUGH THE X OXO STRETCH MOVE HOLD RELEASE

    CREATE~RHYTHM SHAME ABOUT ALL THE SYMBOLS TO MASH THROUGH, COS AUTO PILOT IS NEARLY ONLINE:)~ DYSLEXIC AS HELL FOR UP N DOWN NO LEFT TO RIGHT AS OF YET

    MEMORY HOLDS TO ITSELF, AS IF GLUE TO HOLD A FORM REMEMBERED THROW MORE WOOD ON THE FIRE MY DEAR FOR MY BODY AILS ME TO BE WARM SWEET APPLES OF PRESS FOR OF BREATHS SHORTNESS I BE~ OF TO FEEL THE EARTH

SHAKING, AS BOULDERS RUMBLE EMOTION THOUGH HALLS OF ONES TEMPLE LIKE CURTAINS, N FLAGS OF REDS N YELLOWS BLOWING IN THE WIND

RIVERS FLOW AS IF IN MURKY POOLS OF SWIRLING MUDS ARMIES MARCH AS SHOD EN OF FOOT SANDLE AMONGST POOLS OF MANY CRABS THE LADY LOOKS N SMILES MEEKLY, SOMEWHAT OF CONCERN, BUT STILL OF WHATEVER, FOR SHE HAS SEEN IT ALL THE BODIES UPON N IN THE LAND WAY TOO MANY SPEARS MOVING AGAINST THE THREATENING SKY QUESTIONS OF WAR ONE SIDE OR GROWING IN THE SUNLIGHT OF THE GLORIOUS PALACE PLANTING OF ONES IMAGINATIONS SEEDS OR HOLDING OF SWORD N SPEAR, AGAINST OF EACH FOR RIGHTEOUSNESS FACE LIKE A BANNER GRINNING DEFIANCE TO THE HEAVING SEA

NOW THE QUESTION BEGS TO DIFFER OF WHY THE BLATANT PRIDE IS NOT YOUR COAT COVERED SPECKLED ENOUGH WITH ALL THE STARS OF THE HEAVENS "YES I CAN NOT HOLD THEM ONLY SEE THE BEAUTY OF THEM SHINE, AS I STRUTT AMONGST THE WOVE OF MY COAT MY HANDS HAVE NO SUBSTANCE TO HOLD OF THESE DIAMOND BEAUTIES

SO YOU ARE WANT OF DESIRE THEN THIS FACE OF PRIDE YOU TREASURE SO TO SHOW

YES OF ALL TO BE AS OF MINE TO HOLD

WHY?

BECAUSE IT IS SO BEAUTIFUL

EVEN IF IT IS NOT YOURS TO HOLD

YES!

AH SIR PRIDE YOU ARE VERY HARD TO SEE YOU MAKE OF FIVE TO HOLD HEADSTRONG CANT YOU SEE THE BEAUTY IS FREE

PRIDE DISSOLVES TO THE ETHER AS HEART LOOKS TO THE SKY OF CLOUDS POINTS ROLLING FLUFFY PINK OF EVENING SUNLIGHT

SO THE DARKNESS IS NOT FAR AY ALWAYS LURKING UPON THE HORIZON OF ONES CONSCIENCES CONSCIOUSNESS~

THE VOID IS DEEP~

SO YOU SIT WITH ME NOW EVEN THOUGH I DO NOT EVOKE OF YOU SO

IT IS MY WAY TO SIT N ARGUE OF TO SHOW OF ONLY ONE

BIRDS FLY WHITE BIRDS CIRCLE HIGH AMONGST A VORTEX TWISTING WALLS THUNDERING OF GREY SMOKE ENERGIES, UPWARDS DOWNWARDS, CONVECTION OF PLANTET TO EH SKY RETURNED FEEDING TWISTING COILING UPWARDS DOWNWARDS, PULSING LIKE A GREAT HEART TO LOOK WITHIN IS TO JUST GET PHOTON STREAMED OUT OF CONSCIOUS EXISTENCE

AS BREEZES OF SHOCKED AWE SHATTER ONES SIGHT LIKE A TRILLION ROLLS OF WALL PAPER HOLDING OF PATTERN EVEN THOUGH TWISTED THROUGH THE VORTEX OF CREATIONS SPIRAL REFLECTED BOTH WAYS

ATOP IT NOW LOOKING DOWN THE GREAT GAPING VORTEX THROUGH OF WHAT I CAN ONLY SLIGHTLY FATHOM TO UNDERSTAND LOOKING A TO OF THE TUBE OF MY OWN EXISTENCE TWISTING MIRRORED OF TUNNEL TOP TO BOTTOM HA HA THE GRIN OF FEAR SHOWS HERE HEAD YES WHAT DO YOU WANT IS IT SAFE FUCK OFF IS IT SAFE HOW WOULD I KNOW

YOU MADE IT SHE WHISPERS GENTLY, RIAL LING FINGERS THROUGH MY HEARTS EMOTION

OK MADAM FEAR, COME WITH ME TO MY MOUNTAIN TOP COME WITH ME N SEE OF YOUSELF AN ALL YOUR GLORY

TRUDGING UP ROLLING DOWN MOUNTAIN SCREE GREY, OMINOUS CLOUDS HOVER ABOVE, PENT ANT OF LIGHTNING STORMS DANGER

"COME ON KEEP GOING

FEAR IS SITTING ON THE MOUNTAIN SLOWPE LOOKING UPWARDS

TAKE OF STAFF N WALK

FEAR RESIGNS N TRUDGES ON H 8.

HOW HIGH YOU FIGURE ON GOING

TO THE TOP

WHAT THE TOP THIS MIGHTY MOUNTAIN?

YES

OH~

STANDING NOW ATOP A LEDGE ONLY SKY N CLOUDS ABOVE MOUNTAIN SIDE, COVERED IN JAGGED GREY SCREE ROCKS BELOW

OK SISTER FEAR, JUMP

WILL YOU CATCH ME IF I DO

YES~

WHAT IF I FALL FASTER THAN YOU

IMPOSSIBLE JUMP

FEAR GRABS HERE COAT N WRAPS IT TIGHT

OF WHAT DO YOU FEAR FEAR

DEATH~

PAIN~

SUFFERING

LOSING ALL THE TREASURE

AH SO YOU ARE MEMORY THEN ATTACHMENTS, LIKE A SUIT CASE FULL OF BODIES ATTACHMENT MEMORIES

YES

AH WOW THROW ALL THE CLOTHS OUT I SHALL MAKE OF YOU KNEW MORE BRILLIANT GARMENTS TO WEAR

YOU WILL?

YES I SHALL~

OK FEAR HOLD MY HAND YES N WE SHALL JUMP TOGETHER WE WILL?

YES WE SHALL~

ON THE COUNT OF THREE

WHY THREE?

ON THE COUNT OF THREE

BREATH ONE

BREATH TWO

BREATH

HOLD ON!!!

AH FOR THE LOVE OF ALL SACRED WHAT?

WILL IT HURT

A LITTLE

SO WHY DO IT~

COS YOU SHALL FEEL BETTER AFTER

BETTER OF WHAT

OF LOSS OF ALL THE SUIT CASE OF ATTACHMENTS

I LIKE MY PHOTOS N MEMORIES

KEEP THEM THEN, JUST THROW AWAY THE SUITCASE THAT CONTAINS ALL OF THEM

BUT I WILL LOSE THEM

YOU SHALL NO LOSE ANYTHING

JUMP!

YOULL HAVE TO DRAG ME

WHY?

YOU SAID IT HURTS

A LITTLE

THEN WHY DO IT

BECAUSE IT WILL MAKE YOU LIGHT ENOUGH TO FLY N NOT FALL

FLY LIKE THE EAGLE

YES~

OK LETS GO

HA HA HA

WEEEEEEEEEEEE LOOK AT ME I AM FLYING

SHUT UP FEAR, ENJOY THE RIDE

OH I SHALL~

MMMMMMMMMMMMMH FOOD~

HE HE HE MONKEYS!!!

MORE WOOD ON THE FIRE I AM STILL FREEZING OF THROWS OF DEATH MY BODY SHAKES LIKE, VOLCANOES WISPERING, TO LET GO OF FUME N BLUME THEIR DUST ROCK SMOKNE TO THE SKY

HOT BATH~

MUSIC

OUT~

IN~

SOAPY SUDSY WATERS ROLLING WARM REFRESHING SPARKLES LIKE NEW RAIN, THROUGH MY AURA DANCING BEHIND MY EYELIDS LIKE MIRRAIDED ICECREAM CONES ALL TOUCHING, N CHANGIND PLACES AS THEY DANCE

AWE

FENCE POST TEA BAG DROOLE

I ENDED UP KIPPING IN MY BROS GREENHOUSE, SAMPLING HIS MANY EXOTIC NUGS ALL NITE

"SWEETNESS N CITRUS FRUIT ROLLS

ESSENCE OF CINNAMON N LEMONS

SWEET LITTLE "DOOB" THAT I SUCK ON

ROLLING N FOLDING SPARKLING TESTICLES THROUGH MY MIND

FLOATING N ENDLESSLY SMILING

ONE MILE HIGH

JET STREAMED N LOADED

NUMB N CONTENT

CATAPULTED LIKE A JET

SITTING WITH MY SWEET ROLL,

SLURPING A MUG OF SWEET TEA

THE LADY "WHITE WIDOW

OF MINDS EYE INVENTION

WRAPPED N FOLDED WITHIN YOUR CARESS

3 MILES HIGH

"SMILING"

STILL

"SMILING"

3 SMILES HIGH !

WATER

I HOLD A SHELL IN MY RIGHT HAND (OYSTER LIKE) N AS I LIFT N OPEN THE TOP, RED GLISTENING WINE IS GLIMPSED WITHIN.

THE WHITE OF THE SHELL N THE RED OF THE WINE.

WITHIN A TINY DROPLET FALLS N CREATES RIPPLES UPON THE SURFACE, MIRRORING LIGHT UPWARDS, CASCADING OFF THE INNER PEARL FLANKS OF THE SHELL.

TO STOP THE DROPLET BEFORE IT HITS THE SURFACE IS TO KNOW OF WHERE IT CAME N WHERE IT IS GOING, CONSCIOUSNESS EXPANDS AS TIME CEASES TO EXIST.

THE ENERGIES AS IF LIKE WATER FLOW BACK FROM THE RIM OF THE SHELL, BACK TO THE CENTRE.

THE DROP JUMPS FREE

BECOME THE DROP.

SEE

GOD TOLD ME TO WORK AS A HEALER THIS GIVES ME AN INABILITY OF SENSE OF RESPECT, FOR TO BE GIVEN THIS WORK TO WORK FOR ANOTHER MAN, IT HOLDS ME BACK FROM PARTAKING OF THIS WORLD AS IT STANDS I DO NOT LIKE THIS WORLD N ALL THE POWER STRUGGLES, IT SICKENS ME TO THE VERY SOUL OF MY EXISTENCE, TO SEE OF ALL THE TREASURE BEING USED WRONGLY BY THIS I MEAN ALL THE MATERIAL IS TREASURED OVER LIFE

OATH OF ONLY WATER LIGHT FOOD LOVE OF GROWING, IN THE KINGDOM, WITH THE WORLD THAT MADE ME I HAVE DEEP DEPRESSIONS, THAT COME OF MY INEPTITUDE TO DEAL WITH THIS WORLD ON ITS TERMS, SO I MAKE OF RITUAL TO BE ABLE TO SIT WITH MY GOD I KNOW ME I KNOW THE WORLD I LIVE IN EVERYONE THAT KNOWS ME, KNOWS THIS IS WHY THEY LOVE ME KILL ME OR LOVE ME, JUST DONT PUSH ME COS BY SURE HAIL OF ANGELS UPON THY HEAD, BY GODS CREATION I SHALL STAND RIGHTEOUS IN THE FACE OF ADVERSITY AS LONG AS IT DOES NOT INVOLVE MATERIAL GAIN, OR A POWER STRUGGLE OVER MATERIA I FIGHT FOR OUR RIGHT TO BE ANIMALS LIVING IN THE KINGDOM I MAKE A LOT OF FUCKIN NOISE WITH BIG SOUND SYSTEMS N STAND N TELL ESTABLISHMENT TO THEIR FACES IF THEY LIKE, THAT THEY ARE WRONG COME SEE, WITH ME, THE ANIMAL LIVE WITHIN THE KINGDOM SEED TO GROUND, HERB TO MOUTH, SMOKE OF SPIRIT TO THE SKY---- NOW JUST LOST IT ALL IN TONGUES FOR THE SWEET LOVE OF LIFE ALL IS HERE N NOW ALL IS AS IT SHOULD BE A FLOWER OPENING TO THE GOLDEN MORNING SUN

I NOW SEE THE DEW FROM THE PREVIOUS NITE, GLISTEN IN THE SPARKLES OF SUNLIGHT TEARS UPON MY CHEEKS, N KNOW THAT ALL IS GOOD OF THIS LAND THIS MOTHER WITH THE FATHER(F) SPIRIT GUIDING, MOTHER TEACHING OF THE FIRST DUALITY SPIRIT EARTH AS TO ALL THE MANIPULATION SHIT, FUCK IT, RE-PROGRAM THE MACHINE WE LEARN OF OUR TRUE SELVES THROUGH MOST POWERFUL PLANT ENTITIES OF WHICH TRUTH, THEY SCARE THE FUCKING SHIT OUT OF ME SOMETIMES, N SOMETIMES, TAKE ME SO SWIFTLY OVER TO GLORY, AS IF TO HOLD OF ETERNITY OPENING~ THAT I AM LEFT STUNNED FOR THE REST OF MY LIFE WITH THE KNOWING OF THE MOST AWESOME AWESOME, FANTASTIC CREATION OF IT ALL

I LOOK TO PSYCHE N SEE, AS PUFF DRAGON PEOPLE, WEARING TURBANS, SMOKING SPICE~ ONLY HEADS FLOATING IN A VOID, EVERYTHING CURLED, ANGEL ANGEL THE PROGRAM WE RUN OF SPIRIT THROUGH MIND

THIS IS MY GIFT GIVEN TO HAVE OF THIS KNOWLEDGE N PASS IT ON I CANT TELL FOLKS "TURN ON TUNE IN N CHANGE THE PROGRAM BY GOD THEY WOULD RUN TO THE HILLS, JUMP IN CAVES N POOR ROCKS N SOILED ASHES ON THEIR HEADS N SCRABBLE ABOUT LOOKING LOOKING LOOKING, FORWARD IS THE ONLY WAY ALWAYS TO REMEMBER OF GRACE

SO I SHALL GROW MORE PLANTS WE HAVE NO MONEY WHATSOEVER WE HAVE A LITTLE FOOD FOR EACH DAY GOD ALWAYS PROVIDES WE HAVE SHELTER, N OUR LOVE MY WIFE HAS HERE CAR N A LITTLE JOB SHE LIKES TO WORK AT THE REST

IS ME N THE PLANTS PHEW SWEATING NOW NOT OFT DOTH ONE GET OF THE CHANCE TO OPEN THE GATES OF TRUTH TO SOMEONE/FOLKS N KNOW OF THAT THEY SHALL SEE THEM, IN ALL OF THEIR UGLINESS N BEAUTY CUP OF SWEET TEA///////// VERY TEARFUL TODAY, IT IS ALL FLOODING OUT THIS IS GOOD, AT LAST THE DAMN IS BROKEN IT HAS TAKEN MANY DAYS MANY YEARS IN FACT I SHALL BE ABLE TO FLY LATER IN PEACE, WITHOUT ANY PAIN OF BODY COILING TO BOUNCE I SHALL JUST BOUNCE YOU KNOW I KNOW SO I SHALL SHUT UP N KEEP TALKING

AS OF WHEN MY WIFE FOUND ME I WAS IN A WHEEL CHAIR, HA HA HA HA ALL SHOT TO PIECES OH WHAT A WRETCHED WRETCH I WAS, HE HE HE THE GLORY OF IT WAS IMMENSE, UNTIL ONE DAY I SAID FUCK ALL THIS SHIT YOU ARE NOT ME HOW THE HELL CAN YOU FILL ME FULL OF JUNK CHEMICALS N THEN SIT N TELL ME I KNOW HOW THE FUCK DO YOU KNOW, YOU DONT TAKE ALL THIS SHIT SO I JUMPED FUNNY I THOUGHT I AINT DEAD YET TIME TO DANCE ME THINKS, SO FUCK OFF WHEEL CHAIR HELLO LIFE NOW WHAT TO DO WITH THIS MOST CRAZY CONFUSION CALLED LIFE

MAKE A LOT OF NOISE, PRIMAL SHIT, SOUND BEFORE LIGHT, SO I STOOD UP OUT OF MY MIRAGED SIGHT, N SCREAMED AT THE WORLD THAT TORMENTED ME SO THEY WENT FUCKING MENTAL, TRIED TO SHUT ME UP, STICK ME IN PRISON, IN COURT IN COURT IN COURT, BUT I KEPT COMING BACK HA HA HA SO NOW THEY JUST FUCK WITH OF WHAT WE OWN THEY ARE WELCOME TO IT AS LONG AS THEY DONT TOUCH ME N MY WIFE

OF DEATH TO GLORY, ALL IS GLORY, THEY SHALL NOT MOVE ME I AM MI SO FUCK OFF N FIND YOUR MEAT SOMEWHERE ELSE HE HE HE

THEY GO THEY GO N TRY N FIGHT ME WITH OFFICIALS N POLI, THEY ALL JUST GET EVEN MORE FUCKED OFF THAN THEY WHERE IN THE FIRST PLACE, BUT EVERYONE IS MISSING THE POINT OF WHY THEY ARE ALL SO ANGRY, IT ISNT WITH OF WHAT I DO REALLY IT IS BECAUSE THEY CHANNEL THE ENERGIES THE WRONG WAY OH THEY UNDERSTAND FORWARD, TO ATTACK TO PROTECT FACE BUT THEY DONT UNDERSTAND REFLECTION I JUST STAND THEIR N BLIND THE SHIT OUT OF THEM NOT A JUDGE IN THE LAND WILL CONVICT ME FOR BEING MYSELF WITHOUT DISGUISE SO ALL I HAD LEFT IS TO FIND FIND OUT THE FUCKING TRUTH IS WHAT AN BUST ALL THE BAD PROGRAMING SO WITH ANGER ON ONE SIDE N LOVE ON THE OTHER, I RUN HEAD LONG INTO GLORY THE SUN IS SHINNING AGAIN AS I SIT IN THE GARDEN WRITING TO YOU OH SOLAR SO BRIGHT N GOLDEN, RADIANT OF MY MINDS EYES DELIGHT PEER TO ME YOUR PLEASUROUS RAYS FILL ME FULL OF YOUR GLORIOUS LIGHT N FILL ME ALL TO BRIM OF EVERYTHING, FOR THOUGH ART MY CREATOR THOUGH ART MY LIFE, I COME BEARING NO FALSE WITNESS IN THE SHINE OF YOUR FACE

AH TEA!!! HA HA HA

ALL AT BASE IS SYMBOLS HERE IS MY KEY WHY IS THIS SO AS OF WHEN MY FILTERS COME DOWN

THE REST WAS ONE HELL OF A HEADACHE TO CHEW THROUGH WAY WAY TOO MANY FALLS WITNESSES I FINALLY

GOT TO GEOMETRY N THE COIL OF LIFE ALL IS LIGHT IN REFLECTION, HELD BY THE FILTERS OF BODY N MIND, OR ONES ANGEL HA HA HA TIME TO SMASH MY ANGEL N LET GOD REBUILD ME, FOR ALL THE CHAOS WAS OF MY OWN MAKING GOD TOLD ME NOT OF MONEY, NOT OF MATERIA, BUT OF THE JOY OF LIFE, TO RUN FREE AS THE DEER N THE NEW BORN LAMBS FROLIC DRINK THE WATER EAT THE FOOD RUN A SCURRY UPON THY LAND, SEED TO SOIL, HERB TO MOUTH, SMOKE OF SPIRIT TO THE SKY TO COIL AS GOD SO THIS IS ME THIS IS ALL YOU GET

ASTRALED TO THE ORIGINAL SOURCE

ON THE WAY OUT I MEET A FEMININE ENTITY THAT REACHES DOWN FROM THE SKY N WITH LONG TENTICLE ARMS, FOLDS THEM AROUND ME.

THE BEAUTY OF THIS CREATURE IS BEYOND COMPREHENSION.

HAIR FLOWING LIKE SEAWEED, A FACE OF RADIANT LOVE., PIERCING BLUE EYES N A SMILE OH SO SWEET.

WOOOOOOSH!

I AM WHISKED,

ME AWAY,

WAY UP,

UP INTO THE UPPER STRATA.

FOLDED N CUDDLED WITHIN TENTICLE ARMS.

THERE WE SPIN N DANCE N THE WHOLE OF ALL VIBRATES LIKE A TUNING FORK.

PIN DOT CATHRON WHEELS EVERYWHERE.

THEN SHE MELDS N EVOLVES INTO A MOST AWESOMELY INTRICATE DRAGON ENTITY THAT IS CREATOR N I TRANSCEND INTO A BEING OF BLUE SHIMMERING LIGHT N I DISAPPEAR INTO A SEA OF VIBRANT WHITE ELECTRICITY.

MY WHOLE BEING EXPLODING IN RAPTURE OF ORGASMIC LOVE.

AS I START TO COME BACK A BIT I AM MET YET AGAIN FOLDED IN THE ARMS OF AN ENTITY SOMEWHAT LIKE AN OCTOPUS N WE DANCED THROUGH HALLS OF ARCHITECTURES OF SPIRALS, CUBES, HEXAGONS, TETRAHEDRONS, DODECAHEDRONS,

PYRAMIDS, EVOLVING WAVES N DIMENSIONAL TANGENTS.

I FOLD OUT APON A WAVE N BECOME ENVELOPED ACROSS THE TOP BY ANOTHER THAT SPLIT THROUGH A TANGENT DIMENSION N TAKES ME WITH IT.

THIS IS A STRANGE ORANGE LAND, PURPLE CLOUDS N FLAT PLAIN LANDS THAT SEEMED TO GO OFF AT A 60* ANGLE UP LEFT.

I STAND PROJECTED OUTWARDS N AM SURROUNDED BY GOSSAMER WISP ENTITIES WITH GHOSTLY SMILING FACES.

THESE ALSO DANCE N VIBRATE AS I SWIRL N ROLL VORTEXING ACROSS THE SKY.

I LOOP THE LOOP N FALL BACK THROUGH MYSELF ONLY TO BE GRABBED BY A MOST INTRICATE DRAGON ENTITY THAT FLEW WITH ME, HOLDING ME (THE TOUCH OF THIS ENTITY ALMOST EXPLODED MY PSYCHI N I IMPLODE, EXPLODED N BECOME ONCE AGAIN MANY MANY SHARDS OF IRIDECANT LIGHT.

WE FLY SIDE BY SIDE THROUGH GALAXIES N SUPER NOVAS, THE SKY FULL OF GREEN N RED SHOOTING STARS.

I THEN STAND UP N SHAKE MY BODY AS I FEEL LIKE I HAD TURNED INTO THE TREE I SIT BACK AGAINST.

THE SKY ABOVE A MASSIVE ARCHITECTURED CATHEDRAL CEILING, ALL THE GRASS N THE TREES GLOWING VIBRANT WHITE IN THE STAR LIGHT.

MY FRIEND BECOMES A FALLEN WIZARD THE LIKES OF THE BOOK DISK WORLDS, FALLEN N NOT BOTHERED TO USE ANY MAGIC ANY MORE.

HIS PIPE DONE HIM. :)

SWIRLED UPON THE GROUND LIKE A RAG, CLOAK COVERING FROM SHOULDERS TO THE GROUND. A HAT ATOP HIS HEAD, POINTED N FOLDED TO ONE SIDE.

HIS CLOAK COVERED IN SILVER MOVING SYMBOLS, STARS MOONS ARROWS SNAKES ALL MELDING N CREATING A FLOW OF ENERGY SO INTRICATE MY SIMPLE LANGUAGE CAN NOT DESCRIBE.

SUCKING DEEP UPON MY PIPE I FOLD OUT,

UPWARDS LIKE AN EXPRESS TRAIN.

EVERYTHING BECOMES ATOMS OF LIGHT ALL CONNECTED N EVOLVING.

I MELT INTO THIS ATOMISED SPACE THE SKY COMING DOWN N FOLDING THROUGH ME,
TRANSLUCENT SYMBOLS SILVER EVERY WHERE N BECOME AN EVER EVOLVING MANDELA THAT CHASES N CORALS AROUND ITSELF.
THEN I START TO EXPAND LIKE AN ATOM BOMB EXLODING IN SPACE.
WHITE LIGHT FROM A CENTRE ROLLING OUTWARDS ACROSS THE FLAT PLAIN OF SPACE N TIME, LOOPING N VORTEXING THROUGH SYMBOLS N SPIRALS WAVES N DIMENSIONS (WORDLESS FOLKS, I DO APOLOGISE :)
ZAP! POINT!
OUT! LARGER, FLATTER.
OUT! EVEN BIGGER, FLATTER.
NOW LIKE ATOM PAPER FLAT, OUT !

OUT!

OUT GONE!

POP!

DIMENSIONAL TIME N SPACE ALL EXISTENCE GONE.

TRANSCENDED INTO ALL INCOMPRIHESIBLY VAST ENOURMOUSLY FLAT N SPHERED.

EXPLODING SUPER NOVA AS A STAR!

SILVER BLUE YELLOW RED MELDING ENERGIES FOLDED AROUND N THROUGH ME.

I BECOME MANY SPECTRUMS OF LIGHT FRACTALED N PRISMATIZED.

THE ENERGIES ARE SO GREAT I CRY OUT LOUD WITH THE SHEAR FORCE OF RAPTURE.

I ROLL AROUND N WALLOW IN A SEA BLUE SILVER ALIVE WRITHING SIZZLING THROUGH MY EXISTENCE LIKE FRYING OIL, BUBBLING EFFERVESCENT EVOLVING PRISMATIC EXPLOSIONS OF PURE LOVE FOR WHAT SEEMS LIKE A THOUSAND YEARS N THEN SOME.

I SUDDENLY REALISED I HAVE STOPPED BREATHING!

WHOOP I FILLED MY LUNGS.

ROLLING BACKWARDS AS IF FALLING, EACH BREATH BRINING ME CLOSER TO THE EARTH.

IT IS RAINING THE RAIN DROPS SLICE STRAIGHT THROUGH ME N HIT THE GROUND BENEATH.

I BREATH DEEP N OPEN MY EYES.

THE WHOLE WORLD, THE WAY I SEE IT HAS CHANGED.

EVERYTHING CONTAINING SILVER LIFE FORCE ENERGIES SHIMMERING IN THE STAR LIGHT,
EVERYTHING COMPLEX PATTERNS ROLL N DANCE AROUND ME.
MY PSYCHI, MY MINDS EYE, MY EXISTENCE FULL OF INTRICATE PATTERNS N I SEE ENERGIES FLOW AN EBB, LIKE BEING IN A TIDAL WATER BUT ALSO IN THE AIR.

I BREATH IN ELECTRICITY N BREATH OUT.

MY WHOLE BODY ELECTRIC N ALIVE.

I START TO DANCE N WHIRL GIVING THANKS FOR THE GIFT.

I AM NOW LIKE A TUNING FORK IN TUNE WITH A VIBRATION SO PRIMAL N PURE I BECOME CONNECTED WITH THE GROUND THROUGH MY DANCE.

THE LIGHTS AROUND ME FORCEFULLY BY MY MOVEMENTS COLLIDE N RE-EVOLVE AS DANCERS WITHIN ME.

THE STAR STRUNE SKY ABOVE SPINS LIKE CATHRON WHEELS PIN DOTTING N CAVORTING IN MY DANCE.

I WHIRL N SPIN STAFF IN HAND MY CLOAK FLYING HIGH LIKE A FLAT WING.

I AM ABLE TO SPIN LIKE A TOP ENDLESSLY WITHOUT GETTING DIZZY.

I SPIN N JUMP, I HAVE BODY, BUT THE ENERGIES ARE SO INTENSE I CAN ALMOST FLY.

I RUN UP THE FIELD N DIVE IN THE AIR FLUID MOTION (NOT BAD FOR AN OLD MAN)

I DANCED FOR NEARLY AN HOUR SCREACHING N WHOOPING WITH PRIMAL EXSTATIC DELIGHT N THEN COLLAPSE TO THE FLOOR BEATEN.

I CRAWL SOME 35 FEET BACK TO OUR LITTLE BENDER N SUCK DEEPLY ON MY LITTLE GREEN STICK. (A LICK OF WHITE WIDOW FOR MY BODY)

I SAG TO THE FLOOR N FALL DEATHLY ASLEEP FOR ABOUT NINETY MINUTES.

APON AWAKENING SOMETHING HAS SHIFTED.

I SEE MY WORLD IN A NEW LIGHT.

THE SUN CRACKES ACROSS THE HORIZON WITH AN ORANGE BIG BOLD HEAD N SMILES AT ME.

EVERYTHING IS PRISMATIC N ALIVE ALL CONNECTED, AT ONE.

I SIT N FACE THE SUN N OFFER MY PIPE TO OUR GIVER OF LIFE,

TEARS STREAMING DOWN MY FACE.

I HUM CHANT N MUMBLE HUMBLE MY THANKS AS THE SUN RISES, ENEREGIES WITHIN RISING ALSO TO THE NEW DAY.

COMPLETELY SOAKED BEDRAGGLED N EXTREEMLY TIRED WE BREAK CAMP TOTALLY SPEACHLESS.

RETURN TO THE CAR N EXPRESS BOTH AT THE SAME TIME HOW PLASTIC ARTIFICIAL THE INSIDE OF THE MOTOR LOOKS N FEELS.

AH WELL BACK TO THE HUSSLE AN BUSSLY OF OUR NORMAL DAY LIVE.

HOLDING CLOSE TO MY HEART OF WHAT I WAS SHOWN N LEARNT.

SPANGLED!!!

AWESOME AFFINITY WITH MY MONEY PLANT N MANY MORE.

I SIT HERE N THE WORLD IS BUZZING, NOISY VIBRANT N ALIVE.

I WAS SORTING OUT SOME EARTH FOR TO PUT IN POTS. DIGGING WITH A TROWEL. I HEARD/FELT FROM IN FRONT OF ME. SOMEONE/THING, FELT, SAY." ITS DRY, ISNT IT?"

I LOOK UP FROM MY STOOP N PEER AT THE DANDELION IN FRONT OF ME. "DRY YES" I REPLY.

"WE ARE YOUNG, WE WILL GROW, WE WILL FAN, WE WILL FLY, WE WILL MULTIPLY."

AMAZING. SO MUCH SING SONG.

"SUN IS FUN, SUN IS LIFE, SUNLIGHT." WEEEEEEEEEEE ARE MANYYYYYYYYYY. "

THE BUZZING GETS LOUDER AS THE SUN RISES N ITS HEAT RADIATES DAZZLES OF SPIRITUAL GLEE.

SPRING, "WE ARE ALIVE." "MANY, MORE"

I NOW UNDERSTAND.

I SMILE N TAKE THE POT I HAVE JUST FILLED INTO THE LIVING ROOM TO PLACE IT ON THE WINDOW SILL.

I PART THE CURTAINS N LOOK AT THE LUSH GREENERY OUTSIDE N JUST KIND OF DAY DREAM IN THE SUN.

PLANTING MORNING GLORY ON THE WINDOW SILL FOR THE GARDEN THIS YEAR.

FROM THE KITCHEN I COLLECT WATER TO MOISTEN THE SOIL N ALSO A CUP TO SOAK THE SEEDS IN.

AS I POUR THE WATER ON THE SOIL, I HEAR TINY SINGING VOICES.

"US PLEASE." "US PLEASE." "CAN WE HAVE SOME PLEASE."

OH SO POLITE.

I THROW THE CUP OF WATER OVER THE MONEY PLANTS N LISTEN TO THE GLEE OF THEM SHAKING IN THE SUN N WATER.

"WOULD YOU LIKE MORE MY FRIENDS? "OH, YES PLEASE, WATER PLEASE"

I COLLECT ANOTHER CUP OF WATER.

"WEEEEEEEEE GLEE, LIGHT N WATER, WEEEEEEEEEEEE LOVELY WATER.

WATER IS OUR LIFE. WE LIVE LONG ASLEEP, WE LOVE THE WATER.

I TURN TO MY CACTI, "WOULD YOU LIKE SOME.

"A LITTLE, NOT TOO MUCH. NOT NEED MUCH. LIKE SUN, WARM, LIFE."

I GIVE THE ONE ON THE LEFT A LITTLE WATER, THEN TRY TO WATER THE ONE ON THE RIGHT.

"NO THANKS, NONE, NO WATER. SUN, LOVE SUN"

I SIT BACK IN MY CHAIR N LOOK AT MY SUN STRUNE WINDOW SILL N LISTEN TO THE CHATTER OF MY PLANTS ENJOYING THE DANCING RAYS OF SUNLIGHT.

I THANK MY GOD FOR MY LIFE.

A CHATTER ANSWER SUBTLE BUT SURE.

"WE LOVE TO LIVE"

I ANSWER FROM MY HEART.

I LIVE TO LOVE THE LIFE I HAVE.

"WE KNOW, WE SEE, WE FEEL."

"WE ARE MANY, WE ARE ALL, WE ARE ONE.

I SMILE N WATCH THE DROPLETS OF WATER ROLL, LIKE DANCING DIAMONDS IN THE LIGHT, DOWN THE LEAVES N LAND WITH A PLOP APON THE EARTH.

"WE ARE THE SAME"

"MANY, ALL.

ONE.

THE TINY LITTLE VOICES DANCE WITHIN MY PSYCHI. SING SONG, LIKE THE LIGHT.

"WE ARE ALIVE"

AWESOMELY LOVELY SPRING DAY.

I SIT BACK IN MY CHAIR N DRIFT OFF TO THE CHATTER OF VIBRANT LIFE IN THE SUNLIGHT.

A MOST BEAUTIFUL DAY.

SUN LIFE

AWESOME SITTING BY THE SIDE OF 3000 WATTS STACKED IN THE FOREST. COME ON WHERE ELSE COULD YOU GET THE DIVERSITY. EVERYTHING ABOUT HAS THAT HAPPY FEELING.

BANG THOSE TUNES.

WALKING WITH THE MUSIC IN THE SUN.

RHYTHM.

LIFE.

EXCITE.

DESIRE.

BASSE RIFFS DIVULGE GREAT N WONDROUS SECRETS ONLY TO BE TOLD, WHEN THE SNARE CRYSTALLISES THE AIR WITH THE HIT. \NO MISS THERE FOLKS, WAITED, BAITED, FIRED, ALIVE.

RHYTHM THE CRY OF CHAOS WITHIN THE WILD. WOW I DIGRESS.

PEACE!

ALL BEINGS PLANT N TREE, GREEN HERB OF THE FIELD. HERE, FEEL THE SUN RISE. FLOWER SHOW YOUR FACE. TURN TO THE LIGHT YOU SO LOVE. FEED, FILL.

LIKE MUSIC.

ORGASMIC EMULSIONS.

WHEN THE GROUND WRITHES N THE POWERS THAT ARE JUST, RUN WITHIN THE VEINS.

THEN YOU SEE.

SELF NO DISGUISE.

SELF THE WARRIOR IN THE MIRROR RETURNED.

FACE.

SELF.

NO ILLUSION.

JUST IMAGE LOOKING BACK.

MIRROR DANCE WITH ME, MOVE ME TO MY SPIRIT.

FILL WITHIN ME WITH RADIANT LOVE.

WARMTH OF CREATION FILL THE LIFE FORCE OF MY LIFES DESIRE.

BLONDE APHRODITE

IN A GARDEN SHADY,

STOOD A HOLY LADY.

WITH REVERENT CADENCE, A SUBTLE PSALM.

LIKE A BLACK SWAN AS DEATH COMES ON,

POURS FORTH HER SONG IN A PERFECT CALM.

N BY OCEANS MARGIN,

THIS INNOCENT VIRGIN,

COUNSELS IBOGA.

TO ENLARGE HER PRAYER.

N LIKE AN ORCHID,

SHE RIDES QUITE NAKED,

UPON AN OYSTER SHELL,

ON TOP OF THE SEA.

N TO SOUNDS SO ENTRANCING,

THE ANGELS COME DANCING,

DOWN FROM HEAVEN,
INTO TIME AGAIN.

N ALL THE WICKED,
IN HELLS ABYSSES,
HUGE THE FLAME FLICKERS,
N EASE THEIR PAIN.

IBO

MUTUMBA

LAST NIGHT, WHILST WALKING IN MY DREAMS, I MET A LADY/ENTITY, THAT ORDERED ME TO FOLLOW.

SHE KEPT CRYING, "COME MUTUMBA!!! "MUTUMBA "COME QUICKLY".

EVERY TIME I SLOWED SHE CRIED "MUTUMBA" VERY LOUD. LIKE SOMEONE BANGING ON A GREAT TREE IN THE JUNGLE WOULD SOUND.

I FOLLOWED HER THROUGH A VALLEY OF VERY DARK BLACK, TALL TREES. SOMETHING LIKE AN AVENUE. THERE WAS VERY LITTLE LIGHT N NO STARS ABOVE.

AFTER WALKING FOR SOME TIME, ADMIRING THE LADIES COSTUME (PURPLES BLUES REDS N GREENS, THE CLOTH, FLOWING, HOODED CAPE. ALL COLOURS INTERWOVEN WITH THREADS OF GOLD SEEMED TO MELT N MOVE AMONGST EACH OTHER. THE IMAGE WITHIN THE HOODED CAPE WAS THE SAME AS DESCRIBED BELOW. NO FACE.)

WE CAME TO A DOMED GRASS HUT. THE LADY DUCKED THROUGH THE DOOR N DISAPPEARED.

HESITANTLY I FOLLOWED.

I ENTERED THROUGH THE DOOR N INTO A DIMLY LIT ANTI-CHAMBER.

THERE WAS A BIG HOLE IN THE FLOOR, ABOUT 2.5 FOOT IN DIA.

I MOVED AROUND THE HOLE N DUCKED THROUGH A RED, PURPLE CURTAIN. THE SAME AS THE LADIES DRESS.

SUDDENLY I AM IN A LABYRINTH OF ROOTS N TUNNELS.

AS I MOVE ALONG THE TUNNELS ....

.... LIKE BEING THE CENTRE OF A SPHERE LOOKING OUTWARDS AT ALL ANGLES.

I AM STILL THERE.

THIS IS INCREDIBLY OLD.

I FEEL STRANGELY CONNECTED.

AN AWESOME FEELING.

IF IT ALL STOPS NOW IT GOES ON FOREVER, BECAUSE IT HAS ALWAYS BEEN.

I STILL HEAR THE LADY CRY.

"MUTUMBA MUTUMBA MUTUMBA.

EVERY TIME I SAY THE NAME I AM TAKEN OFF N SHOWN MOST AMAZING SIGHTS, OF TREES N BUSHES VINES LEAVES BRANCHES, EARTH VOLCANOES CLOUDS STORMS SEAS. THE VISIONS ARE ENDLESS. EVERYTHING BOILING IN A SWIRLING VORTEX. THERE ARE NO ANIMALS. THERE IS ONLY LIFE. EXCHANGE.

HA HA HA HA HA. I JUST GOT THE ANSWER.

IT IS CALLED THE EXCHANGE, BECAUSE THIS IS WHERE IT ALL STARTED. THE VORTEX, ALL LIFE, CAME FROM THIS CREATION. IT IS LIKE LOOKING AT THE CRAB NEBULAR, REVOLVING SLOWLY IN AN INWARD VORTEX, ABOVE A MOUNTAIN VAST, GRAY N OMINOUS. A VOLCANO. SPEWING FORTH LIFE. CREATION. FILLS. ENORMOUS ENERGIES. LIKE SUNS COLLIDING, MOLDING FORMING. EMULSION. TIMELESS. ROCKS N FIRE SPEW FORTH ACROSS A GALAXY STREWN WITH LIGHTS. EVERYWHERE I LOOK I SEE CLOUDS OF RED N PURPLE YELLOW N GREENS. SHOOTING STARS N GALAXIES FLY BY, ENDLESS.

"MUTUMBA

"OH HOW I AM SO SMALLED.

OF SUCH AWESOME POWER.

THAT SURROUNDS ABOVE N BELOW

I AM HUMBLE.

MUTUMBA

WARRIOR

RIGHTEOUSLY SOUND

COMPLETE WITHIN THE FOLD

STANDING ON THE RIM LOOKING INWARD
AT A UNIVERSE MOST SPLENDIDLY JEWELED.

PAUL

I CANT REALLY SAY THIS WAS A DREAM. MORE A VISION THAT WILL NOW ABIDE WITH ME.

AN EXPERIENCE OF A YEAR, AN ENTITY I CAN COMPLETELY REALATE WITH.

I SHANT EDIT THIS, COS THE SPIRIT OF THE ENTITY THAT WAS WITH ME AT THIS TIME IS STILL VERY CLEAR TO ME. IF NOT THAT I HAVE NOT AS OF YET HAD THE PRIVILEGE TO MEET AGAIN IN THE NOW.

I KNOW THIS ENTITY. FEMININE. LIKE THE ORIGINAL CREATOR.

BUT I AM NOT AS OLD. I AM BUT A BRANCH OF THAT ORIGINAL CONCEPT.

I AM CONCEPTION BRANCHED.

IMAGINATION EVOLVED.

LIFE SEEKING LIFE N COMPLETENESS.

FULFILMENT.

I AM DESIRE..

APE;)~~~

COME SIT PARTAKE!!!

PARTAKE SIT DOWN . YOU NEED THE SPADE. IT IS A TOOL. REMEMBER. PLEASE REMEMBER. NOT TICK TOCK. BUT. FREE LIFE GIVEN. TAKE OF THE FRUITS MY SON. DO NOT WHIP AT THE WIND. HOWL OR GRUDGE FOR MEAT THAT YOU CANNOT FIND. THE FRUITS OF LIFE ARE FREE. I THINK OF OTHER SONG LYRICS N SEE. THE UNIVERSE. EXPANDING. BREATHING. PARTAKE. ARISE SLOWLY LIKE THE MORNING RAIN .NO THE MORNING SUN. YOU ARE A CHILD OF THE LIGHT. DO NOT QUESTION THIS. SITS DO NOT THINK. STAND N BE, FEEL N FILL THE APPLES OF LIFE THE FRUITS ARE FREE. SLOW DOWN. LOOK. DO NOT TARRY. LOOK FEEL PARTAKE. DO NOT TRY TO ORDER. BE. SERIOUS. YES BE.

SLOW DOWN, PEACE. SOW DOWN. EXPAND FILL PARTAKE .REFRESH .STAY COOL .BODY NUMB MIND EXPANDING. FEEL . OH BLESS YOU MY LORD. THE GIFT OF LIFE IS GIVEN FREELY. COMMAND ONLY WHATYOU NEED . NEED ??> QUESTIONS. NO SIT FILL RISE LIKE THE MORNING SUN. FILL RISE ENERGY. KICKECK.

DRINK THE WATER. THE WATER IS YOUR LIFE. YOUR LIFE IS FREE, SIT PARTAKE TRY THE BANANA. SIT IN PEACE N FEEL. EXPAND FILL. SIT IN PEACE. SACRED PEACE. FATHER. DO. YES YOU NOW CAN SEE. OK

FUNNY LITTLE CREATURE DOSE NOT KNOW HOW TO CARE FOR ONESELF. FILL. BANANAN FILL. PEACE. AMINO ACIDS BLAST. I GOT THE HANG OF THIS NOW. GOT THE SUN GLASSES OFFF N SLOWLY RISING FOR THE DAY.BANANAN

??????????????>????>???????????????????>???>>?>
?????OHYAIOYYYAUUII OYYOHAEEHHEOHUYYAY AYYYAYHEE.
PEACE.

SLOWLY FIL EXPAND SIT DO NOT THINK DO NOT TARRY YOUR MIND WITH RUBBISH.THROW OUT THE GARBAGE. SERIOUS. YES. YOU JUST FORT FOR YOUR LIFE N???

YOU HAVE THE GIFT GIVEN FREELY. SLOW DOWN. SLOW DOWN. NO PAIN. ?? WHY. NO QUESTIONS SEE, FEEL RISE. FILL KNOW BE THESE ARE YOUR TOOLS SLOW DOWN. WHY SO FAST. WONDERING DAZZLES. NOT LIKKE NALTREXONE EXPANDING WITH LIFE. WITHDRAWALS NT THERE JUST LIVING FREE. DYSLEXIC. COULD NEVER TYPE. NO MATTER. YOU ARE CLEAN. VALIUM WAS YOUR SLAVE SIT PARTAKE SLOW DOWN. PEACE FILLS. BANANAS? YES BANANA COS? NO QUESTIONS FEEL ONLY MY LIFE FORCE. EXIST. FILL MORE? AH GO FOR IT GARY YOU ROCK THE UNIVERSE. HA HA HA QUESTIONS. YES OF COURSE QUESTIONS. FILL. BE. THANK YOU. YOUR WILL CONTROLS. CONTROLS? HA HA GOD SHUFFLES THE PLANET N? REFRESH. COR. SLOW DOWN UNDERSTAND. DO NOT GRAPPLE YOU ARE THE NATURE THE ANIMAL. FURRY. FREE. SLOW DOWN BE. THANKYOU LORD. BLESS YOU MY SON. FILL PARTAKE BE. AH. MOST BEAUTIFUL. EXIST BE. BUT MY EYES SEE TOO MUCH. THAT WAS WHY I BLINDED YOU. YOUR QUEST FOR MEANING. MY MEANING .YES. GO ORDER N COMMAND WHAT YOU WILL. BE FREE. BUT GOVERNMENTS. HA HA HA QUESTIONS. THE GIFT OF LIFE IS GIVEN FREE. PARTAKE FILL. THANK YOU. NOW

YOU SEE. YES. SLOW DOWN DONT WORRY YOURSELF SLOW DOWN. SO TIME DOSE NOT EXIST. YOU EXERCISE WELL MY SON. YOU LEARN FAST. SLOW DOWN. PARTAKE FILL. YOU ARE A WARRIOR WEARY N EXHAUSTED AGHAST N BLIND. PARTAKE. GO NOW. COMMAND. EXIT GO. DO. NOW. BANANA YES WATER IS LIFE ALSO GO. LIVE. LIVE FOR YOUR LIFE SLOW DOWN DO NOT STOMP FILL. SLOW DOWN. SIT. HA HA QUESTIONS .DO AS YOU COMMAND NOT AS ANY ONE ELSE COMMANDS ELSE. AH , CONFLICT. TIS IS YOU ONLY TASK. YOU ARE DETACHED. NUMB. YES FOR SURE ALIVE YES. THANKYOU LORD. NOW YOU SE THE GIFTS. OF LIFE. YES I SEE SLOW DOWN. TIME IS NOT MY ENEMY. TIME HA HA HA AHA AHJA HA AHA AHA AHA AHA AHA AHA ASHA AHA AAASHA A. DO IT IN THREES N YOU STAY ALIVE. YOU GOT IT N OWOK. YES THATNKYOU. FILL PARTAKE. FILLL GO. NOW? YES GO. EXERCISE YOUR OWN FREE WILL. GO.

AH WHY DON'T THEY FEED THE CHILDREN LORD LIKE THE BIRDS! THE BIRDS N THE BEES ARE FREE. HOW COME MAN IS NOT GOOD QUESTION. THAT IS WHY I MADE YOU SON OF MAN. AHHHHHHHHHHHH SIGH RELIEF. SECURE. FOR SURE. NOW FOREVER. AHMEN BOSHAAAOOOOOOOPOOOOOOOHOOHOHOHH OHOHOHOHOHOHOHOHOHOHOHOHO HOHOHOHGOHOHOHOHOHOHKLKJJKKJKKJK, KKKKKKKKLKKKKLK NOT KICKECK SLOW DOWN. FILL PEACE DO NOT TARRY WITH YOU R HASSLE SLOW DOWN PEACE FILL. WHY DO I FEEL LIKE THIS? YOU HAVE BEEN ASLEEP FOR

MANY YEARS N NOW> ALIVE YOU LIVE FOR SURE. YOU LIVE. PARTAKE. PARTAKE FILL DO NOT COMMAND. TIME IS NOT YOUR ENEMY. FUNNY LITTLE CREATURE. SIMPLE. BUT LIKE A JIGSAW. GROWING. B UT NOT. WHY QUESTION. YOU NOW CAN SEE SON OF MAN. GO EXERCISE YOUR RIGHT TO BE FREE. IN A MODERN WORLD. BE YOU. GO. PARTAKE FILL. BUT HOW DO I HOLD ALL THIS TOGETHER LORD. YOU ASK TO MANY QUESTIONS. FILL GO YOU LIVE. EXIST. THANK YOU. REMEMBER. FILL WHAT YOU NEED TO FEEL. IF YOU WANT TO STAY SLEEPY, EAT LITTLE N OFTEN. DRINK N BE. BE. EXIST. YOU ARE ANGRY. YES.

THAT IS GOOD. SLOW DOWN. TRY NOT TO UNDERSTAND. BUT EVERYTHING IS BLASTED N WARPED. YOU THINK. SO YOU SEE. WOW. PRAY WHY. THAT IS WHY I MADE YOU IN MY IMAGE. THANK YOU RELIEF. WOW. COSMIC. COWBOYS. REALLY DO KICK ASS. YES THEY DO LOLOLOLOL HAAA HHHA SLOW DOWN. USHA SLOW DOWN FILL. DO NOT COMMAND UNLESS YOU NEED. NEED? QUESTIONS. BE FILL. REFRESH. SLOW DOWN. YOU ARE A COMPLEX CREATURE. SIT PARTAKE BE. SIT N PARTAKE WITH YOURSELF. DO NOT GRAPPLE. JUST BE. BE ONE N NO ONE SELF AS YOU CAN ONLY SEE. BLIND, BUT? SEEING. REFRESH GO. WOW YOU ARE PETULANT. SLOW DOWN. YOU HAVE SO MANY FITS IN LIFE THAT YOU NEED ONLY TO PARTAKE OF WHAT YOU WORK FOR HONESTLY N KNOW THAT YOU ARE A CHILD OF THE LIGHT

SIT. PARTAKE. REFRESH. WOW SARDINES. BALANCE? QUESTIONS. YOU STOMP. TOO MUCH. YOU WORRY. DO NOT TARRY YOUR MIND WITH QUESTIONS ONLY DO WHAT YOU NEED

TO DO TO EXIST. AH DISCIPLINE. UNDERSTOOD. EXERCISE FREE WILL EAT WHAT THOU WILL THAT IS CLEAN. PARTAKE ONLY THAT WHICH IS PURE. SLOW DOWN. YOU JUST FOUGHT WITH YOUR OWN ENEMY. HAVE WON. YES FOR NOW. WHY. DO NOT QUESTION. FILL. REFRESH, GO EXERCISE YOUR OWN NATURE. NOW YOU KNOW THE NATURE OF THE BEAST. GO.

YOU KNOW. DOGS ARE GOOD TOOLS. TO HAVE. COS. IF YOU ARE MESSED UP. YOUR DOG IS TO. BRING BACK BALANCE N A SELF-FORM OF STYLE N BE. PARTAKE. REFRESH KICKECK.

GO. EAT DRINK THE WATER GIVEN FREELY FOR LIFE GIVEN DO NOT TARRY OR TITTLE GET WHAT YOU NEED FOR NOW DO NOT BE GREEDY TAKE OF THE FRUITS OF LIFE. QUESTIONS LATER. EXPAND. FILL. STILL JUMPING ABOUT LIKE A MONKEY IN THE ZOO. YOU ARE A WILD ANIMAL MY SON. YOU ONLY HAVE TO KNOW N BE FREE. PARTAKE FILL. BURT SLEEP, DON'T WORRY, WHY WORRY, THAT IS YOUR SIN. WORRY IS YOURS FOREVER COS. THAT IS ALL YOU GOT FEELINGS. YES. DO NOT COMMAND. BE. EXIST BE ENJOY. ENJOY WHAT YOU HAVE, I HAVE NOT TASTED THE MELON YET GO. NOW LOOK SEE TOUCH FEEL DO EVERYTHING IN THREES N LIVE LIFE GIVEN FREELY. YOU BATTLE WELL. WOW GASP I KNOW I SHOULD GET THE MELON. BUT MY MIND IS COSMIC BLASTED FORMED N MOULDED. PARTAKE FILL GROW LEARN SEE. YOU NOW HAVE THE KEYS TO THE GIFT OF LIFE. GO. DO NOT EXERCISE; GO IN PEACE N COMPASSION N GRACE JUST AS YOU PRAY. FILL FROM WITHIN BE SEE. FEEL GO . DO. DO NOT WORRY. HOW COME AH DO NOT TRY TO MOVE

BEFORE YOU CAN THINK. THINK, DO NOT BE. JUST BE, EAT REFRESH N SEE. SLOWLY TIME IS NOT YOUR ENEMY.

GO. DO BE. WOW THE SWASH, I ATE ARE SWELLING MY SKIN. THIS IS ONLY NATURAL. YOU ARE THE FULL SUM. OF WHAT YOU PUT IN. PLUS A FEW OTHER CRINKLES AROUND THE EDGES. AH SUNGLASSES. NEED TO SEE WITH EYES OPEN NOT CLOSED. WOW. ORANGE LIGHT. BEATS IN TIME WITH MY HEART. DESIRE N SPACE HAVE BEEN THROWN OUT OF THE WINDOW. BE FILL BE FILL GO REFRESH GO NOW .EAT OF THE MELON. IT IS YOUR LIFE GIVEN FREELY. ANGER IS GOOD CONSTRUCTIVE BUT REMEMBER PEACE THAT PACES ALL UNDERSTANDING. DO NOT LABOUR YOU LIFE. SOMEDAY SOON. I AM GOING TO BE ABLE TO WRITE THIS PROPERLY INSTEAD OF KIND OF LIKE DAYTIME DREAMING TRYING NOT TO FILL OR RISE TO FAST AS WEARY. IMMENSELY TIRED. GONE SPACED BLASTED COSMIC AQUAMARINE ENFOLDS FEEL N BE. GO GET THE MELON. MUNCHECK. GO.

REMEMBER. THOU. RESPECT FOR THIS IS FREE AS IS COMPASSION LOVE N PEACE LIFE IS GIVEN FREELY. DO NOT TARRY OR WORRY BE. THE ENERGY FOR LIFE COMES FROM WITHIN. GO N BE. WOW THE MELON. BURNS MY SKIN. SLOW DOWN. FILL FEEL. WOW MY BODY FEELS LIKE ROAD TRASH WOULD IMAGINE ITSELF TO BE. HORRIFIC BUT STILL. AT ONE. BUT NOT EXERCISE WHAT YOU ONLY KNOW HOW THAT IS THE WAY TO GET OUT OF ALL THIS CRAP. AH MUSIC. FLOWERS THE SUN. LOVE OF LIFE GIVEN FREELY GO. MELON. FILL. GO.

EXERCISE WHAT YOUR WILL. CHICKEN FEED, YOU KNOW YOUR NEED.

    GO. MUST REMEMBER TO TRANSFER FILES FROM TOSH TOO LEO. COS. NEARLY TRASHED TOSH. KNOCKED THE KEYS. J N P OUT OF THE DECK. SO CAN'T USE IT PROPERLY AS DYSLEXIC AS HELL N HAVING TO HAVE TO STOMP. EVERYTHING LIKES A MONKEY IN A CAGE AWAITING TO BE FED N FILLED. CHILL PARTAKE REFRESH GO. CURRY TONIGHT. KICKECK. NOW WHAT YOU ARE THAT IS THE NATURE OF THIS BEAST THAT YEA FIGHT. GO REFRESH LIVE. WOKO SELA BUSHAKA MEDITATE. SEE. FEEL .LIVE BREATH. EXIST ONLY FOR THE MOMENT OF THE GLINT IN YOUR EYE. AMUSE YOURSELF. LOVE YOURSELF, AS ONLY YOU KNOW HOW. BE N LIVE. WOW I AM TIRED. BUT LIKE TO WRITE. I AM COMING BACK TOGETHER SLOWLY LIKE A SHATTERED JIGSAW. REFRESH GO. WOW SOME NIGHT. FEW. JUST LOOKED IN THE MIRROR. LIKE WHAT I SEE, BUT WHAT ONE HELL OF A FREAKING BATTLE. THE FIRE N ANGER HAS BEEN EXTREME MORE THAN REALITY SHOULD OF ALOUD. BUT NOW I HAVE DISCIPLINE. THIS IS GOOD. CONSTRUCTIVE. HA HA HA HA I READ WHAT I HAVE READ N SEE SO CLEARLY. I WOULD LOVE MOST DEARLY ADDICTS OF OPIUM N SUCH LIKE SUBSTANCES. STOP. YOU ARE ALREADY IN HELL. COMING BACK TO THE LIGHT IS LESS PAINFUL. I NOW KNOW. THANK YOU LORD I BODY.

THE SCARS ON MY BODY I HAVE GIVEN TO GOD AS REMINDER OF WHAT I AM AN ANIMAL. NO PAIN. JUST GAIN. THEY GOT THAT WRONG AT SCHOOL ALSO. THEY SAY NO PAIN NO GAIN NOT TRUE, I KNOW NOW. THE DARKER SIDE OF MY INNER SELF GAVE ME THE COURAGE TO FIGHT WITH PURE LIFE FOR OF LIGHTNING SEE WITH. LIKE WHITE HORSES CRASHING THROUGH THE HEAVENS STOMPING. GRACEFUL, RE-MINDFUL

OF GRACE. PURE EMULATION OF BEING AT ONE WITH NATURE. WOW I GOT A HEAD ACHE .LOLOLOL

AH ONE HELL OF A NIGHT. SHALL TELL OF MORE LATER. SUFFICE TO SAY. I HAVE MANAGED TO TURN MY HAIR WHITE OVERNIGHT. INCREDIBLE. WOW I TELL YOU FOR SURE YOU THINK YOU ARE SECURE. WELL N LIVING YOUR LIFE THE RIGHT GIVEN. CRAP. YOU ARE ALL SO SHOVED UP EACH OTHER'S APPLES EYES WITH MONEY THAT YOU DON'T EVEN GIVE TIME TO LOOK AT THE PROBLEMS CREATED IN THIS SOCIETY TODAY. YOU DO NOT LIKE THE TRUTH. WELL WHAT THE HELL. I BEEN THERE DONE THAT WORN THE CLOTHES N GRABBED THE BULL BY THE HORNS N WRESTLED WITH MY OWN SELF TO TRY TO UNDERSTAND THE MEANING OF MY EXISTENCE. N THE ONLY THING I CAN REALLY THINK OF THAT WOULD MAKE YOU REAL SECURE N HAPPY WOULD BE FOOD ALL SORTS OF EVERYTHING CLEAN NO DIRTY MEATS NO UNCLEAN HERB, KIND OR DRUG. YOU ARE BLIND. DOCTORS, GOVERNMENTS, AGENCIES. TOOLS OF CONTROL. CONTROL OF THE OPIUM ADDICT, WITH SLAVERY TO METHADONE. I CLUCKED OF SMACK MANY TIMES BUT NEVER IN MY LIFE WRESTLED SO HARD FOR MY LIFE AS COMING OFF METHADONE. NOW THAT TOOK FOUR HOURS N NOW JUST CRUISING.

HAD TO EAT ABOUT 2000 CARBS OF DIFFERENT MEATS N FISH. AH GRAPES. WELL AT LEAST I DON'T WASTE FOOD ANYMORE .I SIGH N LAUGH AT THE GLOW OF MY INNER BEING. AT BEING TO STILL BE ABLE TO TYPE, LAUGH, CRY N SING. WITHOUT

COLLAPSING INTO SHOCK WITHDRAWAL. TOOK A WHILE TO GET HERE. COS. I HAD TO WORK OUT HOW TO GET OFF THE BENZOS. THEY DON'T AGREE WITH I, I, I, I KNOW COS. THAT AIN'T KNOW NO BODY'S FRIEND. SELF-EXAMINATION JUST GIVES WEIRD N STRANGE NUMBNESS OF BODY. CLARITY OF MIND N HEARING. SIGHT REALLY MASHED, BUT ON THE OTHER HAND NOT. WOW POWER THE HERRING HAS. PURE FIRE. I FEEL HER RISE. THAT'S BURNING WITHIN. RADIATING LIKE A DIAMOND ACROSS THE BACK OF MY EYELIDS. SHAME YOU COULDN'T JUST LOOK AT THE ATOMIC EXPLOSION WITHIN YOUR MIND'S EYE, FOR 15 DAYS + INSTEAD OF ALL THE BODY CRAP. BALANCE. MEDITATE. WATER. I HAVE A HEAD LIKE A PEANUT. SPLIT OPEN N THE LITTLE CURL OF THE TAIL ROOT IS SLOWLY GROWING OUT OF THE TOP OF MY HEAD. TREED LOLOLOLOL WOW ON FOOD.

WOW I MUST BE CRAZY COS. SOMEONE TOLD ME ONCE TO EAT N I TOLD THEM THEY WERE FULL OF CRAP. I WAS FULL OF CRAP. LOLOLOL

I HAVE TO NOW RETIRE TO MY BATH CHAMBER N PONDER NOTHING IN MY BATH. FOR I HAVE FOUND THE SISTER SENSE OF HOT SOAPY WATER MOST INVIGORATING N RESTORANT AFTER EATING ALLOWING ME TO SLUMBER A WHILE. I BID YOU AL A FAIR N MOST WONDERFUL DAY N SHALL CALL IN ON YOU ALL AGAIN REAL SOON. TIMOTHY LEARY GOT IT WRONG. IT WAS NOT TURN ON TUNE IN N DROP OUT IT IS TURN ON TUNE IN N CHANGE THE PROGRAM. BEING A COMPUTER MECHANIC FOR

SOME YEARS NOW TAUGHT ME THIS. WE GET FREAKED OUT SO MUCH BY WHAT OTHER PEOPLE SAY THAT WE DONT EVEN CONSIDER OUR OWN THOUGHTS, FEELINGS. DESIRES SENSES. THIS THING DESIRE. PEOPLE THINK OF IT AS WANT. THIS IS WRONG. DESIRE IS THE CENTRE ESSENCE OF THE LOVE OF LIVES EXISTENCE. TO BE ABLE TO PLAY LAUGH CRY N SING FREELY. WITHOUT, REGARD FROM OTHERS N HUMILIATIONS. PEACE IS A PROCESS OF SMASHING DOWN THE WALLS OF ONE MINDSET N REBUILDING ANOTHER.

REPROGRAM THE MAN. THE INNER BEING EVOLVES. ROLES OVER THE COUNTRYSIDE LIKE GREEN GRASS N ALL KINDS OF ANIMALS N ROOT VEGETABLES OF THE FIELD. IT MUST BE A GOOD JOB TO BE A GROCER FOR YOU MAY ALWAYS HAVE ENOUGH N SUFFICIENT FOR THE DAY. WOW!!! DARWIN'S THEORY OF RELATIVITY IS DEFINITELY CORRECT IN THE FACT THAT MAN, A CREATURE, NON-NOCTURNAL OR NOCTURNAL, RELATIVE TO STASIS CORRECT REM PATTERN DREAM STATE SHALL BE IN ORDER. OF BODY MIND N SOUL. MAN IS A MONKEY BY DESIGN. IF HE HAD THE CHANCE HE WOULD JUST LOVE TO TURN INTO A MONKEY N HANG UPSIDE DOWN IN A TREE ALL DAY BY HIS TAIL, N WRAP HIMSELF WARM IN HIS FUR N FEED HIS DESIRES IN GRACE N PEACE N LOVE. MAKING BABIES N REGENERATING THE GENETIC CONSTRUCTION OF A SOCIAL N VIABLE COMMUNITY.

WOW. ROCKA MUST MEDITATE.

AWAKE FOR SPRING

WHILST SITTING IN THE FOREST THIS WEEKEND GONE, WRITING N LISTENING TO MUSIC. A LIZARD RAN UP MY JEANS LEG N SAT ON MY KNEE, LOOKING INTENTLY AT ME.

I HAD JUST GIVEN SALUTATIONS TO ALL BEINGS PLANT N TREE N HE JUMPED OUT OF THE GRASS FOR A BETTER LOOK.

"TINY DINOSAUR I GREET YOU."

"THANK YOU I AM GLAD."

"OF?"

"AWAKING IN THE WARMTH OF THE SUN."

"AH IT IS A MOST BEAUTIFUL DAY, NO?"

"THAT IT IS GIANT, FOR SURE. NO MORE SLEEP, PLENTY TO EAT."

THIS CONVERSATION BEGAN TO AMUSE ME.

THE LITTLE LIZARD HAD GREAT CHARM.

AS I SPOKE SOFTLY HE LOOKED N BLINKED INTENTLY, KNOWINGLY UNDERSTANDING THE FEEL OF MY VOICE.

OTHERS CAME TO SEE N HE SCURRIED UP MY SLEEVE.

"CLUMSY! CLUMSY!" HE CRIED.

SO I AROSE FROM MY CHAIR N WALKED WITH HIM IN HAND INTO THE WOODS.

"THANK YOU" I HEAR FROM BENEATH MY PALM.

I COME TO A GRASSY GLADE WITHIN TALL PINE TREES N SIT WITH MY BACK AGAINST ONE.

I AM NOW IN THREE SPACES N THE CHATTER IS EXTREME.

MYSELF LOOKING OUT AT TREE N LIZARD. LIZARD LOOKING OUT AT MYSELF N TREE, TREE LOOKING OUT AT MYSELF N LIZARD.

I LOOK DOWN AT MY LIZARD FRIEND N HE SMILES.

"NOISY BUNCH EH?"

"THEY ALL WANT TO BE HEARD ALL AT ONCE. HARD TO JUST GET A STORY FROM ONE TREE."

I LAUGH.

"SO YOU HEAR THIS ALL THE TIME."

THE LIZARD BLINKS IN AGREEMENT.

"I GET USED TO IT. MOST OF THE TIME THEY JUST CHATTER ABOUT BEING SO STRONG N LOVING THE RAIN N SUN."

"AT THIS MOMENT THEY ARE CURIOUS AS TO YOU."

"THEY FEEL YOU FEEL, AS THEY WATCH OUR CONVERSATIONS."

"RATHER NOSY ARENT THEY"

"IT IS THERE WAY. THEY STAND IN ONE PLACE ALL THE TIME N COMMUNICATE THROUGH THE GROUND. SO THEIR STORIES ARE VERY ELABORATE N COLOURFUL."

"SUBTLE VIBRATIONS"

"YOU FEEL THESE THEN BEING SO TINY."

"YES N SO DO YOU, BEING OF SPIRIT."

THIS WAS AMAZING, NOT ONLY COULD THE LITTLE CREATURE UNDERSTAND ME BUT ALSO ALL OF THE LIVING THINGS AROUND HIM.

I SIT N CLOSE MY EYES, THE SUN BURNING SOFTLY ON MY FACE.

THE LITTLE LIZARDS IS STILL, NOT MOVING IN MY HAND.

I SEE ME, VERY CLOSE, LOOKING BACK.

WOW! THAT MADE ME JUMP. I OPEN MY EYES N LOOK AT MY LITTLE FRIEND. HE BLINKS ACKNOWLEDGEMENT N I CLOSE MY EYES AGAIN.

I SEE EXTREMELY TALL GRASSES N TINY INSECTS SCURRY EVERYWHERE.

AN ANT HILL.

I RUN N SCURRY. GRABBING AT THE TINY SOLDIERS, MUNCHING WITH SHEER DELIGHT.

I LAUGH N OPEN MY EYES.

YOU HAVE PLENTY OF FOOD NOW THE SPRING HAS COME.

"THAT THERE IS."

I PLACE MY LITTLE FRIEND UPON THE GROUND N BID HIM A FAIR WELL.

HE DOES A LITTLE DANCE, LIKE THE GROUND IS TO HOT FOR HIM TO STAND ON.

"ENJOY!"

"OH I WILL I WILL," THE LITTLE CREATURE RETORTS N SCURRIES OFF TO FIND THAT DINNER HE SO GRACEFULLY SHOWED ME.

VERY STRANGE PERSPECTIVE LOOKING THROUGH THE EYES OF OH SO A TINY DRAGON.

STAFF N SPEAR

LIFE IS VERY MUCH LIKE OWNING N USING TRADITIONAL HUNTING TOOLS. WEAPONS OF A REFINED ART.

THE STAFFS, ARROWS N SPEARS, TAKEN FROM CHOSEN GREEN TREES N TAUGHT TO TAKE SHAPE.

A DAILY PROCESS OF OWNING A SPEAR IS TO TEACH IT TO REMAIN TRUE N STRAIGHT. THIS IS DONE SEVERAL TIMES A DAY BY GENTLY BENDING N APPLYING PRESSURE, RELEASED AT THE RIGHT TIME, SO AS TO REALIGN A WOOD, DAMP OF SAP, BUT SHRINKING. DRYING OUT N BECOMING HARD N USEFUL FOR HUNTING.

LIKE AS IN LIFE, WE WANDER, TO SEE. WE TAKE WRONG PATHS N REQUIRE TO BE REDIRECTED BACK TO THE TRUE SELF. THE STRAIGHTNESS OF THE SPEAR, THE CURVE OF THE BOW N GENTLE CURVE OF STAFF. THESE ARTS LOST TO MOST IN GENERAL, BUT ONCE LOOKED BACK INTO A RECONNECTION WITH SELF N NATURE CAN BE ATTAINED.

SO MY FELLOW WARRIORS, GO SEEK THE WOODS FOR TO TEACH YOU ABOUT NATURE N YOURSELF. TEACH YOURSELVES TO BE TRUE N STRAIGHT AS NEEDS BE THE SPEAR N ARROW.

LEARN TO FLY SWIFT N TRUE.

FOR ALL ELSE IS DISTRACTION FROM SELF-QUEST.

THE PATH OF THE WARRIOR IS TO FOCUS UPON INTENT N CAUSE CHANGE THROUGH THAT INTENT.

APPLY THOSE PRESSURES N REMOULD, WITH CARE N GRACE N SELF-APPRECIATION OF EXISTENCE N LIFE GIVEN FREELY.

TAKE, FEED N FILL.

ALLOW YOURSELVES TO GROW.

ACCEPTING THAT LIFE WILL TAKE ITS COURSE, NO MATTER HOW MUCH YOU CARE N WORRY IS A LOT BETTER THAN TRYING TO BUILD AN ARCH FOR EMOTION.

TO HOLD WITHOUT RELEASE SAID EMOTIONS N EXPRESSIONS IS AS IF TO IMPRISON THE IMAGINATIONS OF SAID EXPRESSIONS N NOT ALLOW THEM LIFE.

LIKE NOT BELIEVING IN THE FAIRY STORY, THE CARICATURES DIE.

WE DIE WITHOUT ALLOWING OUR CREATIVE IMAGINATIONS TO EXIST N BECOME REAL N ALIVE.

LOVE OF SELF N SELF-EXPRESSION OF ALL IS THE KEY.

ENJOY THE LOVE. THE LIGHT. THE FOOD. THE FEELING N THE FILL.

FOR DESIRE IS FULL EXPRESSION OF SELF WITHOUT SELF-RECRIMINATIONS.

SEEK SELF, SEEK LOVE.

SALT IS THE PAIN OF TEARS OF WHAT COULD BE LOST, LOVE IS JUST SIMPLE, LIGHT IS OUR LIVES. ENERGIES OF AWESOME COMPLEXITIES ALL ROLLED INTO ONE.

LOVE.

ALL SHOWN ME BY A VERY TINY LIZARD, WITH SPIRITUAL FRIENDS SO ALMIGHTY THAT NOT EVEN DINOSAURS COULD COMPARE.

THE CROSSING

LOOKING BACK OVER MY RECENT EXPERIENCES I CAME ACROSS A VISION/DREAM I HAD, WHERE I MENTION THE FOLLOWING.

SUDDENLY I AM IN A LABYRINTH OF ROOTS N TUNNELS.
AS I MOVE ALONG THE TUNNELS ....
.... LIKE BEING THE CENTRE OF A SPHERE LOOKING OUTWARDS AT ALL ANGLES.

THEN ON ANOTHER OCCASION I WRITE,

I SEE MANY SNAKES, GREEN, BLUES, SLOWLY SLITHERING. I FOLLOW THEY EVOLVE, SCALES PRISMATIC EXPLOSIONS.

SO I ASK N SEE WITH MIND'S EYE CLEARLY OPEN.

GARDEN WILD

LEAVING EVERYTHING TO NATURE THIS YEAR IN THE GARDEN HAS HAD AN ENORMOUS IMPACT ON PLANT N ANIMAL AS A WHOLE.

GRASSES FLOW UPON GENTLE BREEZES, BUFFETED N DINED ON BY HEDGE SPARROWS.

THE LITTLE BROWN FLECKED BIRDS DOING THEIR OWN IMPERSONATION OF A HUMMING BIRD.

DIVING OFF FENCE N LAUNCHING AT THE SEED HEAD OF GRASSES N BACK PEDDLING MADLY, SO AS TO JUST GET HOLD OF ONE SEED.

FOR OVER AN HOUR NOW THE LITTLE BIRDS DANCE N FLING THEMSELVES AT THE STEMS, STEMS TOO THIN TO SUPPORT THE WEIGHT, SO HAVING TO FLAP TINY WINGS AS IN A PANIC, HOLDING SLOWLY GETTING HEAVIER, BODIES.

THE GRAIN THEY EAT FILLING THEM LIKE DOUGHY LEAD.

EXHAUSTED, SATED NOW, SIT UPON THE FENCE N PREEN.

OH WHAT A MOST WONDERFUL SIGHT TO BEHOLD!

I WOULD NEVER HAVE SEEN THE LIKES HAD I CUT THE GRASS THIS YEAR!

"THANK YOU MANTON FOR THAT SHARE, MOST BEAUTIFUL STUFF.

WAIT UNTIL THEY BRING THEIR OFFSPRING.

TEACH OF WHERE THE JOVIAL GIANT ABIDES. LOL

I DO LOVE THE LITTLE BIRD.

WHEN I WAS A CHILD THERE USED TO BE SO MANY OF THEM, BUT FARMERS N AGRICULTURE TOOK AWAY THE HEDGE ROWS, SO IMPORTANT FOR THE LITTLE BIRD TO BE PROTECTED IN.

THEY WERE NEARLY ALL WIPED OUT.

IT IS GOOD TO SEE THEM THRIVING AGAIN.

TOO MANY FEMALES, BUT POSSIBLY THEY ARE NOT MONOGAMOUS.

THE LAND LEFT TO ITSELF ALWAYS FINDS A WAY TO HEAL THE SCARS OF MAN.

"BLESSINGS"

RHODIOLA ROSEA
OK FOLKS, THIS IS AN INCREDIBLE HERB.

I INGESTED 50MG BEFORE BREAKFAST N FELT THE LIFT IN MOOD N BODY LETHARGY IN TWENTY MINUTES.

I INGESTED ANOTHER 70MG ABOUT AN HOUR AGO N JUST ATE DINNER.
MY WHOLE BODY IS GLOWING N CHARGED WITH ENERGY.

USUALLY AFTER EATING I FEEL TIRED AS THE BLOOD SUGAR LEVELS INCREASE, BUT NOT WITH THIS LADY.
ROYAL SACRED MAJESTIC HERB,
VISIONARY OF INNER N SPIRIT'S EYE,
CLOAKING ME IN ROYAL ROBES
OF FOLDED CLOTH CAPES,
RED RUBY,
AZURE N DIVINE,
LIKE GOLDEN LIGHT SHINING THROUGH CRACKS,
ENVELOPING THE SEER IN TRANSIENT LIGHT.

LIKE WATER THAT CHUCKLES N DANCES WITHIN THE BROOK OF MY THOUGHTS,

A FURNACE BURNING BRONZED COALS UPON A CHALICE FOR MY HEART TO WARM,

WITH BOOTS N ARMOUR THIS HERB GIVEN,

THE WARRIOR IS REBORN.

OF GRACE OF THOUGHT N STRENGTH OF ARM.

A SPICE FIT FOR GODS.

RHODIOLA ROSEA,

LADY,

WARRIOR,

STRONG.

IBOGA?

MUCH RESPECT TO THIS HERB PEOPLE, I FEEL PHYSICALLY AS IF I HAVE RECOVERED FROM A JOURNEY WITH IBOGA, MY BODY, STRONG, ELECTRIC N VIBRANTLY ALIVE.

I SHALL BE WORKING VERY CLOSELY WITH THIS LADY, SHE HAS MUCH OF WHICH I CAN LEARN.

ALL IMPATIENCES ARE GONE, RECHANNELLED ENERGIES THROUGH MIND N BODY ALLOWING SPIRIT TO FLOW LIKE A MIGHTY RIVER, THE DEPTH OF THE EVENTUALLY REACHED OCEAN, LIKE A GREAT CUP THAT ONE CAN DRINK OF AT ANY TIME N BECOME REFRESHED.

IN SALUTATION

STRENGTH,

POWER,

HONOUR.

SOMEONE WROTE THAT IBOGAINE CAUSES BRAIN DAMAGE. DAMAGE TO THE CEREBELLUM. DAMAGE HAS BEEN RECORDED IN PRIMATES, BUT ONLY IN EXTREMELY HIGH DOSES. ONE PRIMATE OUT OF SEVEN. WITHDRAWAL CAUSES DAMAGE TO THE CEREBELLUM N SO DOES EVERYDAY WEAR N TEAR.

RATS COULD BE MORE SUSCEPTIBLE TO CELL DAMAGE. ALL EARLY STUDIES OF IBOGAINE WERE CONDUCTED ON RATS N THEY SUFFERED CELL NECROSIS ON DOSES OF 25MG/KG N HIGHER. THIS WAS PART OF THE MAIN REASON THAT STUDIES WERE HELD BACK SO LONG.

THE AMANITA PANTHARINA IS STRONGER THAN THE AMANITA MUSCARIA, BUT BOTH WORK EXTREMELY WELL FOR WITHDRAWAL. START WITH 6 GRAMMES N SLOWLY WORK UP. I ATE 30 GMS EVERY FIVE HOURS. WEED IS GREAT FOR THE NAUSEA THAT SOME EXPERIENCE FROM THESE MUSHROOMS.

SOMEONE WROTE THAT AYAHUASCA WILL SMASH OPIATE WITHDRAWAL AT 100ML EVERY THREE DAYS. I ORDERED N BREWED THE SAID BREW N DRANK IT 100ML.

I USED IN MY FIRST BREW 150GRMS OF BANISTERIOPSIS CAAPI AS AN INHIBITOR N 100GRMS OF CHACRUNA (PSYCHOTRIA VIRIDIS) FOR THE DMT.

IT TOOK ME AWAY FROM MY BODY FOR ABOUT 90 MINUTES N SHOWED ME MANY OF MY FAULTS, BUT AS IT STARTED TO WEAR OFF THE PAIN OF WITHDRAWAL RETURNED. IT DID GIVE ME SOME RELIEF, ABOUT FIVE HOURS, BUT THE NAUSEA WAS EXTREME. WHEN I GOT TO THE POINT OF MEETING ALL MY DEMONS, I CHUCKED UP FOR NEARLY TWO HOURS. IMMENSE VISUALS.

MY SECOND BREW WAS STRONGER.

I USED 200GRMS BANISTERIOPSIS CAAPI N 150GRMS OF CHAGROPANGA (DIPLOPTERYS CABRERANA) N WAS VERY RELUCTANT TO DRINK IT. I SPLIT THE DOSE INTO THREE N DOWNED THE FIRST TWO DOSES, TWO DAYS AFTER MY FIRST ATTEMPT.

IT WAS HORRENDOUS.

I LAY UPON MY BED N SLOWLY THE KALEIDOSCOPE OF VISUALS STARED. THEN THERE WAS A BLINDING WHITE FLASH N THE RIGHT SIDE OF MY SKULL SMASHED OPEN LIKE I HAD BEEN STRUCK BY LIGHTNING N I FELT AS IF I HAD BEEN HIT BY A TRUCK. THERE WAS NO PAIN THOUGH. JUST A FEELING OF MY SKULL BEING CRACKED OPEN FROM THE INSIDE.

I THEN GOT CAST INTO WHAT I CAN ONLY PERCEIVE AS MY OWN HELL. MY OWN CREATION OF DANTE'S INFERNO. BEASTS OF ALL MANNER, DESCRIPTION N KIND ASSAULTED ME. I WAS TORN N RIPPED BY MANY EXTREMELY DISGUSTING CREATURES WITH RED, GREEN N BLUE EYES. I LAY ON A SLIDING CLIFF OF MUD BEING MAULED N GRABBED BY APPENDAGES FROM BELOW, LIKE THE CREATURES HAD AROSE FROM THE DEPTHS

OF THE DEAD N WERE TRYING TO DRAG ME DOWN WITH THEM. I SURRENDERED N ACCEPTED N FORGAVE AS MUCH AS I COULD, BUT THE ASSAULT WAS COMPLETELY BEYOND ME.

I WAS HURLED N WRENCHED BY DEAD ARMS LEGS, BEAST OF IMMENSE N GROSS CONSTRUCTION. THEY SLAVERED ON ME, BIT ME, ATE LUMPS OF ME, SCREAMED IN TORMENT AT ME N WOULDN'T LET ME GO. I COULD SMELL THE DEATH N DECAY EVERYWHERE. I GAVE UP MANY MANY TIMES N JUST WISHED TO DIE. I WAS PICKED UP N HURLED THROUGH A BLINDING VORTEX OF SCREAMING HEADS N UPPER TORSOS. THE BODIES OF THESE APPARITIONS STOPPED AT BELLY BUTTON LEVEL N SEEMED TO JUST MELT INTO THE MUD WALLS OF THE SPINNING VORTEX. ALL GRABBING AT ME N HITTING ME. I CURLED UP IN A BALL N EVENTUALLY POPPED OUT OF THE END, LIKE BEING SHOT OUT OF A CANNON. FOR A SHORT SPACE OF TIME I WAS EJECTED OUT INTO A WARM BUBBLE OF GOLDEN ROSE LIGHT THAT BATHED ME N KIND OF TOLD ME THAT EVERYTHING WAS OK. THEN THE CHAOS STARTED AGAIN. FROM SOMEWHERE BELOW RED BROWN TENTACLES REACHED UP N POPPED MY BUBBLE N SUCTION SUCKERS HELD ME N DRAGGED ME DOWN TOWARDS THE BEAKED MOUTH OF A GREAT OCTOPUS. I WAS EATEN N DISSOLVED IN A GREAT VAT OF PUTRID GREEN YELLOW PUSS. THE SMELL WAS SO OVERPOWERING THAT I THREW UP MANY MANY TIMES N THE TASTE N SMELL OF PUTREFACTION LINGERED WITH ME FOR NEARLY FIVE DAYS.

I DIED MANY MANY TIMES THAT DAY, ALL I COULD WISH FOR WAS THAT MY BODY N SPIRIT WOULD DIE N JUST LET ME GO N LEAVE ME IN PEACE.

IT DID NOT BEAT THE METHADONE I WAS ON.

AFTER ABOUT 6 HOURS I BEGAN TO RECOVER. I WAS A SWEATING SHAKING MESS FOR MANY HOURS AFTER N COULD ONLY LIE IN A HOT BATH N MUTTER TO MYSELF.

(WHAT THE F---K) OVER N OVER AS I REMEMBER. LOL

IBOGA WAS A LOT LESS PAINFUL.

BUT ALSO EXTREME TO THE EXTREME.

I AM NOW CLEAN 11 MONTHS FROM OVER 150ML METHADONE 500MG METH,150MG VALIUM, 40MG SERTRALINE, 1600MG GABAPENTIN. I WAS ALSO TAKING LOADS OF CODEINE N OVER A GRAM OF HERION EVERYDAY TWO BOTTLES OF VODKA A BOTTLE OF WINE N TWO SPECIAL BREWS.

I HAD TO WEAN MYSELF OFF ALL THE STUFF VERY QUICKLY. I INGESTED 5GRMS OF IBOGA 5 TIMES EXTRACT N IT SLAUGHTERED THE WITHDRAWAL FROM THE SAID METH IN ABOUT 12 HOURS. I THEN FELT BLANK FOR ABOUT FIVE DAYS,

THEN TRIPPED VERY HARD INDEED, A BIT LIKE ON LSD FOR OVER 10 WEEKS. SOME ELEVEN WEEKS AFTER I COULD STILL FEEL THE IBOGA N GET UP ON GOOD FOOD N WATER.

IBOGA IS A MOST AMAZING TOOL N A VERY COMPASSIONATE TEACHER. I WOULD BE DEAD WITHOUT HER.

I HAVE SINCE USED AYA MANY TIMES, BUT HAVE NEVER EXPERIENCED ANYWHERE NEAR THE HELL OF THE TIMES I WAS ADDICTED.

MY EXPERIENCES OF AYA NOW ARE EXTREMELY ECSTATIC.

I GUESS I KILLED ALL THEM DEMONS ONCE N FOR ALL.

ASE

BAS BAS BASSE

I WILL LOVE TO FEEL U NEXT TO ME...

N LISTEN TO YOUR BREATHING N SWEET LITTLE MURMURS N THE WAY UR BODY SPEAKS WITHIN THE PEACE O' SLEEP..

WHILST THINE EYE A MULTIMENSIONAL SNAKE GOES HUNTER GATHERING CHI.. THROUGH TANTRIC INVOLVEMENT SO SUBLIMELY ENTWINED...

ONE'S INNER ESSENCE MAY SHUDDER N MAKE SOULS FLY...

ONWARD THRUST UNTO THY FIRM FORM N ESSENCES OF THE DEEPEST DREAM THAT CARRIES ME TO YOU..

AGAIN N AGAIN...

FOR TO BE BEHOLDEN O' THINE PRESENCE N LOVE WILL BE O SO DEAR N TREASURE CHESTED WITHIN MY HEART ...

MY BODY BENDS N TWIST N BURNS..

MAY U FULFIL MYDESIRES...

TO CARRESS N FONDLE N STROKE N KISS ONE'S SUBTLENESS..

O TENDERNESS O MY HEART DOES SPEAK AS MUSIC WITHIN HARMONIES OF DELIGHTS...

MAY U SLEEP DEEP N DREAM WITH ME N CAST ONE'S EYE TO FLAT PLAIN INFINITY...

N DRAW THE COSMOS TO THE CENTRE O' ME

ARISE O BRIGHT N SHINING STAR... BEDAZZLE WITH UR SAVOURS..

N ALWAYS REMEMBER DEAREST TREASURE THEE MOST SURELY ARE ♥♥♥♥♥♥♥♥♥♥

1 IN 1 COSMOS-BODIES AS ONE...

COME MELT INTO I ARMS N EMBRACE THE FORCE O LOVE ♥

O SUCH A SWEET VIVACIOUS N GENTLE SOUL WITH VERVE N ADVENTURE WITHIN THINE EYES DO SMILE..

I AM LIFTED 1 TRILLION MILES... AT YOUR SMILE.

BE LOVED... BELOVED BE

O DEAREST ONE...

SWEET DREAMS FOR ME N I WITH A GENTLE TOUCH N BREATH O' LOVE SO DEEP...

GOOD MORNING BELOVED,

SUN IS BRIGHT N WIND IS SPEEDY BRISK N THERE BE HEAVY DANCE RAIN CLOUDS, BLUE SKY ELECTRIC N LACED WITH MATRIXES GEOMETRIES.

O LET'S ALL PUT OUR 🖐S TOGETHER N GIVE A GOOD HEARTY WARM WELCOME TO

THE RIGHT HONOURABLE MR SAN PEDRO

YEAH ☺ 🖐CLAPCLAPCLAPC LAPCLAPCLAPCLA CLAPCLAPCLAPCLAPCLAPCLAPCLAPCLAP CSCSCS CCSCSCS WOOHOO🖐AYIIA WOO 🌵

N ON OUR SOUTH SEATED UPON THAT BIG SWIVEL ARM CHAIR THERE IS ------------- WAIT FOR IT.

HERE WE GO

HERE HE IS

TO THE SOUTH,

THE MIGHTY HON OUR TABLE

THE KING OF WOODS!

THE HON OUR TABLE MR IBOGA GAME PLAYING LETTER NUMBER N WORD ☺ALL LIFE

LETS HAVE A WARM WELCOME PLEASE ☺

🖐CLAPCLAPCLAPCLAPCLAPCLAPCLAPCLAPCLAPCL APCLAPCLAP CLAPCLAPCLAP CSCSCSCCSCSCSCSCSCCSCSCSW OOHOOMR IBOGAWOOHOO🖐LOVE YOU WOOHOO🖐 HAHAHAHA

N TO OUR NORTH IS THE NW BY NORTH THE GREAT N MIGHTY RADIANT ARK IT ETC.

THE UP RIGHT N CENTERED,

THE PLINTH STONE,

THE HON OUR TABLE

MR TATA NGANGA NOBUNONI HERA SHEREA ...

LET'S HAVE A WARM WELCOME PLEASE 😀👋👋👋👋👋CLAP CLAPCLAPCLAPCLAP CLAPCLAPCLAPCLAPCL APCLAPCLAP

👋👋👋👋👋CSCSCSCCSCSCSCSCSCSCCSCSCSCSCSCS CCSCSCS

RAUCOUS APPLAUSE N CACOPHONY OF HOOTING CLAPPING N YEAH'S OF YEARS. WOOHOO👋👋👋

PA

WORK TO DO.

RUN DOGS

GET SOME CEREALS MILK

N GET THE HOOVER OUT.

HAVE A WONDERFUL BRIGHT SIDE SHINY DAY.......

BASSIIIII I

BELOVED

BE LOVED

SUNSHINE BLISS

LOVE IN THE LIGHT OF THE MOON

THE GREAT N MIGHTY LORD OF THE NORTH,

THE GREAT ARK ETC,

THE NW BY NORTH

THE HONOURABLE SHE O THE COSMOS ...

LET'S PUT OUR 🖐'S 10 FINGERS 5 ON THE EAST 5 ON THE WEST TOGETHER.

BRING 👣RUN 👣 DANCING UPON THE FLOOR, LET'S HAVE A HO DOWN N GET SOME PSYCHE N EMPATHY SHARING, WARM OF HEART N FULL OF THE SUN, WITH THE MOON IN THE BELLY FOR BALANCE N NO WOBBLE THE VESSEL UPON THE HIGH SEASONS OF LIFE.

JUST A COSMICATION OF THE QUALITIES EXPRESSIVE OF THE ETERNAL SPIRIT OF G.O.D THROUGH THE ETERNAL SOUL ...

NAMASTE

GOOD DAY ☺.ALL LIFE

THE SHE LIGHT OF THE WORLD WILL KEEP UPGRADING YOUR DNA ... MEMORY/MIND/THOUGHT/IMAGINATION LESS OR NO.

ANIMAL HAS NO MIND.

THAT THING IS BODY MEMORY PROGRAMED AT SCHOOL BY 26 LETTER 9 NUMBER N A 0. TAL MEN TAL STATE OF BEING ..

T(TOWER TEMPLE) A(CONSCIOUSNESS OVER MATTER)

LIGHT LAID LAW TO INFINITY OF CONSCIOUSNESS OF BE ING.

FALSE PROGRAMING BY THE HIERARCHY OF THE RIGHT ANGLE OF G.O.D.(GRAVITY ORDERED DENSITY OF 21 EMPATHIC PATHWAYS OF BE ING.

MIND IS A BLUNT USELESS TOOL THAT IS FORCED ON CHILDREN TO CREATE A MENTAL STATE OF BEING SO AS TO USE THE RESULTANT OUT OF BALANCE TEMPLE OF GRAVITY ORDERED DENSITY AS A SLAVE FOR MATTER ISMS...A TOOL CREATED 4300 SUN CYCLES TO CUT BODY MEMORY RIGHT SIDE N CREATE EGO CENTRIC THINK THAT WRITES EMPATHIC ENERGIES TO RNA TO DNA CODING ....CREATING INTERNALISED CONSCIOUSNESS.

A CHILD IS BORN WITH NO STATE OF MIND ...BLIND TO THE WAYS OF FREEMASON CONTROL ...THEN IS PROGRAMMED TO BE USED TO MAKE ILL U SION MONEY FOR SIONIST CONTROL OF A BEAUTIFUL BEING THAT IS AN ANIMAL N IS CUT WITH TAL N TAUGHT TAL K(TO OPEN COSMOS DOOR ...SOUND TO LIGHT ...NO SUCH THING AS MENTAL HEALTH....IT IS CREATED BY THE TAL..

USELESS DUMB NON INSTINCTUAL TOOL OF INFINITY OF CONSCIOUSNESS TO INTERNALISE CONSCIOUSNESS IN THE POT HEAD...N PUT THE TEMPLE OF G.O.D. RIGHT SIDE BODY MEMORY HEAVIER THAN THE LEFT..

EGO CENTRIC TICK TOCK HEAD. SO AS TO USE BEING AS A SLAVE FOR MATERIALISTIC BOX 3D WORLD.

THERE IS NO RIGHT ANGLE IN NATURE N BEING IS AN ANIMAL NO A. M A N....

ALPHABET PROGRAMING OF A BEAUTIFUL ANIMAL OF EXTERNALISED CONSCIOUSNESS OF (H)EARTH.

ORIGINALLY VENETIAN INBREEDING 75000 SUN CYCLES 200000 STRONG IN 200 SHIPS LAND N ALL MALE BREED WITH ANIMAL SO AS TO SAVE THE VENETIAN RACE FROM EXTINCTION. BEING IS A HALF BREED OF VENETIAN N AN I M AL EL O HIM G.O.D (GRAVITY ORDERED DENSITY OF 12 RAY LIGHT 21 EMPATHIC PATHWAYS 7 ABOVE THE HEAD = 28 = 1 TEMPLE OF COMPLETE ENLIGHTENMENT 0= INFINITY OF CONSCIOUSNESS N ETERNITY WITHIN MATTER .

CENTRAL GALAXY SUN IS MALE THE REST OF THE GALAXY SHE LIGHT WITHIN GRAVITY ORDERED DENSITY ...MATTER .

NO REQUIRE A BLUNT TOOL OR A UNIVERSE MADE OF 144000 WORDS.

IT HAS NO EMPATHY OR INSTINCTUAL STATE OF BEING.

RELIGION ENTROLLS OF INFINITY OF CONSCIOUSNESS.

CREATED BY EGYPTIAN PRIEST 4300 SUN CYCLES SO AS TO USE HUMMING BEING AS A SLAVE TO MINE METALS GOLD SILVER COPPER 4 PHAROAH N THE ELITE OF THE HERD SO THEY CAN SHINE THEIR CONSCIOUSNESS OF INFINITY OF PYRAMID.

IT IS CALLED PYRAMID.

A TOOL TO CUT 10 FINGERED BEING INTO 9.

CUTTING EMPATHIC PATHWAYS OF THE BODY TO CREATE OF MIND ILLUSION THINK.

EGYPTIANS USED MERCURY TO CUT HEART CHAKRAS EFFICIENCY FIRING N PROGRAMED SLAVES WITH ALPHABET METAL.

C(CUT) O(STAR) V(DNA) I(AWARENESS) 3RD EYE D(DENSITY OF LIGHT OF EMPATHY) 19 = 1 TEMPLE BEING 0 = 3RD EYE ....VAX TO CUT DNA WITH MRNA TO LOWER HEIGHT OF EMPATHIC PATHWAYS OF ANIMAL ...BECAUSE CENTRAL GALAXY SUN... REVOLVE UPGRADES DNA EVERY 2125 SUN CYCLES.

ROMANS USED CRUCIFIXION 2128 SUN CYCLES ...THEY TAKE MERCURY FOR FURY N WAR N RAISE MARS ROOT CHAKRA (MARY) CALL VENUS J(HEART HOOK JUPITER) E(LIGHT) S(SHE DNA) U(CUP) S(SHE DNA) SHE THE LIGHT OF THE WORLD...

VACCINES ARE TO INJECT BABIES WITH HEAVY METALS TO LOWER FREQUENCY OF HEART CHAKRA N LOWER HEIGHT OF CONSCIOUSNESS SO AS TO MAKE METAL EASIER TO PROGRAM INTO RIGHT SIDE BODY MEMORY N CREATE SLAVES FOR MATT H(TEMPLE) E(LIGHT) W(WAA...WATER OF THE BODY OF G.O.D(GRAVITY ORDERED DENSITY OF 12 RAY LIGHT WITHIN FIRM FROM DNA

ROMAN PRIEST TAKE C(CUT)H(TEMPLE)R(RAISE CONCISENESS) I (AWARENESS 3RD EYE) S(SHE LIGHT T(TEMPLE TOWER) CONSCIOUSNESS 4700 SUN CYCLE PRIEST OF TEMPLE OF AN I METAL N WRITE THE B(BREAST) I(AWARENESS 3RD EYE) B(BREAST) L(LIGHT LAY LAW TO BODY MEMORY) E(LIGHT OF THE WORLD)

CREATING CHRISTIANITY DITTY RUBBISH FROM EGYPTIAN MANTRA SOUNDS

MATT HEW SLAVERY MARK LUKE N JOHN ...N THE EPISTALS TO THE ROMANS N CRUCIFY ON THE CROSS OF CONSCIOUSNESS

THOUSANDS UPON THOUSANDS TO PREVENT DNA UPGRADE FROM CENTRAL GALAXY SUN.

HENCE ALL THE NONSENSE NOW...

I AM AT A LOSS FOR WORD TO DESCRIBE OF WHAT HAS HAPPENED TO I.

SUFFICE TO SAY.

I AM COMPLETE SPHERE OF CONSCIOUSNESS.

6TH DENSITY.

THEN I DROP ID N DISAPPEAR STRAIGHT THROUGH THE 7TH DIMENSIONAL SELF TO 8TH FLAT PLAIN OF INFINITY 8TH DIMENSIONAL SELF.

THEN I AM SUCCEED WITHOUT VOLITION INTO A NEW SPHERE OF CONSCIOUSNESS N THEN BECOME 10TH MULTI-DIMENTIONAL, THEN EVERYTHING BECOMES CREATIONS SPHERE, MULTI-DIMENTIONAL

NO JUST WRITHING WITHIN GOLDEN THREADS IF VINES, LEAVES FRUIT, VALLEYS RIVERS, MOUNTAINS, WRIGGLING DIAMOND, MORPHING ELECTRIC BLUE SKOESTROGEN FINELY WOVEN OF GEOMETRIES EVOLVING. DEEP PEACE, IMMENSE REVERENCE N CHUCKLING, IF ONE ATTEMPTS TO TAKE ONES ATTENTION OF WHICH IS MESMERISED BY STUNNING BEAUTY N ENORMOUS GREAT DRAGON OF WRITHING THREADS OF GOSSAMER GOLDS N PINKS YELLOWS ORANGES PURPLES HUE REDS AZURE SPARKLED SAPPHIRES, PLUMPS PUROLE N DAZZLING RED SPHERE OF GRAPES N CRANBERRIES, BLACKBERRIES, AS IF

ONE HAS BEEN SUCKED INTO A GENTLY EVOLVING WASHING MACHINE MADE OF THREADED VINES OF WHICH RIPPLE N MOVE IN HARMONY WITH HEART N BREATH.

IF ONE ATTEMPTS TO SPEAK I GET SUCCEED BACK THROUGH INFINITY TO THE 6TH DIMENSIONAL SELF N THEN REALIZING OF MINDS I SPLIT DOWN THE MIDDLE WITH EGO I DROP THE BOX OF MANY THINGS N GET SUCKED BACK THROUGH TECHNOLOGY 7TH DIMENSIONAL STRAIGHT INTO THE 10TH OF WHERE BREATHING IS ONLY REALISED AS EXPLANATION N CONTRACTION OF A LIVING WRITHING ALL-CONSUMING/CREATING DRAGON OF CREATION.

OF WHOM CHUCKLES AT THE LITTLE EGO BOUND DANCES THAT I DO.

LAUGHS N ROLLS N ROARS AS THUNDER WITHIN DISTANT CANNONS DEEP RAVINES, SOUND VIBRATIONAL EDIFICATION OF THE VESSEL TO REACH THE CORRECT FREQUENCY OF HEMISPHERICAL BALANCE OF THE BRAINS.

THREE PROCESSORS MUST BE WITHIN HARMOMY, COUPLED BY PERFECT FREQUENCY OF WHICH BRINGS BEING TO ONE WITH GOD IN GOD.

FROM THE 6TH COMPLETE SPHERE OF CONSCIOUSNESS.

THE EYE OF SELF-AWARENESS THE 3RD INNER EYE IS OPEN...

THE HEART BRAIN N THE TWO HEAD BRAINS THROUGH SELF-EDIFICATION OF VIBRATING THE VESSEL AT THE CORRECT FREQUENCY BRINGS THE TRUE TRINITY OF TEA BREATH IF GOD ONLINE.

THE 3 PROCESSORS BECOME ONE ENTITY

ONE DARK OF LIGHT

ONE LIGHT OF LIGHT

ONE OF HEART LIGHT.

I STAND ABOVE MIND.

CONSCIOUSNESS BECOMES UN-ATTACHED FROM EGO TRAVEL ARROW BETWEEN HEAD PROCESSORS N EMPIONS OF THE HEART.

THE HEART TAKES OVER THE LIGHT TWIN IN THE HEAD N 3D THINKING BECOMES MY FEELING OF 4TH DIMENSIONAL SELF THE FORCE OF LOVE.

THE DARK TWIN THAT IS NEVER BEGUILED BY THE LIGHT TWINS PROGRAMING STEPS TO THE FORE N EVERYTHING EXPLODES WITHIN THE NOW FULL OF LIFE FORCE ESSENCE EXPERIENCED THROUGH THE FEELING, I BREATH OF GOD.

THE LIGHT TWIN IS BEGUILED BY PROGRAMING OF WHICH MAKES THE LIGHT TWIN PUSH THE DARK TWIN N CLOSE THE 3RD EYE WITH 3D FORCE DISCONNECTING ONE FROM THE FORCE OF LOVE OF CREATION.

UNIVERSE IS DEFUNCT.

WITHIN A LOGOS LANGUAGE VIBRATIONAL FEELING A PROCESSION OF TRANSPOSED LIGHT SYMBOLS OF WHICH CONNECT 3 INTO ONE BEING WITH LOVE AS THE BINDING FORCE TO GIVE OF PERCEPTION OF LIGHT OFF THE 5TH DIMENSIONAL LIGHT COILED OFF DNA.

COIL 5TH

SPHERE 6TH

7TH RELEASE OF ID.

8TH INFINITY OF CONSCIOUSNESS

9TH FROM INFINITY TO A NEW SPHERE OF HIGHER CONSCIOUSNESS.

10TH AT THE GATE OF CREATION

11TH WITHIN CREATION.

N THERE IS NOTHING TO BE DONE.

THERE IS ONLY THE RAW PRIMAL POWER OF NOW

AYIIA

5TH 6TH 7TH TO HEAVEN N ONE HAS NO FREE WILL IN THAT IT IS IMPOSSIBLE TO TURN THY FACE AWAY, IF I ATTEMPT GOD STARTS BELLY LAUGHING N CALLING ME A SILLY LITTLE MONKEY LIVING WITHIN A CUBE HOUSE N SHOULD BE LIVING IN TREE.

COLLECTING OF THAT WHICH IS REQUIRED EACH DAY.

AHHA

FOLKS STOCKPILE TOILET PAPER HAHHAHA!

GOD SAYS THAT IS DANCE, HAS FINGERS N WATER N CANNOT EAT BOG ROLL RICE WOULD BE BETTER

OOH OOH!

CANNOT WIPE MY BUMB WITH WHOLE GRAIN BROWN RICE ☺ ALLIFE

IT HURTS REALLY REALLY REALLY X 500 TIMES BAD TO DELETE BODY MEMORY, MIND PROGRAMMED INTO DNA AS A CHILD.

BUT THAT WHICH ONE LEARNS OF WHAT THEE REALLY IS, IS ABSOLUTELY ASTOUNDING .

CONSCIOUSNESS EXTERNALISED OF THE BODY.

NO HEAD.

NO INTERNAL DIALOGUE .

NO BODY MEMORY OTHER THAN THAT WHICH ONE CAN SEE N TOUCH WITH FINGER ..TASTE N SMELL NOW.

MENTAL STATE OF BEING IS AN ILLUSION PROGRAMMED INTO DNA AS A CHILD.

PAST N FUTURE NO EXIST N TIME CONSTRUCTION IS INFINITY OF A STRAIGHT LINE AROUND A SPHERE COILED 😄

ASE ATU.

SILENCE FOR ME NOW .

I BLOW MY NOSE OFF MY TEMPLE ☺

NOSE SINGS OIO, I AM I.

LANGUAGE IS POINTLESS 😄

IT HAS NO EMPATHIC PATHWAYS .

N IS CONSTRUCT TOOL OF CONTROL OF BEING THAT ONLY FEELS EMPATHY LIGHT N WARMTH OF BEING ....

36 TONNE METAL ☺☺☺ K ☺☺☺ TO OPEN COSMOS DOOR TO OIO…INFINITY OF EMPATHIC LIGHT

BEING DEEPLY N COMPLETELY LOVED BY A LOVER BRINGS ONE STRENGTH

N LOVING A LOVER UN-CONDITIONALLY, FOR THEIR STRENGTH N FORTITUDE OF REPOSE GIVES ONE COURAGE TO CONQUER MOUNTAINS N OCEANS VAST. I AM NO BODY (GROSS, ONLY FEELING)

I AM NO THING (I HAVE NO MIND)

I AM THE BREATH OF GOD, (BODY SPEAKS FEELING TO THE FORE)

BODY SPEAKS, FLOWS OF RISING TO GREET THE COSMIC WAVES THAT SING VIBRANT COLOURS,

WRAP N CLOAK, N WEAVE OF BREATH THROUGH THE BODY ESSENCES OF LIFE

LOVE N LOVER SIT AS "CUPS" AWAITING TO BE FULL N FILLED OF EACH N DEEPLY DRUNK OF.

INHALED, ABSORBED, RECEIVED N TRANSMUTED OF PURE FIRE, THAT BURNS OF LOVE N PASSIONS RISING FROM WITHIN ONE'S CORE.

BELOVED N LOVER, KNOCKING UPON THE DOOR OF EACH OTHER'S HEARTS TO OPEN!

SWOONED N INTOXICATED OF THEIR LOVE WITHIN LOVERS' GRASP, THEY GASP FOR ATOM, OXYGEN, THEIR BREATH

COMBINED, OUT, IS BREATHED IN, N IN IS BREATHED OUT, CARRY LIFE FORCE N FIRE OF LOVES NECTAR, PASSIONS UPON THE BREATH, COMBINE THE RHYTHM RISE N FALLS GENTLY WITHIN CHEST OF HEAVING BOSOM. PURITY OF LOVE IS SURE N SECURE AS PADLOCK UPON IRON GATE. MELDED AS ONE BEING, VIBRANT OF APRICOTS N YELLOWS PINKS LIGHTLY TICKLES N BODIES TOUCH N BRUSH SOFTLY DOWN HAIRS. BREATH LIGHT, ESSENCE OF BIRD IN FLIGHT, SOARING TWISTING THERMALS WAY UP HIGH THE "EYE" EXPANDS OF INERTIA OF CONSCIOUSNESS, RELEASED FROM RESTRAINT N GIVEN OF G.O.D BREATH. BODY LIGHT, FEELING LOVE, INTOXICATES N LIFTS THE SOUL TO CLEARER KNOWINGS UNTETHERED OF "FORM" THE BODY IS NO MORE. I AM BUT DUST, COILED, SELF-LUMINESCENT LIGHT, ETERNAL FIRE OF THE RADIANT SUN INFINITELY SHARDED OF EXUBERANCE OF GOLDEN PINK HUE LIGHT. FEELING SEVEN RAINBOW DANCE THE CODE OF LIFE! TO RECEIVE OF BEAUTIFUL BOUQUET OF FLOWERS, SETS BUTTERFLIES TO THE HEART, RISE OF 11 PURPLE ROSES WITHIN THE "PRESENT" ILLUSION, TIME STANDS STILL, GENTLE RAIN THEN FALLS ON THE CHEEKS, TEARS, AS JOY, DOES OVERFLOW, ONE'S "CUP" COMPASSION.

    THANK YOU MY DARLING THE BODY SAYS,

WITHIN, FLUTTERS OF ONE'S HEART CHAKRA ROSE TO
OPEN THE GREAT GATE, N SWINGS TOWARDS THE LOVE THAT

FLOWS DEEPLY WITHIN THE GORGES N CREVICES OF ONES BEING! SUKA!

ET SALUTATION EXCELLENCE

THE BODY SINGS, WITHIN DELIGHTS OF "PRESENCE" RECEIVED I AM, I AM, I AM, I AM, I AM ALIVE OF ECSTATIC FEELING PUMPS THE HEART, HEAT RISING OF PASSIONS FIRE SUKA! THE SOUL CRIES, OH HOW HIGH I, EXQUISITE OF LOVERS PASSIONS FLY. EMBRACE TO FALL AS TWO EAGLES, FROM THE SKY, TALONS INTERLOCKED TWISTING WHEELING, FALLING FEATHERS FLUSTERED TO THE AIR, WITHIN IMMINENCE, THEY PART N GRASP THE AIR N WHEEL TO FLIGHT OF HEIGHTS IMMEASURABLE ONCE MORE:) OH JOY:) DANCE WITHIN, MAKE ME N I FLY, TO BECOME FORGOTTEN OF FORM, REMAINS OF EXUBERANCE N DIVINE INNER LIGHT, AS VAST AS BOUNDLESS SKIES,

HAZE OF OPAQUE FLUFFY CLOUDS

A FRONT BLUE YONDER.

THE BOUQUET OF FLOWERS GIVEN SAYS MY LOVE WILL LAST WITHIN THIS GIFT UNTIL THE DAY THE LAST BOUQUET FLOWERS WITHERS, THEN DIFFERENT COLOURS N FLOWERS WILL EMBRACE ONE'S FORM AGAIN

TO FLY N TICKLE ONE'S HEART N FILL WITH LOVE DIVINE

ALL OF MINE, TO GIVE!

RECEIVE N BE.

JOY♥LOVE♥SELF-LUMINESCENT LIGHT♥ HEART, TAKE TO FLIGHT N SOAR THE LOVERS TO THE SKY, ETERNAL N INFINITE OF THE "PRESENT" GIVEN N RECEIVED WITHIN THINE HEART

O MY LOVE.

CONSUME THE POTION THAT IT MAY FILL YOU FULL OF FIRE, SO QUEEN MAY EXPAND N BECOME GODDESS, GIDDY, OF LOVE, COMPASSION N JOY OF THE TREASURE TROVE OF LOVE NESTING WITHIN ONE'S HEART. I AM THE SUN, RADIANT, PURE OF LIGHT RAYED ESSENCE N DIVINE, INFINITE LIGHT WRAPPED WITHIN ETERNITY OF MATTER. LOVE BINDS, AS ROPE UPON THE HEART N RESTRAINS THE BEING OF THE GROSS N THE SUBTLE EPHEMERAL LOVE ESSENCE FEELING FLIES AS FLOCK GEESE, ARROW POINTING EAST FOR WINTER AS SOLITUDE SHUDDERS AT ONE'S HEART'S BEAUTY♥

I EXPLODE AS COILING EXPANDING VORTEX TO A STAR OF KNOWLEDGE THAT THROWS CONSCIOUSNESS DOWN VORTEX OF COMPLETE UNDERSTANDINGS OF DEEP N SACRED KNOWLEDGE N THE WORLD IS MADE OF INFORMATION ALL WRAPPED N WOVEN WITHIN LIGHT.

N ONE CAN PLUCK THE FIELD OF ANYTHING OUT OF EVERYTHING N MAKE OF THAT WHAT ONE LIKES

BECAUSE ANYTHING LEADS TO EVERYTHING N EVERYTHING IS

NOW ALWAYS JUST IS

N

SOLAR GIVES OF CONSCIOUSNESS N EARTH GIVES OF MATTER

N MOON BALANCES THE FORM

N THE STARS WITHIN THE HEAVENS ARE THE STARS OF THE BREATH OF GOD

I AM THE BREATH OF GOD.

ALL 86 BILLION OF THEM TO KNOW OF HERE N NOW.

EVERYTHING IS N NEVER WAS

IT IS ALL HERE

EVERYTHING

A UN I VERSE EXPLODED EVOLVED N BY REFLECTION, CONSCIOUSNESS CREATION AS A MASSIVE PSYCHIC MOVIE

EVERYTHING

IS

FEELING NOW.

A MULTIDIMENSIONAL VIBRATIONAL FREQUENCY UN I VERSE CREATED N WOVEN OF LIGHT WITHIN DIFFERENT DENSITIES OF VIBRATION AL SPACE.

N SPACE IS INHERENTLY SELF-INTELLIGENT

FOR THE VOID OF SPACE IS BUT THE SPIRIT OF GOD

THAT FIRMS FORMS INTO PLACE.

HERE

THROUGH

NOW.

VERY STRANGE FEELING BEING COMPLETE.

A SOLIDITY N SACREDNESS N HALLOWEDNESS OF RESPECT OF GOD

FOR A MOST STUNNINGLY AMAZING CREATION.

AWE

WITH PURE SINCERITY N GRACE IN KNOWLEDGE OF KNOWLEDGE KNOWING GOD N BEING GIVEN SUCH AWESOMELY STUNNING GIFTS OF THE SIGHT GIVEN UNTO LITTLE OLE ME.

IF YOU PERCEIVE YOU GET THERE COS GOD DOES THE DRIVING, ALL WE GOT TO DO IS DROP THE ID, EGO N BECOME ONE BEING WITH G.O.D

THE BREATH OF G.O.D WALKING THE LAND WITH MULTIDIMENSIONALITY OF PSYCHE FOR THE GIFT

OF SACRIFICE I GIVE TO MAINTAIN OF THE CORRECT ACTION.

PA

WHEN YOUNG I SIT BY THE POND N WATCH NEWTS RISE FROM MUDS DEEP IN SPIRALS FORMED IN MUDS OF THE DEEP PEAT WATERS.

WRIGGLING TAILS N SLIDING THROUGH THE WATERS TO RISE N TAKE AIR.

GREAT CRESTED NEWT.

A MALE RISES FIRST TO GRAB A BUBBLE OF AIR.

POP TO THE SURFACE WITHIN A GLIDE.

TURN N SWIRL N DISAPPEAR BACK TO THE DEEPS.

THEN FEMALE WILL RISE WITH A WRIGGLE OF TAIL.

A TWIST OF BODY N BREAK THE SURFACE OF STILLNESS OF THE POND.

TO RIPPLE, CIRCLE WAVES WITHIN THE LIGHT OF DAY.

N GRAB A BUBBLE OF AIR.

TWIST N RETURN UNTO THE DEEPS OF THE CLEAR WATERS OF THE SURFACE MIRROR PLATED POND.

STILLNESS IN MOTION N SERENITY IN LIFE.

A DANCE OF TWO SIDES OF INTERTWINING COIL.

THE LIGHT OF CREATION SMILING FACE WITHIN THE POND.

WEEDS N WATER BOAT MEN.

A SPARKLE OF SUNLIGHT UPON THE SURFACE.

GLANCED OF THE ESSENCE.

A MIRROR VIEW ON SURFACE OF HEATHERS PURPLE BLOOM.

CRACKLE OF GORSE SEED WITHIN THE SUN.

REFLECTION OF GEESE VEE OF FLIGHT TRAVERSE ACROSS THE POND SURFACE SCREEN.

CLOUDS ALOFT SIT N LAZILY GAZE AT THE MIRROR SURFACE SCENE.

BLUE HAZE OF SKY N BRILLIANCE OF SUN'S REFLECTION SMILES.

IS LIKE LIFE VIEWED THROUGH A MIRRORED GLASS.

OR GLIMPSED THROUGH A WINE GLASS AS A VIEW TO SEE. DISTORTED OF PERCEPTION BUT STILL A VIEW TO SEE. IN THE

END LIFE IS BUT A PERCEPTION OF FEELING WITHIN THE DEEPS OF ONE'S HEART.

THE HEAD BE REALLY EMPTY FOR THE HEART TO FEEL THE ESSENCE OF LIFE; BE FEELING THE ESSENCE N SILENT WHISPERS OF THE HEART; NOT TO BE OF HARSH REPOSE; TO CAUSE OF SMART TO THE PURE N TRUE SERENITY OF ONES HEART TO COME TO REST NO MORE ANOTHER DAY. BE THE ESSENCE OF PURE FEELING OF THE BEING OF ONENESS CREATED OF THE LIGHT OF THE WORLD; BE CHERISHMENT OF LOVE WEAVE N WOVE TO EACH N EVERY TROVE OF BEING. SO AT ONENESS IS COMPLETE OF CHEER N EVERYTHING CAN SING THE BEAUTY N HARMONISE THE LIGHT OF THE WORLD.

MANIFEST AS LIFE BE VIBRANT OF FEELING N NEVER OF THE THITHER THAT BETWEEN THE EARS FOR IT BE ILLUSION OF BODY MEMORY THE THING CALLED MIND.

DEAR DNA PROGRAMMED OF LANGUAGE MAKES THE HEART TO CLOSE N THE ILLUSION OF THE IMAGINATION OF THE REVERE OF THE HEAD TO POSE N PONDER THE WONDERS OF THE TREASURES N BEAUTIES OF THE WORLD. THE LIGHT WITHIN FEELING SERENITY OF EXPRESSION N LIGHT OF TOUCH TO FEEL N EXPRESS THE LIGHT OF THE WORLD, THE CONSCIOUSNESS OF LIFE

♥TREASURE EACH N EVERY BLADE OF GRASS AS THEE TREASURES THINE OWN BODY HOLD OF EMPATHIES TO EACH N EVERY ALL OF LIFE.

NO MORE WARFARE MORE PAIN. SLEEP TO RETURN AGAIN TO A REFLECTION UPON THE SURFACE OF THE WATERS OF THE POND OF LIFE.

THE SEER N THE OBJECT SEEN ARE LIKE THE ROPE N THE SNAKE.

JUST AS THE KNOWLEDGE OF THE ROPE

WHICH IS THE SUBSTRATE WILL NO' ARISE UNLESS THE FALSE KNOWLEDGE OF THE ILLUSORY SERPENT GOES,

SO THE REALIZATION OF THE SELF WHICH IS THE SUBSTRATE WILL NOT BE GAINED UNLESS THE BELIEF THAT THE WORLD IS REAL IS REMOVED.

KILL MIND THROUGH CONSTANT VIGILANCE N PUT A COLOUR N LEASH UPON THOUGHTS.

WITH ONE'S VIGILANCE ONE IS ABLE TO BRING THE WANDERING SEARCHER BACK TO SELF N I AM THE SELF-REALISATION THAT I AM.

IS ALL THERE IS.

I AM THE I THAT I AM, THE I THAT FEELS EVERYTHING, OUTSIDE OF CONSTRUCTS OF MIND.

EYES NO SEE, EARS NO HEAR, IF THOUGHT, BEGUILED OF CONCEPTS OF MIND.

I STAND RADIANT WITHIN SELF, PURE LUMINESCENT LIGHT ABOVE MIND.

SELF-REALISATION VIBRATION, SOUL EDIFICATION NON CONTEMPLATIONS.

NEVER MIND ☺

WHEN THE MIND, WHICH IS THE CAUSE OF ALL COGNITIVE ACTIONS BECOMES MOTIONLESS THE WORLD AS ONCE PERCEIVED WILL DISAPPEAR!   I O I ☺

I AM THE BREATH OF GOD.

I AM THE I THAT INVOKES …

BASSIIIII

ASE

I

BELOVED

I AM U N U R I…

I N I …

OH …

MY BELOVED ONE'S SOUL SINGS FOR ME …

THIS VOICE IN MY HEART HAS SET MY HEART FREE …

BEYOND THE VEIL OF SPACES N DIVIDES …

INTO THE BLISS OF LOVE SO DIVINE.…

OH,

ALL OF THIS LIFE IS JUST BUT A DREAM …

NOTHING IS AS IT EVER MAY SEEM …

U OPENED MY EYE … WHAT A WONDERFUL SURPRISE .. U OPENED MY HEART … ♥

U GAVE ME A SMILE N SKIP IN THE WALK …

I CAN JUMP A MILE FROM A STANDING STALK... INTER-DIMENSIONALLY ☺

I FEEL ... I FEEL ... I FEEL ...
WHO AM I...?

I AM U N U R ME...
U R 1 WITH ME N I AM 1 WITH THEE,
N WITHIN THIS LOVE FOREVER I WILL BE TRUE... ♥

I AM, I AM, I AM,
I AM, I AM,
I AM, I AM, I AM,
I AM, I AM,
I AM, I AM, I AM,
I AM, I AM,
I AM
I AM I N I AM THEE N U R I N I AM THAT I THAT I CAN SEE.
I AM ... I AM ... I AM ...
I AM THEE ...
I.
BELOVED I AM U N U ARE I.
I AM I ... ☺
FOR U R N HAVE BEEN WITH ME ALL ALONG
PLAYING ONE'S DRUM N SINGING MY SONG...

I AM ... I AM ...

I MEAN ...

I AM ...

U HOLD ME IN SECRET N A SWEET SUBTLE EMBRACE ...

U GIVE UNTO ME A GIFT OF LOVE N I CHERISHMENTS ...

I AM ... I AM ...

I AM I AM ..

I AM ...

HAPPY😁

U SHOW ME THE WAY ... U TURN ON THE LIGHT...

FOR I AM ONE WITH BOTH DAY N THE NIGHT ...

BUT ONLY A SINGULAR EXPERIENCE OF THE MOST IMPORTANT THING IS U ...

UR LOVE ...

I AM ONE WITH THE LION ... ☺

I AM ONE WITH THE TWINS ... EGO'S SONG ...

I AM ONE WITH THE WOMAN N THE FLYING EAGLE IN THE SKY...

I AM ...I AM ... I AM ... I AM ...

I AM ...

LOVE ♥

I FEEL ....

I FEEL ...

I FEEL WHO I AM.

I AM U N U R I AS ONE NOW ...

I SEE U R I N I AM U IN THIS LOVE FOREVER ...
FOREVER IT IS TRUE.
COSMOS N TO INVOKE IS ALWAYS GOOD TO ME N ME...

I AM ... I AM ... I AM ... I AM ... I AM ... I AM .. I AM ... I AM ... I AM ... I AM ... I AM ... I AM ... I AM ... I AM ... I AM,
I AM
BELOVED I AM YOU N YOU ARE I.♥

I AM ONE WITH THE SUN N THE STARS N THE MOON.
I KNOW THIS THROUGH THE SWEET FEELING,
OF
I LOVE YOU.
I AM ONE WITH THE EARTH,
I AM ONE WITH ME
TOO
GODDESS BOOBOOH
I DO LOVE N ADORE YOU!

I AM ONE WITH THE PLANTS, THE FLOWERS N TREES, THE SKY LARKS N SPARROWS.
I AM ONE WITH THE ANTS, THE BIRDS N THE BEES.

I AM ONE WITH BOOBOOH WITHIN THE BREEZE.

I AM ONE.

I AM ONE WITH THE COSMOS N GALAXIES.

I AM ONE WITH THE WAVES N THE OCEANS N SEAS WITHIN THE BREEZE ....BOO BOO BOOH ... I FEEL ...

I FEEL WHO I AM.

I AM ONE.

I AM YOU N YOU ARE I N WE ARE ONE NOW.

I SEE YOU ARE I N I AM THEE,

IN THIS LOVE FOREVER,

FOREVER TRUE.

I AM, I AM, I AM, I AM, I AM, I AM, I AM, I AM, I AM, I AM, I AM, I AM, I AM, I AM, I AM, I AM I N I AM YOU.

BELOVED I AM YOU N YOU ARE I.

OH ...MY BELOVED SINGS FOR ME WITH THIS VOICE IN MY HEART,

I HAVE NEVER FELT BEFORE N I AM SET FREE FOR I AM YOU N YOU ARE I...

A LOVER FOR ETERNITY BELOVED I AM...

I AM

OM SHANTI!, I OM TATSAT!
I SAT SHANTI I
HUNG TU TI I
TATSAT! OM!

TATTUI TI I
SHANTI I 💋🖤
BOOBOOH

TI SHANTI I
OMSHANT I 🖤
I N I
I N I
OMSHANTI I 🖤
SUKA
BOOBOOH
OMSHANTI I 🖤
LOVE 🖤

ALL IS ILLUSION..

A CREATION OF FEELING LIGHT WITHIN A VIBRATIONAL STATE..
DNA REFLECTS THIS LIGHT N PERCEPTION OF THE LIGHT CREATES THE ILLUSION OF RE AL ITY.
WHAT IS PERCEPTION?

CONSCIOUSNESS OF BODY, MEMORY MIND.

A PROGRAMME SHOVED INTO THE MEMORY OF A CHILD.

NOTHING IS REAL

CONSCIOUSNESS IS INFINITE.

AS THE MOLECULES THAT REFLECT THE LIGHT WITHIN OCEANS.

UNFATHOMABLE N ETERNAL THE GRAVITY THAT TUGS THE LIGHT WITHIN FORM.

THERE IS NO BEGINNING N NO END TO SPACE.

DIMENSIONALITY IS AN ILLUSION OF PERCEPTION OF 12 RE RA SOLAR.

WHAT AGE IS LIGHT???

WHAT AGE IS SPACE???

FROM NOTHING COMES ALL.

FOR ALL RETURNS TO NOTHING

BREATH

LIGHT

LIFE

ILLUSION WITHIN FIRM FORM

MATTER.

LANGUAGE IS A TOOL OF CONTROL OF EXPRESSION OF EXPERIENCES THAT IS LIMITED TO A DIRECT OUTCOME.

KILL MIND

KILL BODY MEMORY.

ONLY BREATH IS LEFT.

WHAT IS AIR?

BUT LIGHT

BASSE TATA NGANGA NOBUNONI MOBENGO HERA SHEREA!

ONE LIGHT.

ONE SPACE

ONE BREATH

ONE BEING

LIFE

EMPATHIC ONENESS IS ALL BEING.

BE LIGHT WITHIN VIBRATIONAL FIRM FORM AS THE OCEANS FLOW ACROSS THE EARTH DOTH CONSCIOUSNESS FLOW OF MYRIAD FORMS WITHIN INFINITIES SMILE AS SUNSHINE UPON THE WIND RUFFLED SURFACE OF A GENTLE LAKE.

BE

BREATH

WITHIN

LIGHT DANCING TO THE SONG OF CREATION

BASSE

EGO IS CREATED OUT OF BALANCE PILLARS OF TEMPLES CUTTING THE HEART CHAKRA FROM THE 3RD EYE.

IS DONE WITH PROGRAMMING BODY MEMORY WITH LANGUAGE.

NO THINK

FEEL.

EMPATHY HAS NO LANGUAGE .

THE HEART BEATS TO ITS OWN RHYTHM.

IT IS BODY MEMORY MIND THAT CLUTTERS THE HEAD.

BE STILL N KNOW

ALL IS LIGHT.

ALL IS BREATH.

ALL IS HEART .

THERE IS NO LANGUAGE WITHIN EMPATHY'S SONG.

LET THE HEART N THE BREATH GUIDE.

ALLOW FEELING TO WALK INSTEAD OF BODY MEMORY MIND.

I AM BREATH

I AM NO MORE

I AM NO BODY

I AM NO THING

I AM BREATH

I AM THE LIGHT OF THE WORLD.

BASSE ♥♥♥

WONDERFULLY N FOR A WHILE A BUTTERFLY DANCES.

BRIGHT OF WINGS UPON THE AIR. OF CURRENTS THAT FLITTER N FLUTTER AS MUSIC DANCES.

TRANCE N THROUGH GENTLE MEADOW GLADES WITHIN LAZY SUMMER'S HAZE OF SUNSHINE REFLECTED THROUGH GENTLE CLOUDS OF A VAST BLUE N YONDER SKIES.

BE GENTLE AS A BUTTERFLY TO SKIP N DANCE THE PRANCE OF LIFE ☺

AS THE LIGHT FADES N SHE IS GENTLY SWAYED WITHIN THY HEART, MY DARLING .. I LOVE YOU.

THE TREASURE YOU HAVE GROWN N EMPATHIES SHOWN. YOU ARE WONDERFUL N BEAUTIFUL TO EYE, TO FEEL.

EVER WARM N EVER BRIGHT.

GIVE ME SWEET DREAMS ALL THROUGH THE SHADOWS OF THE NIGHT.

YOU MOVE N FLOW N MAKE ME GROW FROM BABY INTO BOY.

THEN YOU CARRY ME UP HIGH ALOFT N TURN ME INTO BEAUTY OF A BEING, LIVING GOD.

YOU CARESS N TICKLE N CALM OF FRIGHTS.

N CARRY I ONWARDS INTO THE LIGHT EACH NEW N WONDROUS DAWNING OF DAY...

YOU LAUGH

YOU SMILE

YOU CRY

YOU SING

YOU CARRY ME UPON YOUR WINGS OF SPIRIT THAT SOARS HIGH.

YOU EAT THE BANQUETTE N GUZZLE THE WATER N THE WINE.

THE VINE YOU ARE

DIVINE YOU ARE

YOU ARE MY TREASURED STAR.

THE LIGHT YOU SHOW TO EVER GROW FROM OVUM TO BIG HAIRY GUY 😀

MY DARLING TEMPLE YOU ARE A DEAR N WONDROUS MIRACLE OF CREATION.

I THANK YOU MY DARLING ONE FOR ALL THE EXPERIENCES KNOWN.

INFINITE SMILES FOR A MILLION MILES, EACH SPACE YOU BEAT N TAKE BREATH.

THANK YOU, YOU BEAUTIFUL ANGEL FOR CARRYING ME SO FAR INTO THE NIGHTS N THE LIGHT OF DAYS.

TREASURED ARE YOU MY DARLING HEART.

MY BLESSED BODY OF THE EARTH

YOU ARE WONDROUS N BEAUTIFUL

A SONNET OF COMPLEX RHYTHMS TO PLAY.

THE SONGS OF LIFE.

MY DARLING TEMPLE.

MY LOVE YOU.

YOU ARE MY TREASURED STAR.

BASSE TATA NOBU 🖤

LET US EAT NOW DARLING

YOU N I ARE HUNGRY

YES ☺

BIG PROBLEM WITH THE WORLD.

NO ONE TEACHES CHILDREN TO FOCUS ON THEMSELVES.

TOO BUSY LOOKING AWAY FROM SELF BEING N BECOMING SOMETHING INSTEAD OF LIVING AS A BEAUTIFUL N SHINING STAR.

EDU CA TION SUCKS 😂😂😂😂😂😂😂😂😂

KNOW THY SELF.

BE

BREATH

BE

LIGHT

BE

LOVE

❤❤❤

WOW 😁

ROCKING THE

COS I MOS SORC E ART HE ARTY I BAKA...

LANDED 😁

AH SHE ❤

LUSH FUCKUN DUCKING SHE AH LUSH BUSH AWESOME FREAKING TREES... ❤

UNRA RA RA RA RA RA RA RA RA RA RE RE RE RE RE RE RE RE RE RE AL A DUCKING DITTY LITTLE DANCE. 😁

BANG

I AM I AM TATA N GANG A NOBU NO N I I I I O AL I O EL (SMOKEY JOE HOLE 😁) HIM GOD. ❤

TEMPLE OF LORD GOD STANDS 😁❤❤❤❤❤❤❤❤❤❤❤❤❤❤❤

YAKA SHE

AH WOW

.LUSH MASSIVE CLOUD OF LIVING FIRE 💧💥💥❤❤❤❤ I ☀ I ❤

ROAR ROAR ROAR

CRY.....HITS....THE SKY..

Y I HOLE E SMOKEY JOE E ART HE ART Y I GO GO GO GO GO GO GO GO GO GO COS I MOSIS SORC E ART HE ART Y I FOLKS N BASH THAT THAT THAT THAT

COS I MOS SORC E ART HEARTY I DRUM SON OF AN SON OF AL O I SON OF I O EL HIM GOD....😁

YAKA SHE ❤️❤️❤️❤️

RA ROAR

I AM I

I AM I

I AM I

I AM I

I AM I

I AM I

I AM I

I AM I

I AM I

I AM I

YEAH ❤️❤️❤️❤️

HUCKING CHUCKING MASSIVE MOUNTAIN RANGE BEING I IS I 👍❤️❤️❤️❤️❤️

BAKA HOR TROLLS

YAKA SHE ❤️❤️❤️❤️

AYIIA POWER....EARTH CORE ONLINE NOW N SOLAR RA IS DATING OLE E SMOKEY JOE E HOLE HE ADDED 😄 SMOKING MMMMMH

BIG TEETH HAHAHA

BAKA BOOOOR TROLLS.

WATCH THY HE ADDS COS I MOS I GOT GRID EARTH ONLINE NOW NEED TO BASH THEE HE ADDS NEW DE LE TE THEE STUPID ITY PROGRAM TROLLS NOT CRASH THEE HE ADDS IN...😄

BOYS N GIRLS...😄

BIG DADDY HAS LANDED NOW...😊.

N I AM HUGE N RIGHTEOUS NOT EAT TROLLS FOR SNACKS I Y I O I O AL I O EL O HIM GOD WILL BASH THEE HE ADS IN NORTH SOUTH EAST WEST GRID EARTH Y I HEARTIES N STAND TEM P LE OF THE LORD GOD IN ORDER ♥♥♥♥

LUSH MASSIVE SHE CLOUD ROAR ♥♥♥♥

I AM

I 😄

ONLINE EARTH CORE GO GO GO HO HO HO HO NEY MMMMMH HONEY MMMMMH BIG HOMEY HONEY MMMMMH FOLKS ♥♥♥♥

STUNNING 😄

YEAH TEETH 😃

BIG TEETH 😄

TATA N GANG A NOBU NO N I I I I WARRIOR IS HERE NOW N ALIVE 😄😄😄 😄😄😄😄😄😄😄😄😄😄😄😄😄😄♥👍♥

I AM I BEING I AM I ♥♣♥

LORD GOD BLESS THESE BEINGS OF I O RA AN I O EARTH ♥♥♥♥

YEAH 😊

MUDDY MIGHTY AWE. 😊 TEETH ♥

I HAVE ARRIVED BABIES ....😊

HI I ♥

HI 😂😂😂😂😂😂😂😂😂😂😂😂😂😂😂😂😂😂😂😂😂😂😂😂😂😂😂😂😂😂😂😂😂😂😂😂ROAR RA ROAR RA ROAR ♥ LOVERY TEETH L SIRE 😊

OH I WILL 😊😊😊😊😊😊😊😊😊😊😊😊😊😊😊 9.9D GANG I IS I ♥

LOVE AL ♥

YEAH 😊

TEMPLE STANDS

HOUSE IS TRASHED 😊

UNIVERSE IS CONSTRUCTED THROUGH MIND OF THE SUBJECT THAT OBJECTS.

N THE SUBJECTS GET OBJECTS THROWN AT THEM.

PURELY FROM A CONSTRUCTIVE VIEW.

AFTER DUE CONSIDERING TO SUM UP MY RELATIONSHIP, CAN BE ACHIEVED IN TWO WORDS.

SPACE N IRON.

I UNDERSTAND SPACE

N

THE CONSTRUCT OF IRON,

VERY DEEPLY ☺ ALL LIFE

WHAT AN EXPERIENCE LIFE IS, EH?

WOW!

STUNNING EXPERIENCE

DON'T GET TANGLED TOO MUCH WITHIN THY EMOTIONS,

THEY ARE NO' REAL, JUST ECHO FLUTTERS OF MEMORY TRACES EXPLORED N MIND SENDS OUT THE WORM, GRASPS THE BRIGHT STAR OF THE FILING CABINET OF MEMORY, PULLS OPEN THE DRAWER N REACHES IN N GRABS A WEAVE, THE I THAT INSTANT THEE WOVE OF ATTACHMENTS IS GIVEN FOCAL POINT OF CONSCIOUSNESS THE WOVE OPENS N EXPLODES OF A MASSIVE PSYCHIC MOVIE, BUT IT IS NO REAL.

IT IS ONLY A PERCEPTION WITHIN THE HEAD.

BREATH IS REAL.

BREATH.

I SIT TO PONDER OF THY WONDERS OF THE WEAVE N WOVE OF LIFE... A TAPESTRY.. A COSY QUILT.. A PATTERN FULL OF LOVE N STRIFE..

OF ONE TO ANOTHER DAY TO SEE THE ILLUSION OF TOMORROW'S DREAM...CREATED N ACTED OF AS NOW...A TRAGEDY, A REVELATION, A PLEASANTRY OF REVERIES WITHIN

ONE'S HEART. TO LOOK, TO PEER N GUSTFULLY STEER ONESELF OF THE WAVES N CURRENTS THAT FLOW OF ILLUSIONS OF MEMORIES, TINY PICTURE SHOW... OF HOW THIS IS THAT N THAT IS THIS, N OH MY DEAR POOR SOUL I SHOULD HAVE DONE THIS FOR THAT N WORN THAT WITH A GAY ABANDON N A GLARY SHOW..

AS TO DANCE N PRANCE THE GIFT OF LIFE N LET DOWN HAIR WITHOUT A CARE N FROLIC IN THE SANDS OF TIME FORGOTTEN N FILLED WITH INTRICATE PATTERNS AS A PICTURE OF A TINY SHOW..

A CINEMA FRONT ROW SEAT.

THROWING POPCORN AT HEADS N FEET OF ROWDY GIRLS N BOYS FROM ATOP THE BALCONY TO BELOW AMONGST THE CHEAP SEATS.. A GLARE A SCREAM.. A COKE FIZZY STRAWED STREAM ..

ICE COLD BRAIN FREEZE..

A SNEAKY FAG.

OH WHAT A DREAM..!

LIFE WITHOUT OF ANY STRIFE IT CAN ... N SHOULD HAVE BEEN...

BUT ALAS THE MIRRORING IS ALL DISTORTED BY A SYSTEM N NO' A GENTLE SUBTLE CRYSTAL STREAM THAT NATURE HOLDS N SHOWS TO GIVE OF FREELY, TO BE SEEN DEEP WITHIN THE FOREST GLADES OF ONE'S EMOTIONS...

TAKEN HOLD OF N ENFOLDED WITHIN THY BODY'S MEMORY. TO REALIGN N GUIDE THE TIDES TO FUTURE'S ILLUSIVE TIMES YET TO COME..

TO HAVE N TO HOLD.

TREASURE ALL N EVERY BREATH OF LOVE IN LIFE N ALL THE SERENE SCENES OF THE RIDES IN CARS TO SEE STARS SHINING GAILY WITHIN THE MELEE OF DARKNESS'S INFINITE TWILIGHT SKIES.

TO SIT WITHIN ONE'S BODY MEMORY .

A REVERE OF LIFE THAT IS N SHOULD BE CHERISHED N HELD ALWAYS CLOSE N TO ONE'S HEART.

TO GUIDE N SHINE N REALIGN..

ONE .

WHEN..

OF A BROKEN HEART.

NE'ER TAKE OF ANOTHER'S RANT OR ATTITUDE OR GLARE.

EYES THAT PEER N QUESTION THEE WITH A STERNLY STARE..

ARE OF EGOCENTRIC POSTULATIONS N THEY HAVE NO LIFE OR SELF TO OWN...

OR A CREATION TO BE SHARED N SHOWN...

TO BE THEIR WEALTH N STEER THEM CLEARLY ON THE SETTLED PATH TO A PEACEFUL HOME...

THE SACRED SPACE THAT HOLDS N FOLDS THE TREASURES N SERENE SMILES OF THAT WHICH IS WITHIN AN OPEN HEART...

PLACE LOGS WITHIN THE HEARTH OF LIFE N LET THE FIRES GLOW..

BRIGHTLY N FORTHRIGHTLY OF THE TRUTH OF BEING EMPATHETIC ONENESS, TO LIVE N SHARE

THE LOVES OF LIFE

LIVE TO LOVE

THE LOVE OF LIFE.

N LET YOUR PATRONAGES GLOW FORTH FROM THE VERY CORE OF YOUR BEING .. BE THE STAR THAT YOU ARE.

ANGEL S SHINE YOUR LIGHT N GLOW THE LOVE OF LIFE TO SHOW...

BE

BREATH

BE LIGHT ALL DARKEST DAYS TO BRIGHTEST STARLIT NIGHTS

BE EMPATHETIC ONENESS.

LIFE.

PAZULA

TAKE Z N PUT IN U N SPIN AROUND ME N THROWING UP THROUGH A.

CENTRE PILLAR POWER

BY FOUR SERVANTS OF THE EARTH

NORTH SOUTH EAST N WEST

MAY THE SUNLIGHT FOREVER GLOW WITHIN THE MAGNETIC RESONANCE OF THEE TREASURED HEARTS TO GLOW..

A PLACE TO SIT BENEATH THE SPREADING REACHES OF THE STILLNESS OF BEACH TREES BOWS

ERECT N TRUE.

SURE N FORMED OF EVER CHANGING HUES OF SILVERS GLISTENED OF DEW N SPATTERS OF GENTLE SOFTNESS MOSS... OF GREENS N EVEN BROWNS.

AS SMOOTHING OF BARKS DO CURL...

CLOUDS GENTLY FLOW N FURL ACROSS VAST YONDER SKIES..

BLACKBIRD HOPS THE GRASSES NEAR.

A WORM TO BE SPIED N TAKEN OFF FOR HIS CROP N TROT N FLITTER TO A TROT ALONG THE LEAF STREWN LAWNS.

HOP. HOP DOES BLUE TIT DANCE N PRANCE A TROTS FROM BRANCH TO BRANCH N CHIRPS A TINY SHRILLING CALL... ALL A-DANCE.

A SUBTLE PLEASANT SCENE.

UPON THOSE DAYS OF WHEN ONE GAZES, DAY DREAMS THAT GENTLY SING OF FEELINGS INSTEAD OF THOUGHTS.

BELOW THE BOW OF A BEACH TREE... A GRAND N MIGHTY SHOW OF WOOD THAT IS CLEARLY SEEN TO BE THE ONE SERENE, GOOD FORTITUDE OF WOOD, AN EVER PRESENT NATURE'S FLOW OF CREATION WITHIN HER FLOWS

OH ROBIN..

YOU ARE SO FIRM TO BE VERY SO FORTHRIGHT

TERRITORIAL TO A FORE N WHISTLE THE BEAUTY FOR YOUR TUNE.

SOON ALL THE LEAVES WILL COME OFF, FALL FROM BEACH TREE.

STILL TO STAND ERECT N TALL

NAKED OF LEAF WITHIN THE FALL.

SPREAD BOWS ACROSS THE FIELDS ABACK THE EVER DEPTHS OF INFINITE SKIES TWISTED N MORPHED OF CLOUDS AFORE, THE DEPTHS OF VAST BLUES OF AIR N WIND SWEPT SKIES TO VIEW.

OH SIGH!

AS SUNLIGHT GENTLE MARKS HER PATH AS SHADOWS OF THE BEACH TREE BOWS UPON THE GROUND..

AS CLOCK HANDS MOVE..

THE SHADOWS PASS FIRM N GENTLE ALONG THE LEAF STREWN MAT.

TIME A HAT.

EPHEMERAL AN ILLUSION FROWNS

NOTHING TO THE FORE IS COUNTED OF ILLUSION OF PAST AS THE TREE BOWS SHADOWS OF SUN'S SWEET PASSING ACROSS THE SKIES.. MARKED AS SHADOWS UPON THE GROUND.

A MEMORY HELD WITHIN A GLIMPSE OF THE TWINKLE OF ONE'S EYE.

TODAY IS ALWAYS THE ONE THAT RISES TO THE FORE

N YESTERDAY.. A GOODBYE.

A MEMORY OF A MENTAL VIEW OR A SETTING PICTURE WITHIN A FRAME.

AS LEAVES FALL UPON THE GROUND FOR EACH N EVERY DAY.

THE CLOCK OF SEASONS RUNS HER TUNE...N NE'ER DOES MISS A BEAT.

JUST NATURE'S GENTLE COLOURS' CHANGE OF HUE..

HER FACE DOES SOMETIMES WEEP OF RAINSTORMS N GENTLER OF SHOWERS ... UPON THE BEACH TREE

THAT STANDS ERECT WITHIN FOREST DEEP.

SERENE SMILES THE BARK N SHOWS THE PASS OF TIME.

AS A REMINDER OF THE PLEASANT SPACES WITHIN GLADES N FORESTS OUTSIDE OF TIME.

IS EPHEMERAL BEAUTY.

FACES OF NATURE AS SHE SMILES.

OH TIMELESSLY N SO TRUE N SURE.

GRAND TALL BEACH TREE STANDS A STATELY LOOK ..BOWS SPREAD AFORE ACROSS A GENTLE BROOK.

THE LAND.

STILLNESS IS PEACE IS WITH ALL.

AS THE GENTLE SHADOWS OF EVEN TIDES DO CALL..

N SO THE SONG NEVER FADES OF A BEACH TREE WITHIN DEEPS OF FOREST GLADES. ♥♥♥

NATURE'S TUNE A SOMETIMES SET TO GROW

HER FACE UPON THE FOREST GLADES N DEEPS N KEEPS THAT FOLD WITHIN THE LAND.. ♥♥♥

FOR A CAVE IN DARKNESS MAY THE BEAST SLUMBER N NO MORE RUN UNTO THE FIELDS, A SLUMBER NOW OH MIGHTY DRAGON THAT THROWS OF BALLS OF FIRE, IT DIRE NE'ER THE DAWN OF A NEW DAY. BEHOLD THE DRAGON WAKES OF SLUMBERS N MOVES MOUNTAINS FOLDED OF GRANITE, SCARRED BY THE BEAST OF TIME WHEN HENCE THE DRAGONS DIES, PULLED APART N RIPPED ASUNDER OF SOLIDITY OF POWER, BY DRAGGING EASTWARDS TO THE FALLS OF TANRAHOR, OF VEILS N EVIL MIST UPON THE MOORS OF GHOSTS OF DEAD, THE MIGHTY DRAGON ROARS N SLUMBERS FOR NOW THE LIGHT OF THIS DAY DAWNS, THE DRAGON LIFTS TAIL FROM CAVE INTO RADIANT SKY, ONCE MORE, TO STRETCH N ARC SO HIGH OF MAJESTY DIVINE.

WITHIN CRYSTAL PALACES OF MIRRORS' REFLECTIONS MIND, TO FEEL OF SUCH WONDEROUS DELIGHT OF WARMTH

TO BE RELEASED, ONCE MORE FROM THE CAVE OF DARKNESS TO ARC ACROSS THE SKY...

AH

I SEE A STAR ATOP..

A WHIRLWIND DOES TWIST AFAR...

O CRYSTALS N GOLD ...

A SHIMMERING LIGHT

AN ARROW FLASH

AS CROSS BOW FLIGHT...

ARC!

N OWL DOES CALL STIRRING UP A HOOT TO TAKE TO SILENT FLIGHT...

AS RAIN PATTERS GENTLE

UPON GREEN N WETTED LEAVES ...

TO RUN N FALL...

INTO...

THE STREAMS N RIVERS OF THE VALLEY OF MY FEELINGS...

TO SIT GENTLE WITHIN THE POOLS N DEEPS... O MY HEART...

DO STAND N ALWAYS WITH GREAT CHEER...

O MIGHTY MAJESTIC RED WOOD

STAND ... PROUD ...

STAND A CLEAR SPIRE UNTO THE SKY ...

SIT WITHIN THE NEEPS N NAPS N UNDER TO FALL WITHIN THE CRACKS N CREVICES OF STURDY EMOTIONS MOUNTAINS ... N FOLLOW THE PATH OF MEANDERING STREAMS ...

THAT GLISTEN N SPARKLE WITHIN SUNLIGHT'S CHEERY SCENE ...

A COAT CAST OF PURE EFFERVESCENT LIGHT...

COME

UPHOLD ME UNTIL THE NIGHT REMOVES CLOTHS N GIVES BLANKETS DEEP ... SO I MAY SLEEP ...

SO EYELIDS DROP N SLUMBER'S DREAMS DO SPEAK.

BE FOREVER WITHIN THE FOLD OF LIFE ... ALWAYS... :)

MEDITATIONS' ENERGY WORKS N MANTRA CREATES COMPLETENESS N SELF-CONFIDENCE N TEACHES KNOWLEDGE OF THE NATURE OF CONSCIOUSNESS, LIGHT OF SELF IS AWAKENED, OUR SOULS SOAR HIGH N CARRY ALOFT UPON WINGS OF A BREEZE THAT BLOWS GENTLY THROUGH THE BOWS N BRANCHES N LEAVES OF FEELING, FOR ABOVE N AROUND US THE WILD WINDS OF SUCH FEELING ARE CALLING WITHIN, AROUSING TO RAPTURE THE EARTH N THE SEAS AS THE TALL LONG GRASSES DANCE IN SUNLIGHT'S GLANCES,

AS WIND TOSSES BRANCHES OF BOWS UPON HIGH.

DEAD LEAVES FLITTER N FLUTTER DOWN AS GENTLE EMOTIONS OF NATURE SINGING HER SONNET SONG,

AS WHITE CLOUDS GO SCUDDING ACROSS THE BLUES OF SKY, TO SEE SUNLIGHT A TWINKLE WITHIN ONE'S EYE, IS MY DELIGHT, TO FEEL SPEAK WITH CREATION OUTSIDE OF TIME, I WILL SPEAK WITH ONE AGAIN N AGAIN EACH SPACE WHEN THE SUN ARISES.

NOW I SLEEP N TIGHTLY HOLD A DARLING TREASURE TO ENFOLD WITHIN WHEN I SURVEY SUCH WONDEROUS BEAUTY HELD WITHIN A NANO BAR OF INSTANTANEOUS LIGHT, AN ARROW TO THINE EYE, TO GAZE UPON ALL THE ANGLES OF DELIGHTS GIVEN NOW N ONLY NOW IS ETERNAL PRESENCE N POWER OF THE INWARD FORCE OF A COSMOS EVOLVED OF VIBRATIONAL LIGHT.

GOOD BRIGHT DAY, FOLKS N A HUG TO KEEP ME COMPANY, SNUG WARM N FULL O' LIGHT ☐

WALKING THE ROAD TO SELF-ENLIGHTENMENT BEGINS LIKE A BEING A GROSS FAT BABY WHO GRABS EVERYTHING N STICKS IT IN THE MOUTH, THEN SPITS EVERYTHING OUT BECAUSE IT LOOKS SWEET BUT TASTES BITTER.

THE BABY GROWS THIN, THE GROSS ROLLS OF FAT FALL OFF, LEANNESS N GAUNTNESS APPEAR, THE WARFARE OF THE TWINS HAS BEGUN.

IT IS MINE

NO IT IS MINE, MINE I HAD IT FIRST, IT IS MY ATTACHMENT N MY STORY BUILDING THAT I SUPPORT TO SUPPORT ME.

IF I LOSE SIGHT OF THE BUILDING I WILL NO' KNOW WHERE I AM N THEN I WILL LOSE MY IDENTITY N SURELY DIE.

I WILL NO' EXIST, WILL I? CAN I EXIST WITHOUT THE IDEA OF MY LIFE?

THE GROUND UNDER FOOT TURNS TO JAGGED FLINTS N THE SUN TORMENTS THE SHRIVELED BODY N ASSAULTS THE BLOOD SHOT EYES.

VULTURES CIRCLE HIGH.

WALKING ON, THE REST OF THE BODY SLIPS OFF LEAVING WHITE BONE SKELETON STANDING UPON PEBBLES ON THE GROUND, DRIED N BURNT CRISP BY SCORCHING NOON DAY ARC OF THE SUN.

ONE WALKS ON.

FLINTS TURN TO PEBBLES N OPEN TO BOULDERS N VAST OPEN SANDS OF WHICH THE GRAINS OF EXISTENCES ARE SOULS, MINGLING N JOSTLING GENTLY THE GRAVITY OF THE WIND SWEPT DUNE AS GRAINS OF FEELING FLY INTO THE SUN STREWN AIR.

NONCHALANT BLACK MOSQUITO BUZZES BY ADDING TO THE FREQUENCIES OF DANCING LIGHT.

ONE WALKS ON.

THE BONES DISSOLVE N BECOME THE DUNES OF DRIFTING SANDS, ALL THE SAME ME, BUT OF DIFFERENT IRIDESCENT REFLECTIONS AS THE HOUR GLASS OF WHAT WAS ONCE TIME ... MIND SPINS ON TO THE ORDER OF THE SOLAR

SYSTEM N THE FINAL WORMS OF DEAD CHILDHOOD LEARNT RESPONSES PROGRAMMED FAIL ...

N THE SKELETON OF SELF DISSOLVES TO DISAPPEAR N MELT INTO THE SHIFTING SANDS THAT ARE WASHED GENTLY BY THE SEAS OF TRUTH OF INTUITIVE REASON.

IF IDEA BETWEEN THE EARS THEN THEY BE THOUGHTS ...

N THOUGHTS CAN ONLY LEAD TO FEARS BECAUSE THE IDEA HAS NO FEELING ...

SO MUST BE AN ILLUSION AS THE GRAINS OF SANDS UPON THE BEACH OF THE MYRIAD MIRRORED PERCEPTIONS OF ONE'S MIND.

THE ONCE GROSS N ROLLS OF FAT OF WANTON BABY BECOME EPHEMERAL OF THE ESSENCE OF BEING N RADIATE THE PURE LIGHT OF CONSCIOUSNESS UNFRAMED N UNFED UNFORMED, UN-MOULDED, UNTETHERED BY A DIRECTOR CALLED MIND.

FROM GROSS UGLY BABY TO SKELETON WALKING SHARDED ROCKS OF ONE'S EGO'S KARMIC WAVES.

THE SKELETON DISSOLVES N MANY PERCEPTIONS BECOME ONE.

I OBSERVE

ALL HAVE A WONDERFUL N BRIGHT N SELF-FULFILLING DAY, SHARE SOME LIGHT N FLY YOUR KITE HIGH INTO THE VAST BLUE YONDER OF EARTH BOW AURA N SUN DAZZLED WIND SWEPT SHOWER STREWN RAINBOWS ... O WHICH.. .ALL..

GET BLASTED OUT N LEAVING ...

SILKS OF SILVER N FINE THREADS OF GOLD N LEAVES GENTLY FALL... THE LEAVES OF THE VINE OF LIFE,

THE ONCE FAT GROSS WANTON BABY OF IDEAS N SNAKES OF ATTACHMENTS DISSOLVE LEAVING INTUITIVE KNOWING OF N ANSWER TO.

WHO AM I

WHAT AM I

FIND THE NATURE OF ME...

FIND N KNOW THINE BEACH SAND VINE OF SELF...

KNOW THINE IS BUT A GRAIN OF SAND ...

A VERY VERY VERY SUBTLE N BEAUTIFUL GRAIN OF INFINITY FOCUSED FORCE WITHIN ESSENCES OF LOVE THE POWER OF NOW ☺

BASSIIIII

BIRDS ARE CHATTERING.

BREEZE IS BLOWING GENTLY THROUGH THE TREES N THE VINE IS SHUFFLING HER HEARTY SONNET SONG.

INCREDIBLE ENTITY THE BODY OF THE BREATH OF GRAVITY ORDERED DENSITY.

B

MIGHTY N GREAT EMPATHIC G.O.D. O COSMOS THE ART THE ART OH! SHE I SHE.

EMPATHIC ONENESS MESSAGE ONE LIFE.

LOVE

ASE

ATU

ALL ELSE IS ILLUSION OF A THING CALLED MIND.

DELETE THAT IT

ONE BEING ALL

BASSE TATA NOBU LOVES U AL AN I M AL EL O HIM 🖤

YOU HAVE LIFE.

LOVE THAT.

WHAT MORE DO YOU REQUIRE.

BE GRATEFUL...

THE SUN N GRAVITY OF LIGHT MADE YOU.

REJOICE..

GIVE PRAISES TO THE SUN.

THE EYE OF THE WORLD

BE EMPATHIC ONENESS

ALL ONE LIFE TO BE.

AT PEACE N KNOW CONSCIOUSNESS IS INFINITE N ETERNAL WITHIN MATTER OF SHE I SHE GANG O GRAVITY ORDERED DENSITY 12 RE RA SOLAR REEL O HIM AN I M AL.

STOP THINKING

START FEELING THE BREATH N HEART OF LOVE SPEAK HER EMPATHIC SONG.

LET GO OF THE IDEA N EMBRACE THE EMPATHIES OF THE ONE HEART OF LIFE

LOVE ♥

BE

STILL

N KNOW

LIFE IS AWESOMENESS INDEED.

BE

BREATH

BE LOVE

BE THE LIGHT OF THE WORLD

I AM THE I THAT I AM I AM.

PURE AWARENESS IS.

I IS THE LIGHT OF THE WORLD.

BECOME THE I OF CREATION

BASSE TATA NOBUNONI HERA SHEREA 12 RE SOLAR SON OF THEE SUNS OF G.O.D.

ASE ATU SHE I SHE IS THEE I ♥ O THE WORLD ♥♥♥

BLISS!

IF YOU CAN NO GO TO THE MOUNTAIN BRING THE MOUNTAIN TO YOU :)))

IF THERE IS EVER ONE ...

WHO WHEN U R A-SLEEPING ...

WILL WIPE AWAY TEARS ...
WHEN IN DREAMS U R WEEPING ...
WHO WILL OFFER SPACE ...
WHEN ALL L DEMAND;
LOVE DOES LAY MORE INFINITE ...
THAN GRAINS OF SANDS ...
O OCEANS DEEPS ...

IF THERE IS EVER ONE ...
TO WHOM U CAN CRY ...
WHO WILL GATHER EACH TEAR ...
N BLOW IT AWAY DRY ...
WHO WILL OFFER HELP ...
UPON THE MOUNTAINS OF TIME ...
WHO WILL STOP N LET EACH SUNSET
SOOTHE ONE'S JADED SUBTLE BODY ...

IF THERE IS EVER ONE ...
TO WHOM ...
U CAN RUN ...
WILL PUSH BACK THE CLOUDS ...
SO U R BATHED IN THE SUN ...
WHO WILL OPEN THEIR ARMS ...
IF U WILL FALL ...

WHO WILL SHOW U EVERYTHING ...

IF U LOST IT ALL ...

IF THERE IS EVER ONE ...

WHO WHEN U ACHIEVE

WILL BE THERE BEFORE THE DREAM ...

N EVEN THEN STILL BELIEVE ...

WHO WILL CLEAR THE AIR ...

WHEN FULL OF LOSS ...

WHO WILL COUNT LOVE ...

BEFORE THE COST ...

IF THERE IS EVER ONE ...

WHO WHEN U R COLD ...

WILL SUMMON WARM AIR ...

FOR UR HANDS TO HOLD ...

WHO WILL MAKE PEACE ...

WITHIN UR POURING PAINS ...

MAKE LAUGHTER FALL ...

WITHIN FALLING RAINS ...

IF THERE IS EVER ONE ...

WHO WILL OFFER U THIS N MORE ...

WHO ...

WITHIN KEYLESS ROOMS ...

CAN OPEN ALL UR DOORS ...

WHERE IN OPEN DOORS ...

OFT ONE CAN SEE ...

OPEN FIELDS ...

N WITHIN OPEN FIELDS ...

ALL HARVESTS YIELD ...

THEN SEE ONLY MY FACE ...

WITHIN REFLECTIONS OF THESE TIDES ...

THROUGH CLEAR WATERS ...

BEYOND RIVER SIDES ...

ALL I CAN DO IS GIVE MY LOVE TO YOU ...

WITHIN ALL THAT THIS IS ...

IS ...

A POEM ...

A NECKLACE ..

O AN INFINITE N INVISIBLE KISS ... 🫘

IF I AM THE CAT... I GET TO PURR N CHASE BUTTERFLIES N YOU THE MOUSE... EAT CHEESE N SCRUB YOUR WHISKERS N WIGGLE YOUR NOSE... N SQUEAK ☺ ♥ ALSO YOU GET TO SNUGGLE UP IN BALLS OF FLUFF SNUG N COSY N WARM.

WHIST I GO ON THE PROWL EACH NIGHT ... N SLINK ABOUT IN DARK ALLEYS ...MEOWING AT THE TOMCATS' FIGHT.

N THEN I COME HOME N CURL UP ON THE WINDOW SILL IN THE SUN N SLEEP ALL DAY ♥

YOU THE MOUSE TAKE BUTTERCUPS FOR UMBRELLAS N DAISIES FOR SKIRTS … N HAVE WILD PARTIES IN MEADOW LANDS N BURROW HOLES … LEFT BY MOLES … THAT YOU TAKE OVER SQUATTERS' RIGHTS.

YOU SIT ON REEDS N NIBBLE AT SEEDS N CHASE DANDELION TUFTS IN AUTUMN'S FAIR.

I, THE CAT, SIT BIG N FAT N LICK UP ALL THE CREAM ♥

WOW!

I

LOVE ME

I AM A BEAUTIFUL MAN N I LOVE ME UNCONDITIONALLY, N I CAN ACTUALLY SAY

"I CAN FEEL MY LOVE FOR ME" N I CAN FEEL SPACE IMMENSE INWARD VASTNESS OF DEEP VIBRATIONAL FREQUENCY OF AWESOME POWER OF LOVE N AN INCREDIBLE FORCE OF INSTINCTUAL LIFE ENERGIES FOCUSED WITHIN ONE'S BEING.

A SILVER SPHERE OF EVOLVING FOCUSED ON FREQUENCIES OF ALL …

EVERYTHING IS WITHIN A GLIMPSED SEDUCTIVE PERCEPTION OF WHICH IS NO' REAL.

MIND MANIPULATES THROUGH PERCEPTIONS THAT WHICH I EXPERIENCES.

SO IF IT IS OF MIND THOUGHTS THEN IT IS NO' REAL.

THE ONLY THING REAL IS FEELING.

IF ONE CAN TOUCH IT WITH A FINGER THEN FEELING SAYS THAT FINGER TOUCHES LIGHT OF A DIFFERENT DENSITY TO ONE'S FINGER.

MIND N THOUGHTS FEEL NOTHING.

EMOTIONS ARE FALSE MIND-FIRED ENERGIES OF THOUGHTS PUSHING ENERGIES AROUND THE BODY.

EMOTIONS ARE BUT RESULTS OF FEELING THE I OF THOUGHTS N THOUGHTS ARE BUT FEELINGS RISING FROM I.

I NO' THINK

I FEEL I EXPLORED WITHIN THE STARS OF HEAVEN OF WHERE ALL OF THIS IS CREATED.

THERE IS NO OUTER WORLD.

NOTHING AT ALL.

IT IS ALL MANIFEST OF THE ENERGIES OF I EXPLORED.

THE BODY IS BUT AN IMAGE AS IS THE WORLD BUILT WITHIN N PROJECTED OF WHAT APPEARS TO BE OUT.

BUT THERE IS NO OUTSIDE ANYTHING.

EVERYTHING IS A PERCEPTION.

N IF NO' ATTACHED TO FEELING IT IS ILLUSION.

WELCOME TO NOWHERE.

I CAN MAKE THAT WHICH I LIKE.

IT IS BUT A HOLOGRAM CREATED BY ME

N I AM I ☺

BASSIIIII ♥

THE LAND WALKING...

THINE EYES DO SHINE AS EXOTIC STARFISH STARS IN BLACK PITCH SKIES... OF ESSENCES SO SWEET N DEEP. ONE GETS LOST WITHIN THE MYRIAD VIEW OF WANTON DREAMS...

LIKE OCEAN WAVES THAT LAP UPON A GENTLE MORNING'S SHORE.

YOUR FACE SHINES OF LIGHT UPON THE EARLY RISING DAWN...

SPARROW HOPS BOW TO BOW.

N LAZILY ONE'S EYES LOOK DESIRE INTO THE DEPTH OF OCEANS DEEP.

DO NO' WEEP THE LOSS OF A WAVE THAT TRAVERSES THE SURFACE OF A SILVER LAKE...AS WHITE SWAN GLIDES...

A MEMORY IS BUT A GLANCE INTO THE LOOKING GLASS OF A RAIN FILLED SKY...

SAY GOODBYE TO THE FLOW N FORM THAT CREATES OF STORMS THAT FROWN UPON THY BROW.

LET THE HAIR FLY SOFTLY ACROSS A WANTON SKY.

MY DEAR ONE SHINES AS SPRING SUNSHINE N FRESH RAINS UPON THE LAWNS OF THY VERY LOINS...

THY EVER REFRESHING PRESENCE HOLDS ME... N MY DEAR N CLOSENESS BE...

AS EVENINGS LIGHT BLANKETS THE SCENE OF FIELDS N TREES OF PASTURES THAT SIGH AMONGST THE LANDS.

COME QUICK MY DEAR N FOLD INTO MY ARMS N HEART...

HARKEN QUICKLY TO MY CALL...

THERE BE NO FINER TREASURE FOUND THAN THE COMFORT OF ONE'S SWEET CARES, THAT CRADLES MY EVER FLEETING SOUL....

AS SHE FLIES AMONGST THE FRESHNESS OF EMPATHIES' CALL OF A HEART OPEN TO THE LIGHT OF LOVE.

CHERISH EACH N WITH EVERY BREATH AS ONE'S BOSOM HEAVES A GENTLE SIGH OF OH SUCH FEELINGS THAT FLIGHT THE MIND.

BE LIGHT N FREE..SO AS TO FEEL THE EARLY RISINGS OF THE SUN N END OF DAY ONE CAN ALWAYS SAY.

LOVE IS SEEN UPON THE GENTLE FROWNS OF MEADOWS THAT ROLL SOFTLY ACROSS THE MOORS.

THE LAND THY BODY..

OH SUCH SWEET DELIGHTS TO FEEL..

N PLEASURES THAT OFT DO DANCE WITHIN THE EDGES OF MY FEELING ... ☺

GOLDEN BROWN,

TEXTURE AS SUNSHINE,

YOU ARE MY LOVE

SO SWEET N ALIVE

COME SIT WITH ME,

GIVING ONE'S DIVINE N RADIANT LIGHT.

FLOWING WITH LOVE,

HOLDING N KNOWING YOUR LIFE GIVING ESSENCE

OF PURE N ILLUSTRIOUS DELIGHTS.

HONEY,

OH BEAUTIFUL HONEY,

OH!

ONE

BRINGS SUCH POWER WITHIN ONE'S BEING

OF BEES 🐝 BRINGING HOME NECTAR N POLLENS IN SPLENDOUR,

TO SET A PICTURE TWINED WITHIN ONE'S HEART,

OF HONEY'S HOMELY DELIGHTS ▨

AAASAAAH HONEY!

AWESOMELY SPLENDID

WHOLESOME

SEDUCTIVE

OF RAYS

OF GOLDEN BROWN SUNSHINE

ESSENCE

SO DIVINE ☼

BASSIIIII

SELF-TRUTH N TRUTH WITHIN OTHERS CREATES COMPLETENESS N SELF-KNOWLEDGE.

OUR LIGHT IS AWAKENED

OUR SOULS SOAR HIGH N CARRY ALOFT UPON WINGS OF A BREEZE THAT BLOWS GENTLY THROUGH VALLEYS N DALES OF ONES MIND'S EYE THROUGH THE I OF GOD.

FOR WITHIN IS THE WILD WINDS OF FEELING N THEY ARE CALLING,

AROUSING TO RAPTURE THE EARTH N THE SEAS AS THE TALL LONG GRASSES DANCE IN SUNLIGHT'S GLANCES,

AS WIND TOSSES BRANCHES OF BOWS UPON HIGH.

DEAD LEAVES FLITTER N FLUTTER DOWN AS GENTLE EMOTIONS FIRED OF THOUGHTS OF FEELING NATURE SINGING HER SONNET SONG,

AS WHITE CLOUDS GO SCUDDING ACROSS BLUES OF SKY,

TO SEE SUNLIGHT A TWINKLE WITHIN ONE'S EYES, IS OF A DELIGHT.

WATER WATER OF SPLENDOR FLOWING TO BRING OF SUCH DELIGHTFUL

HAPPY LITTLE BROOKS FULL OF FEELING,

TINY SILVER FISH THAT FLIT WITHIN SHOALS,

MANY OF I BUT AS ONE MIGHTY FISH.
SWIMMING AMONGST THE WATERS OF LIFE,
BRINGER OF LIFE FORCE,

WATER WATER I SING
SWEETLY OVER YOU
YOU ARE MY DELIGHT
I SING TO YOU WITH MY
BLESSINGS,
MAY YOU QUENCH ME
REFRESH ME
N .ALL.. RENEWED

WATER WATER I DANCE, I SING
SONNETS THAT SPLASH WITHIN SUNLIGHT.

BRINGING SWEET, SWEET, BEAUTIFUL REFRESHING BLESSINGS

TO THE OBSERVER OF LIGHT WITHIN ONE'S LIFE'S LOVE VIBRATIONS,

I AM JOYED
I AM ECSTATIC
I FILLED WITH DELIGHT.
YOU ARE BUBBLING OF JOY

POOLS OF DANCING LIGHT

BLESSINGS

WATER

SWEET BLESSINGS

WATER

THANK YOU FOR THE LOVE THE JOY N THE DELIGHT

I LOOK AT THE SKY

IT IS COVERED IN MARSHMALLOWS.

YEAH!

BASSIIIII

I AM BEAUTIFUL ... UNCONDITIONALLY AN IMMENSE INWARD VASTNESS O' DEEP VIBRATIONAL FREQUENCY THE AWESOME POWER OF LOVE IS AN

INCREDIBLE FORCE OF INSTINCTUAL LIFE ENERGIES FOCUSED WITHIN ONE'S BEING...

www.ingramcontent.com/pod-product-compliance
Lightning Source LLC
Chambersburg PA
CBHW052011070526
44584CB00016B/1706